Boosting Pharmaceutical Innovation in the Post-TRIPS Era

Boosting Pharmaceutical Innovation in the Post-TRIPS Era

Real-Life Lessons for the Developing World

Burcu Kılıç

Public Citizen's Global Access to Medicines Program

Edward Elgar

Cheltenham, UK • Northampton, MA, USA

Published by
Edward Elgar Publishing Limited
The Lypiatts
15 Lansdown Road
Cheltenham
Glos GL50 2JA
UK

Edward Elgar Publishing, Inc.
William Pratt House
9 Dewey Court
Northampton
Massachusetts 01060
USA

A catalogue record for this book
is available from the British Library

Library of Congress Control Number: 2013958022

This book is available electronically in the ElgarOnline.com Law Subject Collection, E-ISBN 978 1 78254 413 5

ISBN 978 1 78254 412 8

Typeset by Columns Design XML Ltd, Reading
Printed and bound in Great Britain by T.J. International Ltd, Padstow

Contents

Figures

Abbreviations

AAI	American Antitrust Institute
AER	*American Economic Review*
ANDA	abbreviated new drug application
API	active pharmaceutical ingredients
BMJ	*British Medical Journal*
CGKD	Centre for Governance of Knowledge and Development
CIPR	Commission on Intellectual Property Rights
CMAJ	*Canadian Medical Association Journal*
CMS	Carnegie Mellon Survey
CRS	Congressional Research Service
CSIS	Centre for Strategic and International Studies
CTIETI	Committee on Technology and International Economic and Trade Issues
DRL	Dr Reddy's Laboratories
FDA	Food and Drug Administration
FDI	foreign direct investment
FTA	free trade agreement
FTAAP	Free Trade Area of the Asia Pacific
GAO	Government Accountability Office
GSK	GlaxoSmithKline
IFPMA	International Federation of Pharmaceutical Manufacturers and Associations
IIC	*International Review of Intellectual Property and Competition Law*
IJIO	*International Journal of Industrial Organization*
IP	intellectual property
IPAB	Indian Intellectual Property Appellate Board
IPRs	intellectual property rights
JEI	*Journal of Economic Issues*

JGE	*Journal of Generic Medicines*
J.Int.Econ	*Journal of International Economics*
JKM	*Journal of Knowledge Management*
JLAT	*Journal of Law and Technology*
JPE	*Journal of Private Enterprise*
JWIP	*Journal of World Intellectual Property*
MEXT	Ministry of Education, Culture, Sport, Science and Technology
MIT	Massachusetts Institute of Technology
NBER	National Bureau of Economic Research
NGO	non-governmental organisations
NIERC	Northern Ireland Economic Research Centre
NIH	National Institutes of Health
NIS	national innovation system
NRC	National Research Council
NSF	National Science Foundation
OCS	Office of the Chief Scientist
OECD	Organisation for Economic Co-operation and Development
OSIPP	Osaka School of International Public Policy
PharmSci	American Association of Pharmaceutical Scientists
PhRMA	Pharmaceutical Research and Manufacturers of America
R&D Law	Law for the Promotion of Industrial Research and Development
R&D	research and development
RAND.J.Econ	Rand Journal of Economics
S&T	science and technology
SME	small and medium enterprise
TTIP	Transatlantic Trade and Investment Partnership
TPP	Trans-Pacific Partnership Agreement
TRIPS	The Agreement on Trade Related Aspects of Intellectual Property
TWN	Third World Network
UNCTAD	United Nations Conference on Trade and Development
UNECE	United Nations Economic Commission for Europe

USTR	United States Trade Representative
WHO	World Health Organization
WIPO	World Intellectual Property Organization
WTO	World Trade Organization

Preface

The process of globalisation and the emergence of a rules-based multi-lateral trading system pose significant challenges to local pharmaceutical industries in developing countries. With the advent of global patent protection for pharmaceuticals, developing countries are facing a significant dilemma. It is necessary for these countries to comply with international intellectual property standards while simultaneously protecting their local industries and, thus, ensuring an affordable supply of drugs. A better understanding of the nature of the Agreement on Trade Related Aspects of Intellectual Property Rights (TRIPS) and its components could help to raise awareness of the need for a comprehensive innovation policy. It is widely accepted that intellectual property rights (IPRs) are economic assets. Furthermore, they are necessary to develop world-class standards of innovation and creativity. This book argues that innovation is not driven by the presence of strong IPRs alone; it has many other components going far beyond the IPRs regime. Nonetheless, designing policies for the promotion of R&D and the building up of innovation capacities in developing countries requires a well-constructed patent regime. However, it also requires the implementation of broad-based science, technology and innovation policy initiatives aimed at promoting and facilitating capacity building for the enhanced absorption of new technologies.

To this end, this book investigates the concept of innovation and illustrates the crucial role that patent strategies play within processes of pharmaceutical innovation. Drawing on extensive country and company case studies, the key issues relevant to the revival of local pharmaceutical industries have been identified. Based on an understanding of the post-TRIPS environment and case studies of national innovation strategies, the following question has been addressed – to what extent can lessons from national experiences be transferred to current policy developments for innovation in the pharmaceutical industry in a developing country context?

The research findings aim to contribute significantly to the body of knowledge in relation to new developmental policies. Overall, it is hoped that these findings will promote innovation and ensure the sustainability of the local pharmaceutical industry in the developing world.

Acknowledgements

This book was produced with the support and assistance of many different institutions and individuals to whom I remain indebted. Without the benefit of these contributions its completion would not have been possible.

First and foremost, I owe a debt of gratitude to my PhD supervisor, Dr Duncan Matthews, for all of his encouragement, guidance and feedback from the beginning of the research project to the completion of my PhD thesis. His constant enthusiasm and never-ending support has enabled me to produce this book.

I am grateful to the Centre for Commercial Law Studies, Queen Mary, University of London for believing in my research and for financially supporting my studies. I would also like to express my gratitude to the Central Research Fund, University of London for the research grant that I received for my fieldwork. I would like to extend my thanks to the British Council and to the Swedish Institute for financing my master level studies in the UK and Sweden.

I am grateful to all the staff and my colleagues at the Centre for Commercial Law Studies for their support and assistance. As a loyal and regular user of the Intellectual Property Archive, I would particularly like to thank Malcolm Langley for his valuable assistance. I am indebted to my colleagues and friends in the Intellectual Property Archive for all the feedback and friendship that I have received over my doctoral studies. Finally I am grateful to all my family and friends for supporting me throughout my doctoral studies.

To my parents Necla and Cengiz Kılıç
for everything they have done for me

and to my sister Buket Kılıç Aslan
for her ongoing support, tolerance and affection

1. Introduction

Science is the most reliable guide in life

Mustafa Kemal Atatürk

BACKGROUND

The origins of pharmaceuticals can be traced back to ancient times. The practice of medicine was at a relatively advanced stage in ancient civilisations. Naturally occurring substances were often used to heal wounds and to relieve pain and treat infections. Medicines were compounded from a variety of substances including the remains of animals, plants, and minerals, as well as from other traditional sources, for example, honey.

The urbanisation process, which occurred following the Middle Ages, contributed to the development of the specialised field of apothecary, a method of formulating and dispensing *materia medica*[1] for healing purposes. The process of drug manufacturing was associated with apothecaries, who specialised in preparing and dispensing drugs according to recognised standards. In the centuries that followed, these apothecaries became known as 'chemists' and 'druggists', many of whom initiated the process of drug discovery in their back-street shops.

The Industrial Revolution, which began in the 18th century, changed the way of doing things dramatically. There was a clear shift from manual home productions to machine-based manufacturing that took place in factories. The development of new industries and factories coupled with the usage of new machinery contributed to the rising level of economic growth in Europe and North America.

The Industrial Revolution began initially in Great Britain. It then spread throughout other European countries such as Germany, France and Switzerland, and also reached North America. At this time, a significant amount of technology transfer took place, moving from Great Britain to all the latecomer countries. This technological and economic catch up was based on borrowing, copying and modelling. Flexible legal systems

---

[1] 'Materials of medicine' in Latin.

and supportive government policies appreciably contributed to the industrialisation process.

In the late 19th century, German dye companies emerged as the vanguard of a new generation of pharmaceutical companies. German companies initially transferred knowledge and technology from Great Britain. These companies imitated British manufacturing methods. Nevertheless, the German companies invested heavily in research and development (R&D). Importantly, the companies established research collaboration agreements with the universities. When compared to their British rivals, the German companies were more successful in using their capital efficiently and avoiding legal wrangles regarding patents. The German companies expanded their R&D activities into the chemistry area. The firms developed techniques in relation to synthesising and the development of chemical compounds. These efforts later led to the nucleus of the modern pharmaceutical industry. By the early 20th century, the German dye industry had become a global powerhouse that effectively dominated the world chemical and pharmaceutical market.

The rise of the German dye industry was a turning point in the history of the pharmaceutical industry. It prompted the investment of tremendous resources in pharmaceutical R&D in other countries. The discoveries of penicillin and insulin revolutionised the course of drug discovery. The emergence of new technological opportunities for drug development and increased R&D activities enabled American companies to grow into pharmaceutical world powers.

Over the course of the 20th century, most European countries as well as Japan had completed their industrialisation process. These countries made remarkable achievements in the areas of drug discovery and development. The pharmaceutical companies in the US, Western Europe and Japan became the dominant inventors and suppliers of the world drug market. This Western shift from a position of being a borrower to being an innovator created a global market for intellectual property rights (IPRs) protection. Patent protection, in particular, became vital to the continuation of the innovative pharmaceutical company model. The high profit margins associated with pharmaceuticals lent consistency and continuity to the industry. The respective national governments soon realised the industry's huge potential in creating an attractive growth market for investment, employment and exports. Thus, the pharmaceutical industries in developed countries started to play an influential role in developing social, political and economic issues of national and international importance.

During the last quarter of the 20th century, the social and economic distinction between industrialised developed countries, and the non-industrialised developing countries became much clearer. The scientific and technological gap between these two categories of country became apparent, particularly in the area of life sciences. Some of the developing countries invested a great deal of effort towards narrowing this widening gap by building up their local capacities. These countries explored alternative approaches as a means to close the gap and they pushed hard on the development side. At that time, it appeared that the best option was to follow the traditional development path taken by most of the developed countries. This traditional process includes a learning process that largely involves imitation. Over the course of the industrialisation process, all developed countries have ultimately relied heavily on imitation in order to build up their own technological capacities and to assimilate knowledge. At the time, conventional wisdom suggested that imitation was a stepping-stone to innovation. In fact, industrialised country experiences suggest that imitation or free riding is indeed an essential and primary part of the catching up process. Hence, as part of this process, the first thing for a country to do was to establish a legal environment conducive to the development goals of the country. Most of the developing country economies at the time were unable to deal with the increased population and health care costs. Due to an increasing number of health crises, access to affordable medicines emerged as an important policy issue. There was a constant public interest in serving national supply requirements.

To a certain extent, in an effort to facilitate imitation and borrowing and to cut increasing healthcare costs, most of the developing countries opted not to grant patents for pharmaceuticals products and/or processes.[2] The absence of patent protection assisted the progress of local pharmaceutical industries in developing countries. Companies within these countries specialised in generic medicines and built up capacities in drug manufacturing. Certain countries such as India and China became the exporters of generic drugs to Africa and other developing countries/continents.

Soon enough, the Western pharmaceutical companies experienced a significant decline in their global market sales. This led to trade deficits

---

[2] According to the study of WIPO in 1988, among 98 members of the Paris Convention for the Protection of Industrial Property, 49 members excluded pharmaceutical products from protection. *See,* Drahos P. (2002) 'Developing Countries and International Intellectual Property Standard-Setting', *JWIP,* V.5, pp. 765–89.

for developed countries, and the US economy was particularly affected. Eventually, what became known as the 'other drug war' came to the forefront of US policy. Using its strong lobbying power, the pharmaceutical industry wanted the US government to take measures against developing countries and the generic companies therein. Thus, the US government initiated trade sanctions against certain developing countries in order to force them to introduce and enforce IPRs protection for pharmacduticals. By then, the good policies of the past became the bad policies of the present day. Although the US was once itself an imitator country, in recent times the US industry has vowed to take a zero tolerance policy towards borrowing and imitating. The outcome of the bilateral dialogues was not successful. In other words, it was not sufficient enough to protect the global market for IPRs. Hence, the developed countries, led by the US, took the issue to the multinational setting in order to create an ambitious and comprehensive agreement on standards for the protection of IPRs of all kinds.

The Agreement on Trade Related Aspects of Intellectual Property Rights (TRIPS) was a package deal, whereby countries made certain concessions in exchange for trade benefits. It stands as the first multilateral treaty that sought to use IPRs as commodities in the area of international trade law. TRIPS set the standards for the global market of IPRs and it established the minimum standards for protection.

The placement of IPRs in trade agreements has led to strict restrictions on knowledge diffusion and transfer. The historical record of industrialised countries shows that traditionally knowledge was transferred freely across national borders, during the period when the developed countries were themselves developing countries. Nevertheless, after TRIPS, knowledge became a trade-related commodity, subject to strict rules. To put it differently, TRIPS changed the nature of the game to one where the winner takes all.

It was particularly controversial that TRIPS made patents available for pharmaceutical products. The advocates of the agreement have claimed that strong protection of pharmaceutical products is necessary to ensure greater technology transfers and foreign direct investment (FDI) in R&D in developing countries. Undoubtedly, such a confrontational approach ruled out the possibility of catching up using the traditional process of industrialisation through imitation and adaptation. This process is historically proven to be an effective strategy for developed countries.

Another emerging problem was the foreseeable negative consequences of a strengthened patent regime on healthcare costs and access to medicines. This was one of the unique circumstances that characterised the TRIPS negotiations. The developed countries stayed totally indifferent in relation to addressing the negative outcomes of a strong patent regime on developing countries. Even though there were attempts to overcome such problems, the global solution has remained elusive. Arguably, the solution is still at the mercy of developed countries and multinational pharmaceutical companies.

Nevertheless, this does not necessarily mean that developing countries have run out of options. At an individual country level, a degree of optimism still exists. Some developing countries have encouraged a sustainable local pharmaceutical industry. This provides heartening evidence that developing countries may yet be able to change the nature of the game to one where the winner does not necessarily take it all.

The relationship between patents, innovation and developing countries is a complex, multi-faceted and multi-disciplinary one. The impact of the IPRs regime on local innovation and economic development has been an issue of controversy in recent years. The role of IPRs in the innovation process has recently been challenged by economic studies. These studies have demonstrated that patents do not act as a determinant of R&D investments in many industrial fields. Moreover, the post-TRIPS experiences of developing countries have made it evident that the global IPRs alone have delivered little more than broken promises to developing countries.

Nevertheless, developing countries still have a number of options for surviving the post-TRIPS period and the potential to boost their current levels of pharmaceutical innovation. The research on IPRs and TRIPS to date has tended to focus on legal issues rather than practical issues, that is, the national innovation strategies and systems.

The national innovation system greatly contributes to the growth of the economy. This contribution includes increasing the flow of technology and knowledge and raising levels of socio-economic development. It has become evident that unless IPRs are well supported by other complementary socio-economic essentials, the existence of an IPRs regime is unlikely to support innovation and development within a country. Thus, countries are well advised to create effective innovation strategies that utilise the relevant TRIPS flexibilities, enhance their local capabilities and prioritise technology transfer and information flow.

To this end, this book sets out a number of recommendations on how this can be achieved. This is done in relation to the key development objectives of promoting the technological and scientific advancement of the country, enhancing local pharmaceutical innovation capacities, providing wide access to medicines and knowledge, safeguarding public health interests and fostering innovation.

2. Innovation

Over the last few decades, innovation has become a widely used concept. It is frequently associated with globalisation and economic prosperity. The current rules-based, multi-lateral trading system presents innovation as the global way forward. It is often stated that encouraging innovation is key to economic growth and sustainable development, especially for developing countries. Furthermore, with the emergence of the Agreement on Trade Related Aspects of Intellectual Property Rights (TRIPS), a great deal of attention has focused on the role of intellectual property rights (IPRs) and their impact on innovation and technology transfer. Patent rights, or IPRs more broadly, have become central to many issues surrounding innovation. The debate in this area has created a constant need for developing countries to enlarge their understanding of the concept of innovation including the necessary trade-off between innovation and patents.

Taking this into account, this chapter outlines the issues surrounding the concept of innovation. The objective is to highlight and present the economic rationales of patent rights and to discuss how these rationales apply to the context of innovation. The familiar argument is that patents create incentives to innovate; yet little is known about how those incentives work in practice. It is still an open question in the literature as to whether patents actually encourage and promote innovation. Although the empirical evidence is to some extent ambiguous, it might be interpreted to indicate a positive correlation in favour of the pharmaceutical industry.

Thus, this chapter, describes and critically appraises a number of studies reporting on (i) innovation, (ii) innovation and patents, and (iii) the economic effects of patents and how efficiently they work creating optimal incentives. Furthermore, the present chapter details the research methodology undertaken to identify and assess the relevant economic and legal literature.

THE CONCEPT OF INNOVATION

It is widely recognised that innovation is central to the welfare of humankind because the social returns to innovation exceed the private returns. In other words, the benefits of innovation to society as a whole greatly exceed the benefits to the firms that develop the innovative processes and products.[1]

The basic definition of innovation can be simply described, as making changes to what already exists. Innovation can, therefore, be considered as an interactive process in which the later steps are linked back to the earlier ones.[2] It encompasses a new idea brought to the market or into the production strategy. Successful innovation makes a significant contribution to economic growth. In a narrow sense, innovation can be characterised as the act of starting for the first time and later introducing something new (for example, initial technology that leads to high tech-technology).

To a large extent, the possession of technological knowledge regarding potential production arrangements, in conjunction with knowledge of the technology in use, comprises the given state of the arts. In this context, invention is described as producing technological changes in the knowledge available. However, innovation is defined as the application of existing knowledge to changes in the actual technological arrangements. Historically, the relationship between invention and innovation is usually examined in accordance with the three separate patterns of technological change. Before the Industrial Revolution, it was often the same person who performed both the invention and the innovation. This person also devised new techniques and applied them. With the introduction of labour-saving machinery and the growth of the patent system, separate persons started to carry out invention and innovation, that is, the inventor sold the rights to his invention to the innovator and the innovator manufactured and marketed it. The second half of the 20th century saw a substantial increase in research and development (R&D) investments and a large amount of technological change has originated from industrial

---

[1] Baker, J.B. (2007) 'Beyond Schumpeter vs. Arrow: How Antitrust Fosters Innovation', AAI Working Paper 07–04, p. 2 available at http://ssrn.com/abstract=1103623. *See* Mansfield, E. (1987) 'Microeconomics of technological Innovation' in B. Guile and H. Brooks (eds) *Technology and Global Industry*, Washington DC, National Academy Press, pp. 307–26.

[2] Lundvall, B. (2002) *Innovation, Growth and Social Cohesion*, Cheltenham, UK and Northampton, MA, USA, Edward Elgar, p. 43.

R&D activities. Hence, today, many economic theories assume that the individual firm invents and innovates as a part of normal business activity.[3]

Economists have long argued that there is a sharp distinction between invention and innovation. According to Schumpeter, widely cited as the undisputed godfather of technological innovation, invention and innovation are not synonymous terms because 'the making of the invention and the carrying out of the corresponding innovation are, economically and sociologically, two entirely different things'. He asserts that even though they often interact, they are never the same, and innovations are usually more important than inventions.[4] The Schumpeterian theory focuses solely on the innovator, not on the inventor. While it considers innovation to be a distinctly economic process and a matter of business activity, it places invention outside the economic realm.

Along with the Schumpeterian theory, economists since Schumpeter typically distinguish between invention and innovation. Invention is usually taken as a starting point. It often refers to the act of finding new things whereas innovation is considered as a process of getting new things done.[5] As such, the term invention refers to a technical idea that can lead to new products or that can be used to solve an industrial problem. Nonetheless, innovation describes the process of introducing a new technology – in the usual case, the arrival of an invention in a commercialised form on the market.[6] For Maskus, invention refers to the creation of new knowledge, and innovation, or commercialisation more

[3]   Solo, C.S. (1951) 'Innovation in the Capitalist Process: A Critique of the Schumpeterian Theory' *The Quarterly Journal of Economics*, V. 65, N.3, p. 417; Dasgupta P. (1986) 'The theory of Technological Competition' in J. Stiglitz and G. Mathewson (eds) *New Developments in the Analysis of Market Structure*, Cambridge, MIT Press, pp. 519–48; Merges R. (1988) 'Economic Perspectives on Innovation: Commercial Success and Patent Standards', *California Law Review*, V. 76, I.4, p. 843.

[4]   Schumpeter, J. (1939) *Business Cycles*, V. I–II, New York, McGraw-Hill, pp. 84–6.

[5]   Kingston, W. (2009) 'Why Patents Need Reform, Some Suggestions for It' in C. Arup and W. van Caenegem (eds) *Intellectual Property Policy Reform: Fostering Innovation and Development*, Cheltenham, UK and Northampton, MA, USA, Edward Elgar, p. 22.

[6]   Merges, supra note 3, p. 845.

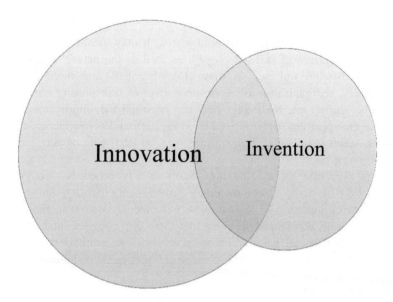

Figure 2.1   Invention and innovation

broadly, includes development of marketable products from that know-ledge.[7] However, this does not imply that the firm that achieves success with an innovation is the first to perfect a particular invention.[8]

Schumpeterian theory describes innovation as the truly dynamic element in the economy, that is, it is the source of credit, interest, and profit as well as business fluctuations.[9] The process of innovation includes several stages such as the gathering of new ideas, and the transforming of those ideas into new marketable commodities. It also includes spreading and, at times, sharing the use of those ideas and commodities.[10] In a broader sense, innovation means establishing a new production function, covering the cases of new commodities as well as those of a new form of organisation, for example, a merger, expanding into new markets, and so on.[11]

---

[7]   Maskus, K., S. Dougherty and A. Mertha (2005) 'Intellectual Property Rights and Economic Development in China' in C. Fink and K. Maskus (eds) *Intellectual Property and Development*, Oxford, Oxford University Press, p. 299.

[8]   Merges, supra note 3, p. 860.

[9]   Solo, supra note 3, p. 427.

[10]   Roberts, E. (1987) *Generating Technological Innovation*, Oxford, Oxford University Press, pp. 3–7.

[11]   Schumpeter, supra note 4, pp. 84–6: Schumpeter, J. (1939) *A Theoretical, Historical and Statistical Analysis of the Capitalist Process*, Vol.1, New York, McGraw Hill, p. 87.

Innovation may entail redesigning goods, altering the production process, the composition of material inputs. It may include assessing the kinds and mixture of skills deployed, as well as the nature of upstream and downstream linkages. It may also offer new and more efficient machinery, reorganisation of work, new ways of transporting inputs and outputs, and so on. No matter how big or small the improvements are across the spectrum, they all lead to innovation and economic activity;[12] 'when taken together ... [innovation] may be [the] true unsung hero of economic growth'.[13]

It is also true to say that innovation usually proceeds through the interaction of many actors including government, industry, universities and research institutions. Innovation simultaneously shapes market structure. Theoretical research indicates that there is a complex interaction of technical and social factors. These factors include market structures as well as the presence of scientific and technological knowledge.[14]

Innovation and Imitation

It is often suggested that there is a trade-off between innovation and imitation. Recent evidence suggests that in order to stimulate economic development and/or maximise social welfare, there exists some optimal mixture of innovation and imitation. This mixture tends to vary, depending on country characteristics and preferences.[15] The trade-off between innovation and imitation highly depends on the demand of consumers, the economic environment, the probability of success and the strategies of rival firms.[16]

The process of imitation includes imitating, copying or counterfeiting. According to Schumpeter; imitation refers to the diffusion of innovation

---

[12]   Trajtenberg M. (2005) 'Innovation Policy for Development: An Overview', STE Program Working Paper, STE-WP-34-200, p. 5.
[13]   Mokyr, J. (2005) 'The Great Synergy: The European Enlightenment as a Factor in Modern Economic Growth', Society for Economic Dynamics, Meeting Papers, 179; Trajtenberg, supra note 12, p. 5.
[14]   Saha, T. (1980) *Research, Development and Technological Innovation*, Lanham, Lexington Books, pp. 116–18.
[15]   Park, W. (2002) 'Patent Rights and Economic Freedom: Friend or Foe?', *Journal of Private Enterprise*, V.18, N.1, p. 89.
[16]   Mohtadi H. and S. Ruediger (2009) 'Imitation, Innovation and Threshold Effects: A Game Theoretic Approach', available at http://www.uwm.edu/~rue diger/Imitation,%20Innovation%20and%20Threshold%20Effects%20A%20Game %20Theoretic%20Approach%20Mohtadi%20Ruediger%202009.pdf, p. 3.

where innovation is defined as the commercialisation of invention, which is a purely physical set of creation and discovery.[17]

There are two main features underlying imitation; first, the imitator may make no payment to the innovator and second, the development costs incurred by the imitator are typically lower than those of the innovator.[18] Economic analysis has suggested that, considering the cost of R&D, it is less expensive for a small firm to imitate another firm's innovative activity. However, another economic study conducted on marginal costs of the imitator and innovator firms shows that the marginal cost of the imitator (non-innovating) company will usually be higher than those of the innovating firm. Because the innovating firm is always a step ahead of the imitator company, although innovating poses a fixed cost for the innovating firm, the marginal cost will be lower.[19]

For example, Mansfield et al. found that about 60 per cent of the patented successful innovations in their sample were imitated.[20] Furthermore, in a survey conducted among industry R&D personnel, Richard Levin et al. found that even major patented innovation could be imitated within three or fewer years.[21]

It should be noted that the relative effectiveness of patents and the subsequent risk of imitation might differ across industries. For inventions that are difficult to reverse-engineer such as aeroplane designs, patents inevitably become costly because disclosure raises the risk of imitation. Furthermore, even the safest patent expires at the end of the statutory term. Nevertheless, for inventions that are easy to reverse-engineer, such as drugs where disclosure is imminent with or without patenting, patents offer great benefits by providing exclusivity at least for a limited period.[22]

In addition to high marginal costs, the empirical evidence shows that imitation reduces rewards. It also has a diminishing effect on incentives to innovate. A weak IPRs regime in developing countries tends to

---

[17] See, Kim, L. (1997) *Imitation to Innovation*, Boston, Harvard Business Press, p. 13.

[18] Katz, M. and C. Sharipo, (1987) 'R&D Rivalry with Licensing and Imitation', *AER*, V.77, N.3, p. 403.

[19] Mohtadi and Ruedinger: supra note 16, pp. 9–10.

[20] Mansfield, E., M. Schwartz and S. Wagner (1981) 'Imitation Costs and Patents – An Empirical-Study' *Economic Journal*, V.91, N.364, pp. 907–18.

[21] Levin, R. et al. (1987) 'Appropriating the Returns from Industrial Research and Development', *Brookings Papers on Economic Activity*, pp. 783–820.

[22] Moser, P. (2005) 'How do Patent Laws Influence Innovation? Evidence from Nineteenth-Century World Fairs', NBER, Working Paper 9909, available at http://www.nber.org/papers/w9909, p. 14.

increase the probability of imitation; furthermore, the introduction of IPRs lowers the profits retained from imitation and places considerable pressures on imitative firms in developing economies.

Typically, IPRs are enforced by restricting the imitation of products. The economic study by Futagami et al. provides evidence of the value of IPRs and their long-term effects on innovation. The study shows that governments in developing countries may promote innovation and technology transfer by strengthening IPRs protection.[23] Nevertheless, there are also some empirical economic findings that identify the economic conditioning factors regarding the relationship between imitation and innovation. Hence, it is required that specific economic conditions should be present in each country in order for the country to benefit from strengthening the IPRs regimes.[24]

Schumpeterian Theory of Innovation: Monopoly or Competition?

With few exceptions, the Schumpeterian theory of innovation has been long neglected by legal scholars and has not received any sustained attention. For Merges, the reason could be that the economic analysis and related legal literature usually focuses on microeconomic modelling. Nonetheless, the Schumpeterian perspective appears to be well suited for examining the relationship and interaction between legal rules, specifically patent laws, and innovation.[25]

Schumpeterian innovation theory rests on three major principles:

(1)   A continuous process of creative destruction in which innovative technologies and organisational structures constantly threaten the status quo, something that tends to characterise the capitalist economies;
(2)   Technological innovation provides the opportunity for temporary monopoly profits, and the Western economies owe much of their existence to this linkage; and
(3)   Large firms are more likely to keep the engine of technological innovation; therefore an industry structure encouraging innovation

---

[23]   Futagami, K., T. Iwaisako and H. Tanaka (2007) 'Innovation, Licensing and Imitation: The Effects of Intellectual Property Rights Protection and Industrial Policy', Discussion Papers 07–05, OSIPP, available at http://www2.econ.osaka-u.ac.jp/library/global/dp/0705.pdf, pp. 2–28.
[24]   Mohtadi and Ruediger, supra note 16, p. 11.
[25]   Merges, supra note 3, p. 845.

and competition among large firms instead of small ones appears to be the best structure for fostering technological innovation.[26]

According to Schumpeter, there is nothing like perfect competition to create optimal incentives for innovation. The concept of perfect competition fits very well with mathematical modelling. However, it neglects the dynamics of creative destruction. He further notes, 'perfect competition is and always has been temporarily suspended whenever anything new is being introduced – automatically or by measures devised for the purpose – even in otherwise perfectly competitive conditions'. He asserts that the economic theory tends to put so much emphasis on the analysis of price that it neglects the essential elements, which counts as the competition from the new commodity, that is, the new technology, the new source of supply, and the new type of organisation.[27]

For Schumpeterian theory monopolies[28] generally favour innovation. However, competitive market structures and innovation processes tend to contradict each other. Schumpeter argued that competitive market structures are not compatible with innovation, as they do not provide the innovator with a market environment in which he can appropriate enough of the returns from innovation to justify his R&D investments.

It is widely known that Adam Smith, usually cited as the father of modern economists, vigorously opposed monopoly power. He saw it as detrimental to the operation of the invisible hand. He was, however, one of the first economists to strongly emphasise the need for limited monopolies to promote innovation requiring substantial up-front investment and risk.[29]

Many economists welcomed Schumpeter's challenge to orthodox competition theory which regards perfect competition as the most conducive

---

[26] Schumpeter, supra note 11, pp. 81–106; Merges, supra note 3, p. 843; Menell, P. (2003) 'Intellectual Property: General Theories', Levine's WP Archive (618897000000000707), p. 135.

[27] Schumpeter, supra note 11, p. 105.

[28] Schumpeter describes monopolists as single sellers whose markets are not open to the intrusion of would-be producers of the same commodity and of actual producers of similar ones or, more technically, only those single sellers who face a given demand schedule that is severely independent of their own action as well as any reactions to their action by other concerns. See, Schumpeter, supra note 11, p. 99.

[29] Mennell, supra note 26, p. 131; Smith, A. (1776) *The Wealth of Nations*, Oxford, Clarendon Press. pp. 277–8.

means of achieving efficiency in the market.[30] Scherer and Ross, however, were critical of Schumpeterian theorists because of their sole focus on powerful monopolies and tightly knit cartels, in relation to the model of dynamic efficiency. According to Scherer and Ross, rapid technical progress entails a subtle blend of competition and monopoly, with more emphasis on competition than monopoly power. Furthermore, the role of monopolistic elements diminishes when rich technological opportunities exist.[31]

It is, therefore, arguable that a short-term monopoly is very likely to encourage innovation. Even for Schumpeter a 'monopoly position is no cushion to sleep on. As it can be gained, so it can be retained only by alertness and energy'.[32] In doing so, a monopolist would be in better position compared to a new market entrant. The empirical evidence shows that a monopolist, by introducing a new product to the market, will also be able to divert profits from his old product. Nevertheless, it should be noted that the gain of the monopolist with the new product would be much higher than the gain of the new entrant, as the monopolist would be co-ordinating the prices of both products and pricing the old product in a way that internalises the effect on the new one.[33]

Thus, in order to stimulate innovation after an invention, IPRs create ex post monopolies. Hence, Geroski observes that it is the promise of monopoly – not its actual existence – that stimulates innovation in this line of thinking.[34]

On the other hand, economic theories based on imperfect competition support the view that much invention is spontaneous. Hence, invention is forthcoming without the provision of a short-term monopoly, or IPRs more broadly. Plant, for instance, argues that first-mover advantages,

---

[30]   'Although economists who study innovation generally accept Schumpeter's first two principles, most empirical studies of the relationship between market structure and research and development expenditures reject the linkage between monopoly power and disproportionately large investments in innovation', Scherer, M. and D. Ross (1990) *Industrial Market Structure and Economic Performance,* 3rd edn, Boston, Houghton Mifflin pp. 614–60; Menell, supra note 26, p. 135.

[31]   Scherer and Ross *Ibid.*; Menell, supra note 26, p. 135.

[32]   Schumpeter, supra note 11, p. 102.

[33]   Chen, Y. and M. Schwartz (2010) 'Product Innovation Incentives: Monopoly vs. Competition', Georgetown University Working Paper, 29 January 2010.

[34]   Geroski, P.A. (2005) 'Intellectual Property Rights, Competition Policy and Innovation: Is There a Problem?', SCRIPTed, V.2, available at http://www.law.ed.ac.uk/ahrc/script-ed/vol2-4/geroski.asp.

imperfections in markets and other factors provide inventors and publishers with sufficient rewards to create and market their works in the absence of IPRs. Patent protection, therefore, would lead to an over-investment in R&D that could result in discoveries that fall within the patent domain. This, in turn, would be seen as wastefully diverting resources from more appropriate endeavours.[35]

Notwithstanding this opinion, an influential 20th century economist, Arrow, argues that it is the competition rather than the monopoly that promotes innovation. For Arrow, in a competitive market environment supported by exclusive IPRs, competitive firms are likely to devote more attention towards R&D efforts when compared to monopolists, who will not process innovations in all cases.[36] Hence, monopolist firms tend to innovate less than competitive firms because they have more to lose. Subsequently, this gives rise to a limitation on the incentive of the monopolist to innovative. This is widely cited as the 'Arrow effect' or the 'replacement effect' to the extent that the monopolist replaces himself rather than developing new business. On the other hand, a competitive firm is likely to be more innovative because it aims to take away much of the business previously conducted by rival firms.[37] However, it must be emphasised that in a market environment where firms compete by offering differentiated products, a competitive firm may also face a replacement effect that reduces its incentive to develop a new product. This is the case even though the effect tends to be smaller than for a monopolist.[38]

In this context, the empirical economic research produced four key principles highlighting the correlation between competition and innovation output. First and foremost, competition itself, specifically in relation to innovation, encourages innovation. That is to say, firms try harder to develop new products or processes. Consequently, these firms benefit from the resulting patent exclusivity. This dynamic gives rise to patent races between the firms.[39] Schumpeter, however, argues that the fact that

---

[35] Menell, supra note 26, p. 132.

[36] Gilbert, J. (2006) 'Competition and Innovation', *Journal of Industrial Organization Education* V.1, I.1, available at: http://works.bepress.com/richard_gilbert/15, p. 14.

[37] Baker, supra note 1, p. 7.

[38] Gilbert, supra note 36, p. 13.

[39] Baker, supra note 1, p. 7.

there is a possibility that a successful innovator will drive competitors out of business always constitutes an obstacle for competition.[40]

The second key principle states that competition encourages R&D investments that are aimed at escaping competition. In other words, competition regarding an existing product market encourages firms to engage in R&D activities in order to lower costs, improve quality or develop better products.[41] Therefore, a firm has less incentive to innovate, if the *ex ante* market is less competitive.

For the third principle, the rate of innovation in fact depends very much on the nature of the market. Innovative activity is likely to arise if the market is more competitive *ex ante* and the less competitive it is *ex post*.[42] Under these market conditions, where more innovation is unlikely to allow a firm to escape competition, and the firm would instead be expected to face higher levels of competition, it would have less incentive to pursue innovations in the first place.[43]

Finally, the fourth principle is based on the idea of a pre-emption incentive. A pre-emption incentive rests on an assumption that a firm will have an extra incentive to innovate new products or processes itself, thereby pre-empting potential rivals. This kind of incentive is found to be stronger than Arrow's replacement effect, particularly for monopolist firms, when compared with competitive firms. Due to the nature of the market, a monopolist firm has a greater incentive to invest heavily in order to pre-empt the entry of his rivals by being the first to patent a new technology. Furthermore, it should be noted that pre-emption is more likely to occur in markets where the dynamics of R&D competition provide a technological leader with an unassailable position in the race to patent a new technology.[44]

Thus, there is still an unresolved question in the economic literature, that is, is it the presence of a monopoly or the presence of competition that does more to promote innovation? While the economists are still debating the issue, it is possible to say that economic research has at least refined our understanding of key interactions. For instance, it has

[40]   Nelson, R. (2006) 'Reflections of David Teece's "Profiting from Technological Innovation ..."', *Research Policy*, V.35, p. 1108.
[41]   Baker, supra note 1, p. 7.
[42]   *See,* Geroski, supra note 34.
[43]   Baker, supra note 1, p. 8.
[44]   'In some circumstances, a small lead in the innovation race can be enough to render competition ineffective, and adding more competitors to the R&D race may have little or no effect on the pace of innovation by the firm that occupies the technological frontier', Gilbert, supra note 36, pp. 14–15.

identified the central role of IPRs to many issues surrounding the incentives to innovate debate. Therefore, before determining what exactly spurs innovation in either case, there is a constant need to define the interaction between IPRs and innovation. Because whether it is the presence of a monopoly or the presence of competition, all the firms must fight in order to be the market leader. In this respect it is vital that firms have a measure of market exclusivity. Thus, it is arguable that patents, or IPRs more broadly, appear as a crucial feature of innovation.

INNOVATION AND INTELLECTUAL PROPERTY PROTECTION

From an economist's point of view, the objective of IPRs is to preserve incentives to innovate. Some utilitarian economists[45] have suggested that IPRs provide the prospect of reward. This, in turn, promotes creative and technological advances by providing increased incentives to invest in invention and to further develop new ideas.[46] These incentives maximise the difference between the value of the invention and the cost of its creation.[47]

Thus, IPRs improve resource allocation by enabling people who create ideas, products, and processes to capture more of the economic value of their creative activity. The protection granted by IPRs is traditionally regarded as necessary to stimulate innovation. The link between IPRs and innovation, therefore, has been the subject of much empirical investigation.

In this context, the 'IPRs-induced incentives to invest' rationale (a widely acknowledged assumption that establishes links between IPRs and innovation) was developed, based on two assertions. First, without effective incentives the invention inducement would be weakened. Second, IPRs are the cheapest and most effective way for a society to produce incentives.[48] Furthermore, it has also been argued that the legal

---

[45]   Including Jeremy Bentham, Adam Smith, and John Stuart Mill.

[46]   Andersen, B. (2006) 'If "Intellectual Property Rights" is the Answer, What is the Question? Revisiting the Patent Controversies', in Andersen, B. (ed.) *Intellectual Property Rights, Innovation, Governance and the Institutional Environment*, Cheltenham, UK and Northampton, MA, USA, Edward Elgar, p. 118.

[47]   West, J. (2006) 'Does Appropriability Enable or Retard Innovation', in H. Chesbrough et al. (eds) *Open Innovation: Researching a New Paradigm*, Oxford, Oxford University Press, p. 111.

[48]   Andersen, supra note 46, p. 118.

protection of IPRs creates incentives to use resources more efficiently through investment in planning and development.[49]

The most obvious defect of this rationale lies in the assumption that IPRs do not necessarily provide incentives to use and allocate resources more efficiently. It has been contended that a system with strong IPRs protection may result in more resources being devoted to expensive inventive and innovative R&D efforts, which are aimed at avoiding a technological region that is occupied by a patent holder. Thus, this kind of concentration could potentially lead to an increase of costs and inefficient technological trajectories.[50] Likewise, Arrow suggested that in some cases the patent system tends to under-allocate available resources for innovation. His argument rests on the assumption that under monopolistic conditions the incentive to innovate will be lower than under a competitive market.[51]

Patents have historically been viewed as the strongest possible form of intellectual property (IP) protection. Furthermore, two important goals are identified as underlying the patent system. First, patents promote R&D. Second, patents encourage the disclosure of inventions, so that others can use and build upon their research results.[52] Therefore, it is widely held by economists that a lack of patents results in under-investment in R&D. Without patents, innovation occurs only via trade secrecy. Accordingly, an extra incentive to invent, disclose and innovate is often needed. A patent right can help to fill this need.[53]

The Economic Rationales for the Patent System

The doctrine of patents is usually presented as part of a widely shared utilitarian baseline. This economic theory provides a viable theoretical legitimacy for the coherence of the patent system. In the course of the wider discussion undertaken here, the perceived economic rationales for

---

[49]   Posner's (1992) 'dynamic efficiency argument' reads that in a world without IPRs, inventors are not encouraged to conduct their inventive activities, as without an IPR they would not be able to recover the costs of R&D or expect any special reward, *See,* Andersen, supra note 46, p. 125.

[50]   Winter states that inefficiencies might occur if patents are granted to inventors at an early stage of technological trajectory. *See,* Andersen, supra note 46, p. 126.

[51]   *Ibid,* p. 127.

[52]   Gallini, N. (1992) 'Patent Policy and Costly Imitation', *RAND: Journal of Economics*, V.23, N.1, 1992, p. 52.

[53]   Granstrand, O. 'Intellectual Property Rights for Governance in and of Innovation Systems' in Andersen, supra note 46, p. 317.

the patent system need to be examined thoroughly. This is necessary in order to reach a better understanding of the role that the patent system plays within the innovation system.

The 'incentive to invent' has been widely accepted as the classic function of the patent system since the 15th century. This theory focuses on the impact of the patent system on invention and R&D.[54] As a virtue of the patent system, the theory holds that in the absence of patent protection, there would be a radical decrease in the number of inventions. According to this theory, increased patent protection leads to increased R&D. Further to this, by granting temporary exclusivity rights to inventors, the government delegates the R&D decision and investment.[55]

The roots of this theory can be found in Schumpeter's notion of innovation. Recall Schumpeter and, of course, his well-known theory that monopolies are necessary in order to create the economic incentive to invent. Schumpeter regards monopoly profits as the only possible way of rewarding innovators for undertaking costly and risky inventive activity. It follows that the incentive to invent is equated with monopoly profits achieved by an invention.[56]

In the context of today's modern, knowledge-based economy some commentators have claimed that Schumpeterian theory is outdated. Hence, today's competitive market necessitates routinised inventive activities, which actually offer many prizes for competitors. Baumol illustrates this with an R&D race between two competing firms. In a two-firm R&D race, the winner receives the highest payoff. This payoff comes usually through the successful patent. Nonetheless, the other firm whose R&D comes close to that of the winner is able to obtain compensation commensurate with the value of its performance.[57]

As such, Kitch's 'prospect system' fits neatly into a theory of 'incentive to invent'. For Kitch, the patent system encourages further commercialisation and efficient use of as yet unrealised ideas. Kitch

---

[54] *Ibid,* p. 319.

[55] Encaoua, D., D. Guellec and C. Martínez (2005) 'Patent Systems for Encouraging Innovation: Lessons from Economic Analysis', available at http://www.uwm.edu/~ruediger/Imitation,%20Innovation%20and%20Threshold%20Effects%20A%20Game%20Theoretic%20Approach%20Mohtadi%20Ruediger%202009.pdf, p. 3.

[56] Pretnar, B. (2003) 'The Economic Impact of Patents in a Knowledge-Based Market Economy', *International Review of Intellectual Property and Competition Law*, V.34, N.8, p. 888.

[57] Baumol, W. (2002) *The Free-Market Innovation Machine*, Princeton, Princeton University Press, p. 4.

applies classic property theory to patents and he argues that patents will provide incentives to inventors just as privatising land will encourage the owner to make efficient use of it. This theory focuses particularly on the role of a single patentee in co-ordinating the development, implementation and improvement of an invention, as in the case of the monopolies in Schumpeterian theory. Drawing on the Schumpeterian tradition, Kitch considers invention as being the first step in a long and expensive process of innovation instead of an activity, which comes close to producing a final product. However, contrary to Schumpeterian theory, he ascertains that the vast majority of IPRs do not confer a monopoly power. Kitch does stress the importance of strong rights as he sees these as necessary to preclude competition and effectively encourage innovation. For Kitch, patents constitute the economic incentive to invent and thus they should stand alone. Further to this, patents should be broad and should also confer total control over current as well as future inventions.[58]

On the other hand, recent analysis by Bessen and Meurer suggests that the patent system provides only a minimal incentive in relation to public R&D. They argue that most public firms, which perform the lion's share of R&D, do not receive positive incentives from the patent system. According to their research, the total investment in R&D was $160 billion in 1999. Of this sum, public firms invested $150 billion. Despite this, only 45 per cent of the patents granted to US residents were obtained by the public firms.[59] The findings of Bessen and Meurer lead them to conclude that 'it seems unlikely that patents today are an effective policy instrument to encourage innovation overall'.[60]

Economic theory has long recognised that the exclusivity provided by the patent system protects innovators and blocks imitators from the invention. This guarantees an innovator the net social return on R&D expenditure. In this context, the 'incentive-to-innovate' theory attempts to establish a link between innovation and competition. It follows that patents induce firms to carry an invention to market. It refers to a post-invention environment and it gives existing patents an ongoing motivational role to spur on commercialisation.[61] In a similar vein,

---

[58]   Burk, D.L. and M.A. Lemley (2003) 'Policy Levers in Patent Law', *Virginia Law Review*, Vol. 89, pp. 1619–27.

[59]   Bessen, J. and M. Meurer (2008) *Patent Failure*, Princeton, Princeton University Press, p. 142.

[60]   *Ibid*, p. 216.

[61]   Summers, T. (2003) 'The Scope of Utility in the Twenty-First Century: New Guidance for Gene-Related Patents', *Georgetown Law Review*, V.91, I.2, p. 492.

Mazzoleni and Nelson have suggested that the anticipation of receiving a patent provides motivation for undertaking useful research. They refer to this as 'invention motivation' theory.[62] However, as a counter argument, the suggestion that there is a correlation between the availability of patents and the incentive to innovate is not simple or universal. The patent system interacts with industries at several points in the innovation process and, thus, there is a complex relationship between patents and innovation. This industry-specific relationship, present at each stage of the patent process, embodies certain stages and motives. These motives and actions include deciding to seek protection, obtaining a patent and setting the scope of the patent in order to decide whether to enforce a patent and determine the litigation process.[63]

All of this supports Arrow's proposition that patents, or IPRs more broadly, are necessary in order to create *ex ante* incentives, as opposed to *ex post* control rights. In the context of patents, adopting a narrower circumscription to particular implementations of an invention is therefore required in order to provide rights that offer less than monopoly control.[64]

Historically, inventions and their exploitations were considered necessary to secure industrial progress. It has been argued that in the event of there being a lack of protection against imitation, inventors are more likely to keep their invention secret. In this scenario, the secret will sometimes die with the inventor and thus, society will lose the new art. Therefore, society must contact the inventor in order to provide for the disclosure of the invention. In this context, the theory of social contract[65] rests upon the assumption that there is a contract between society and the inventor. This agreement grants the inventor a limited period of exclusivity in return for the disclosure of the invention, so that it will be made available to society.[66]

---

[62] Mazzoleni, R. and R. Nelson (1998) 'Economic Theories about the Benefits and Costs of Patents', *Journal of Economic Issues*, V.32, N. 4.

[63] Burk and Lemley, supra note 58, p. 1624.

[64] *Ibid.*, pp. 1653–7.

[65] A 'positive theory of the social contract'. The rationale is basically that justice requires that society compensate and reward its people for their services in proportion to what they cost and how useful they are to society. Those believing in the IPR system here consider that the most appropriate way to secure inventors is by issuing IPRs.' *See,* Andersen, supra note 46, pp. 417–42.

[66] Penrose, E.T. (1951) *The Economics of the International Patent System*, Baltimore, The John Hopkins Press, p. 32.

The legislature establishes patents for both private and public goods primarily by providing exclusivity to the inventors, with the law giving a private-good effect. This leads to Schumpeter's innovation phase, which is based on the presence of a monopoly. At the same time, the disclosure requirement of patents fits well with Schumpeter's diffusion phase. To put it differently, patent information becomes a pure public good for a zero price, irrelevant of whether it is used for generating further knowledge or not. This is called the public good effect of a patent. This public good effect leads to innovation-based competition in the market. The most solid arguments for rewarding innovation are built precisely on an understanding of these simultaneous private- and public-good effects.[67]

In fact, it can be argued that one of the important functions of the patent system is to contribute to the growth of the public domain by encouraging the disclosure of inventions. This disclosure should be sufficient to enable a skilled person in the art to reproduce a patented invention. Thus, 'the incentive-to-disclose' theory rests on the impact of secrecy for the progress of science. It is concerned with the impact of disclosure on R&D as a way of facilitating stimulation, co-ordination and diffusion.[68] In line with this, Mazzoleni et al. have developed the 'invention dissemination' theory in which patents induce inventors to disclose their inventions, when otherwise they would rely on secrecy. Therefore, this theory aims to facilitate expanding both wide knowledge and the use of inventions.[69]

Nonetheless, such economic arguments, which have the aim of justifying the existence of patents on disclosure theory, have been subject to a number of criticisms. For instance, it has been argued that it is not possible to keep inventions secret for very long. Furthermore, even if the knowledge has been kept secret, inventions derive from the needs of the society and the current state of the art. Hence, it is likely that others would come up with similar ideas and inventions. Finally, according to the critics of this kind of economic justification, the excessive litigation which occurs as a result of the patent system, and which is assumed to be an unavoidable by-product of the system,[70] creates a handicap for

---

[67] Pretnar, supra note 56, p. 891.

[68] Granstrand, supra note 53, p. 319.

[69] Mazzoleni and Nelson, supra note 62.

[70] 'The problem of excessive litigation has plagued the patent system in most countries for over a hundred years and many authorities have concluded that it is an unavoidable by-product of the system. It was bitterly complained of in England in the 1850s' Penrose, supra note 66, p. 33.

inventors. Thus, it is argued that inventors tend to apply for patents only in cases where secrecy is impossible.[71]

Mazzoleni et al. propose two additional functions for patents. First, patents induce commercialisation and second, they enable exploration control. The 'commercialisation induce' theory rests upon the assumption that patents on inventions induce the needed investments to develop and commercialise them. On the other hand, the exploration theory considers patents as a means to enable the orderly exploration of broad prospects.[72]

For Penrose, the patent system relies on the assumption that it is desirable to encourage invention for its own sake. Therefore, a monopoly privilege is the best way of doing this, because it does not necessarily require exploitation of the invention.[73]

In this context, the economic rationales of the patent system appear to confirm the received conventional wisdom, that is, the existence of patents promotes innovation. Nevertheless, the differences in the way various industries value patents casts considerable doubt on the effective utilisation of patents in order to optimally encourage innovation.

PATENTS AND INNOVATION: EMPIRICAL STUDIES

Given the important role attributed to the patent regime, as a catalyst for innovation over the centuries, very little is actually known about the economic effects of it. Further to this, little is known regarding how efficient it is as a system for creating optimal incentives. Historically economists have devoted limited attention to the patent system. As a result, economic analyses of the patent system have been persistently neglected although the patent system has developed primarily to promote economic ends.[74] It has long been claimed that economists have virtually relinquished the field, while patent lawyers were glad to see them go. Machlup describes the lack of economic analysis in relation to the patent system as a deplorable situation. Hence, it is not possible to argue the relative merits or demerits of various features of the patent system without undertaking further research to analyse the social costs and benefits involved.[75]

---

[71] *Id.*
[72] Mazzoleni and Nelson, supra note 62.
[73] Penrose, supra note 66, p. 17.
[74] *Ibid*, p.xi.
[75] *Ibid*, p.vii.

Over the last century, economists gradually realised the importance of the issue and this promoted further research. In fact, several studies have been conducted involving different industries regarding the effectiveness of patents as a means of promoting innovation. R&D expenditure is usually used to measure input into innovative activity whereas patent applications are considered to be a measure of the output.[76] Over the past decades, a significant amount of economic research has been devoted to investigating the firms' decisions to use patents in appropriating returns from inventions. Pigou had long recognised the problem of appropriability, that is, establishing a balance between economic returns and legal protection to stimulate further invention. He noted the basic framework of modern welfare economics and asserted that patent laws bring together private net product and marginal social net product. He further noted that 'by offering the prospect of reward for certain types of invention they do not, indeed, appreciably stimulate inventive activity, which is, for the most part, spontaneous, but they do direct it into channels of great usefulness'.[77]

In a similar vein, the data collected from both the innovation surveys and R&D studies showed that patents are judged to be relatively ineffective as an appropriation mechanism. The available evidence further suggests that strengthening patent protection is likely to restrict spillovers and, therefore, diminish subsequent R&D investments rather than increase R&D expenditures.

The first research in this area was conducted by Mansfield, Schwartz and Wagner in 1981, using data from 48 product innovations. Their research estimates that almost 90 per cent of pharmaceutical innovations and 20 per cent of chemical, electronics and machinery innovations would not have been introduced without patents.[78]

The subsequent 1986 empirical study by Mansfield was an industry survey which discussed a 'what if' scenario. The scenario had two elements:

(1)   To what extent would the rate of development and commercialisation of inventions decline in the absence of patent protection?

---

[76]   UNIDO, (2006) 'The Role of Intellectual Property Rights in Technology Transfer and Economic Growth: Theory and Evidence', Vienna, Working Paper, p. 17.

[77]   Pigou, A.C. (1924) *The Economics of Welfare*, London, Macmillan; Menell, supra note 26, p. 132.

[78]   Mansfield et al., supra note 20, p. 915.

(2)   To what extent do firms make use of the patent system and what differences exist among firms and industries and, over time, in the propensity of patents?

Mansfield worked on a random sample of 100 US companies, which had a considerable amount of investment in R&D activities and asked the R&D managers to estimate what percentage of their firm's innovations would not have been developed without patent protection. The results of the survey showed that 60 per cent of pharmaceutical and 38 per cent of chemical inventions would not have been developed in the absence of patent protection. Nevertheless, the absence of patent protection would not have had a high impact on the innovativeness in other industries. Regarding the lack of patent protection, there would have been only 17 per cent less inventions in machinery, 12 per cent less in fabricated metals, and 11 per cent less in electrical equipment. It would not have had any affect at all on the rate of invention in the areas of office equipment, motor vehicles, rubber and textiles.[79]

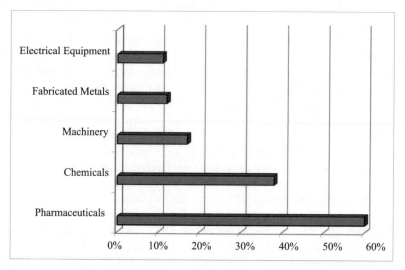

Figure 2.2   What percentage of the inventions would not have been developed without patent protection?

---

[79]   Mansfield, E. (1986) 'Patents and Innovation: An Empirical Study', *Management Science*, V.32, N.2, pp. 173–81.

The study also indicates that patents are infrequently regarded as necessary to the development or commercial introduction of an invention in certain industries such as primary metals, electrical equipment, textiles and so on. However, patents are widely used in these industries. The firms still tend to value some of the more obvious benefits of patent protection such as royalties, the potential use of patents as bargaining chips and the possibility that possessing a patent could delay competitors entering the market. Such a justification offers an explanation as to why the patent propensity, that is, the percentage of innovations that are patented, is about 60 per cent in an industry such as that for motor vehicles, where patents are said to be relatively unimportant. Hence, the results further indicate that firms generally do not make attempts to rely on the law of trade secrets when patent protection is available.

According to Mansfield et al., it is arguable that patent protection often does not affect the rate of market entry significantly. This might be the reason why patents were considered to be relatively unimportant within most of the industries. Assuming such knowledge, Mazzoleni and Nelson argue that the survey evidence might have been unreliable because much of it focused almost exclusively on large, established firms operating within particular industries. However, the significance of patents for new entrants, small firms, or universities and other organisations outside of any particular industry is often different from large, established firms. The evidence collected from the university start-ups, particularly in biotechnology, as well as changes to the US patent policy since the 1980s, appear to support this assumption.[80]

The debate here is part of a wider discourse. It is difficult to say exactly why patent propensity is still high in certain industries where patents are considered to be relatively ineffective in protecting returns to innovation. Cohen, Nelson and Walsh[81] attempt to solve this dilemma. They posed the question of why firms are increasingly employing patents by examining the relevant appropriability mechanisms. The study used data from the Yale survey, collected in 1982, and the Carnegie Mellon Survey (CMS) on industrial R&D in the US manufacturing sector, which was administered in 1994. The authors conducted their own survey of

---

80   Mazzoleni, R. and R. Nelson (1998) 'The Benefits and Costs of Strong Patent Protection: A Contribution to the Current Debate', *Research Policy*, V.27, pp. 273–84.

81   Cohen, W., R. Nelson and J. Walsh (2000) 'Protecting Their Intellectual Assets: Appropriability Conditions and Why US Manufacturing Firms Patent (Or Not)', NBER Working Paper, 7552 available at http://www.nber.org/papers/w7552.

R&D managers in 1994, sampling almost 3000 research labs across the US. The survey results revealed that secrecy in 17 industries, and first mover advantages in 13 industries, ranked as top appropriability mechanisms. In fact, these patents have not been considered as the dominant mechanism for protecting product innovations in most of the industries. Patents only counted among the major appropriation mechanisms in a more sizeable minority of industries such as pharmaceuticals and chemicals. It should be noted that the growing importance of secrecy as an alternative to patents indicates that firms are better able to profit from innovation by maintaining secrecy in the development stages. This can be explained by the short imitation lags even for patented inventions. Once the product is on the market, the relevant patents usually complement secrecy by offering some extra lead-time as well as a competitive advantage to a firm before competitors can respond.[82]

In fact, the results of Cohen et al.'s study indicate that levels of appropriability mainly depend upon the complementarities between product and process protection, in relation to all the mechanisms. These industries do not exclusively rely on patents; even pharmaceutical firms utilise complementary capabilities in addition to patents. The tendency for firms to use patents alongside other mechanisms has led to the realisation that even though patents are considered relatively ineffective, they might add sufficient value at the margin when used with other mechanisms.

Assuming a certain amount of knowledge, the authors have attempted to identify the specific kinds of motivation behind the decision of a firm to apply for a patent. In this respect, the respondents of the survey were asked to indicate which list of reasons motivated their most recent decisions to apply for a patent. The long list of reasons ranged from the prevention of copying, to patent blocking, or even to strengthen the firms' position in negotiations with other firms (regarding cross-licensing agreements, etc.). As presented in Figure 2.3, the prevention of copying has been identified by 96 per cent of respondents as the major motive behind patenting decisions. The motive of blocking rival patents on related innovations ranked second.

---

[82] Arundel, A. (2001) 'Patents – The Viagra of Innovation Policy?', MERIT, Internal Report to the Expert Group, available at www.edis.sk/ekes/patents.pdf, p. 16.

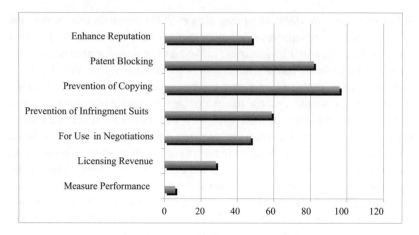

Figure 2.3   Firms' motives to patent product innovations[83]

To probe for differences in the motives for patenting across industries, the authors also distinguished between technologies and industries, by exploiting a distinction drawn in previous literature that focused primarily on differences between complex versus discrete or simple technologies. The key difference between these two technologies was identified upon comparison of the number of separately patentable elements that a new, commercialisable product or process comprises. In this context, as drugs or chemicals typically include a relatively discrete number of patentable elements these are categorised under discrete technologies. However, electronic products, for instance, are comprised of hundreds of patentable elements, and these are characterised as complex technologies. This distinction between the characteristics of industries becomes significant when firms' motives to patent are examined. By way of illustration, the survey results reveal that among the 16 industries in which the use of patents for negotiations motivates 50 per cent or more of the respondents, there were only a small handful of discrete products. Accordingly, a comparison of two-industry groups, and the weighting of cases by volume of patent applications, reveals that, on average, patents are used for cross-licensing by 54.8 per cent of those in the complex product industries. Yet, the usage of patents for cross-licensing is limited to 10,3 per cent in discrete technologies. In the course of the wider discussion, the survey results present the fact that there are

---

[83]   *See,* Cohen et.al., supra note 81, Figure 7 – Reasons to Patent Product Innovations.

common uses of patents that stand apart from the function of protecting the profits directly associated with either the licensing, or the commercialisation of the patented invention. The authors further observe that even where the patents are weak or untested, they can be used either defensively or offensively as a part of a litigation-intensive strategy. However, the high cost associated with such kinds of strategies, and small firms' prejudice against patents due to these high maintenance costs, raises serious concerns as to whether the social value of patenting is actually substantially reduced while the costs of innovation are unduly raised.[84]

On the other hand, in their seminal work, Arora, Cecagnoli and Cohen approached the impact of patent protection on R&D at the firm level by employing data from the 1994 Carnegie Mellon Survey on Industrial R&D in the US. In their research, they initially tried to estimate the proportional increment of the value of innovations realised by patenting them. They did this by what they called calculating the patent premium. They then used the estimated parameters to simulate the effect of changes in the patent premium on both R&D and patenting itself. The results suggest that the expected premium, which is conditional on patenting, that is, the patent premium for innovations that were patented, is considerable. On average, a firm can earn a 50 per cent premium over the no patenting case. This goes up to 60 per cent in the health-related industries. This estimate leads them to suggest that an increase in the mean of patent premium distribution would significantly stimulate R&D, especially in industries where the patent premium is high, such as the drugs, biotech and medical industries. However, they conclude that, irrespective of whether inventions are worthy of patenting or not, patents are a valuable subset of innovation. Hence, it is clear that patents do provide incentives for R&D.[85] Nonetheless; the reverse of this finding concentrates on the value that patents give to products in the real world. It investigates the role of patents in encouraging R&D by examining how easy it is to get a patent and how much protection that patent gives to the product.[86]

In a later piece of research, Lerner assessed the impact of major patent policy shifts on innovation across 60 countries over a 150-year period. His findings indicated a level of consistency with previous empirical

---

[84] Cohen et al., supra note 81.

[85] Arora, A., M. Ceccagnoli and W. Cohen (2008) 'R&D and the Patent Premium', *International Journal of Industrial Organization*, V.26, I.5, pp. 1153–79.

[86] Burk and Lemley, supra note 58, p. 27.

research, that is, that patent policy shifts have a negative impact on innovation. This is particularly evident where a nation already has strong patent protection and when its per capita gross domestic product lags behind other nations. The findings do, however, support the theory that patent protection-enhancing shifts have a number of positive implications for foreign applications. For instance, there was a substantial increase in the number of applications on both the absolute and percentage basis in relation to patent applications by foreign applicants. However, the number of applications from residents fell by significant accounts.[87]

Consistent with the above empirical evidence, Taylor and Silberston noted that the protection afforded by the patent system is assumed to be weak and ineffective in protecting competitive advantage. The results also indicated that the innovator's willingness to invest in R&D does not necessarily depend upon the degree of protection granted by the patent system.[88] For industries such as software or computers, it is, once again, observed that imitation promotes innovation. Hence, strong patents inhibit innovation due to the sequential and complementary structure of innovation in these industries.[89]

The value of patents for a firm is usually associated with the sector of activity, that is, the firm's business strategy, as well as the interactions with the business strategies of the firm's competitors.

Nonetheless, recent economic research demonstrates that the net private return from patents to publicly listed US firms is substantially negative. This is true to the extent that private benefits and private costs have been measured. Consistent with previous research, the pharmaceutical companies are the only outstanding exceptions in the study.[90] In fact, patents have long been recognised as valuable assets in sectors where innovations are easy to copy, such as pharmaceuticals and chemicals.[91] Within these industries, patents are regarded as highly effective for encouraging investment in R&D. The resulting patents in these sectors

---

[87]   Lerner, J. (2002) 'Patent Protection and Innovation over 150 Years', NBER WP 8977.

[88]   Taylor, C.T. and A.Z. Silberston (1973) *The Economic Impact of Patent System: A Study of the British Experience*, Cambridge: Cambridge University Press, p. 396.

[89]   Bessen, J and E. Maskin (2000) 'Sequential Innovation, Patents and Imitation', MIT Working Paper, Economics, p. 3.

[90]   Moir, J.H. (2009) 'What are the Costs and Benefits of Patent Systems', in C. Arup and W. van Caenegem (eds) *Intellectual Property Policy Reform: Fostering Innovation and Development*, Cheltenham, UK and Northampton, MA, USA, Edward Elgar, p. 30.

[91]   Arundel, supra note 82, p. 16.

are more detailed in their claims and therefore, it is easier to replicate the finished product. Hence, the maximisation of patents for an industry is positively correlated with the increase in duplication costs and time associated with patents.

The findings of Cohen et al., do, however, strongly emphasised that the key appropriability mechanisms in most industries are secrecy, lead time and complementary capabilities. Thus, patents are still not the major mechanism for appropriating returns to innovation in most industries.[92] However, both the lead-time mechanism and the availability of a patent are found to be crucial for Japanese firms. The empirical research, however, proved that lead-time and secrecy are considered to be the key means of protecting inventions for most US companies.[93]

For instance, in a study conducted on the aviation industry, where new product lines are complicated, and products have long lasting effects; it was found that both lead-time and the strength of the learning curve were determined to be more important than patents in capturing benefits of the innovation mechanism. There is no doubt that it is very expensive, complicated, and time consuming to duplicate an aeroplane, particularly when compared to the relatively simple methods that exist to analyse a pill and reproduce it.[94] It follows that in cases where imitation is as costly as inventing, or cases where firms have the economic and technical means for protecting their inventions; there is no need for further legal protection.

Assuming such knowledge, the next question that arises is how much IPRs protection is optimal given that firms can also appropriate their investments in innovation through secrecy, lead time advantages and so on. It is often suggested that IPRs strategies should be placed firmly within the context of an overall appropriation strategy. This strategy would also necessarily comprise other factors that are essential to a company's ability to profit from innovation.[95]

In light of the above, it can be said that there is overwhelming evidence that the concept of innovation differs across industries, and that these industries treat patents differently. Nevertheless, it is a common misconception, particularly for legal scholars, to make generalised assumptions on the role of patents in relation to the innovation process. The impact on innovation through patent protection or IPRs more

---

[92] Cohen et al., supra note 81, p. 24.
[93] Granstrand, supra note 53, p. 281.
[94] Schacht, W. (2000) 'Federal R&D, Drug Discovery, and Pricing: Insights from the NIH-University-Industry Relationship', CRS Report 2000, p. 8.
[95] Arundel, supra note 82, p. 3.

broadly, is likely to depend upon a number of factors. Patent protection is not necessarily regarded as the main appropriability mechanism for most of the industries. In fact, it is true that an assessment of the cumulative and sequential nature of these industries suggests that patents tend to hamper innovation activities. The empirical research does, however, demonstrate that patent protection is important for the pharmaceutical industry. Patents, or IPRs more broadly, are considered to be one of the most conducive means of appropriating returns from R&D investments in this area.

Unlike other technologies, there are clear patent boundaries that are regarded as a significant determinant of relative returns in relation to R&D, in pharmaceuticals. The presence of a high level of patent protection dramatically increases the time and the cost of imitation, which are nonetheless, lower than the average. Hence, patent protection is widely acknowledged as the primary incentive for innovation in pharmaceuticals.

What emerges clearly from investigation of empirical data is an effort to recognise the differences in innovation among the industries. It is also important to stress the need for a guide to the practices of pharmaceutical innovation. This is all the more necessary when one takes account of the different needs and experiences of the pharmaceutical industry regarding patents.

3. Innovation and the pharmaceutical industry

AT A GLANCE: PHARMACEUTICAL INNOVATION

Innovation in development of drugs is critical to the survival of a big pharmaceutical business model. It follows that innovation in drug development is a fundamental requirement for a company to establish and maintain a competitive advantage in an increasingly complex world. Pharmaceutical innovation has numerous features and is an ongoing process. The scope of innovation generally ranges from developing, manufacturing and marketing new drugs about which relatively little is known at the time of their discovery, to enhancing existing drugs that have been on the market for some time by making minor changes to them. Between these activities, manufacturers also try to find new ways to increase the safety, effectiveness, and convenience of their products.

Given the relationship between research and development (R&D), industrial innovation and growth, the analysis of the pharmaceutical industry undertaken here demonstrates an extremely important part of development economics. Co-operation across government, universities and industry often combines to provide a high level of expertise, which accelerates the process of bringing new products to the market. The industry maintains a number of patterns, which are linked to two main factors. The first factor can be identified as the nature of the drug discovery process; these are characterised by a low degree of cumulativeness and by quasi-random search procedures. The fragmented nature of the relevant markets is the second factor that shapes pharmaceutical innovation.[1]

Furthermore, on examination of the pharmaceutical industry it is clear that the presence of a high ratio of R&D spending in relation to sales

---

[1]   Malebra, F. and L. Orsenigo (2002) 'Innovation and Market Structure in the Dynamics of the Pharmaceutical Industry and Bio-technology: Towards a History-Friendly Model', *Industrial and Corporate Change*, V.11, N.4, 2002, p. 668.

emerges as a distinct characteristic of the industry.[2] Hence, the cost of R&D has become an important issue in relation to policy considerations such as regulatory requirement and economic performance which are central to the regulation of the pharmaceutical industry.[3] The debate in this area usually revolves around the relatively high R&D expenditure level in the pharmaceutical industry, when compared to other industries. Ensuring the successful development and launch of new drugs is considered to be a challenge for the pharmaceutical industry. High costs coupled with the lengthy process involved constitute obstacles for innovation in the pharmaceutical sector. The average time required to bring a medicine to market is estimated to be about 8–10 years in the US. The proportion of substances that are successful and result in marketable products is one out of 10 000. In addition, only three out of every ten successful drugs bring in enough revenues to meet or exceed average R&D costs.[4]

Further to this, an economic analysis of the industry reveals that apart from the high cost of R&D activities, it is also necessary for companies to control other important complementary assets. In addition, possessing the competencies developed in the management of large-scale clinical trials, obtaining regulatory approval and managing the costs of marketing and distribution appear to be the key requirements for the innovation process to succeed. Thus, it can be said that the costs of the development of a drug also depend on these factors. An economic study in 2003 revealed that the average pre-tax cost of bringing a new drug to the market was $802 million. The data was collected from a survey of ten research-based pharmaceutical companies for 68 randomly selected drugs.[5] However, there are a number of criticisms of this figure, mainly because the relevant data was not made available to other researchers. There was a significant lack of transparency regarding the collection of the data for this study. This makes the data regarding the industry's cost

---

[2]   Scherer, F.M. (2007) 'Pharmaceutical Innovation', Working Paper 07–13, AEI-Brookings Joint Centre for Regulatory Studies.

[3]   Dimasi, J., R. Hansen and H. Grabowski (2003) 'The Price of Innovation: New Estimates of Drug Development Costs', *Journal of Health Economics*, V.22, p. 153.

[4]   Gassmann, O., G. Reepmeyer and M. von Zedtwitz (2008) *Leading Pharmaceutical Innovation*, 2nd edn, Heidelberg, Springer, p. 1.

[5]   Dimasi et al., supra note 3, pp. 151–85.

structures highly ambiguous. It is still unclear what forms of expenditure are included in these figures.[6]

In the context of this wider debate, it should be noted that the majority of the data in this account is primarily collected and collated by the Pharmaceutical Research and Manufacturers of America (PhRMA). There has been much controversy regarding the reliability of the PhRMA's statistics. Doubts have been cast regarding the accuracy of much of the data that the PhRMA has made available, yet it is still a widely accepted fact that the R&D budget of the pharmaceutical industry is substantially higher than other industries.

The relevant statistical data indicates that pharmaceutical R&D/sales ratios have consistently been at a level nearly seven times higher than the ratios of other manufacturing industries. There is a growing consensus that pharmaceutical companies' reinvestment into R&D is disproportionately small when compared to non-R&D expenditure.[7] For instance, a recent study on drug price negotiation mechanisms was conducted by Families USA, a US-based consumer health group. This study found that drug companies[8] typically spend more than twice as much on marketing, advertising and administration as they do on R&D.[9] A more recent study, based on systematic data collected directly from the industry and the medical profession, confirmed the findings of the Families USA study. The more recent study suggested that pharmaceutical companies typically spend almost twice as much on promotion as they do on R&D. The findings showed that during the course of 2004 24.4 per cent (around $235 billion) was spent on promotion, whereas only 13.4 per cent was invested in R&D. This fact led authors to make the critical comment that, contrary to the industry's claim, spending on promotion, such as marketing and advertising, predominates over R&D spending in the pharmaceutical industry.[10] Supporting these views, the US Government

[6] Collier, R. (2009) 'Drug Development Cost Estimates Hard to Swallow', *Canadian Medical Association Journal*, V.180, I.3, p. 279.

[7] Joseph, S. (2003) 'Pharmaceutical Corporations and Access to Drugs: The "Fourth Wave" of Corporate Human Rights Scrutiny', *Human Rights Quarterly*, V.25, p. 432.

[8] The report examined the nine pharmaceutical companies: Merck, Pfizer, Bristol-Myers Squibb, Pharmacia, Abbott Laboratories, American Home Products, Eli Libby, Schering-Plough and Allergan.

[9] 'No bargain: Medicare Drug Plans Deliver High Prices', Report from Families USA, 9 January 2007, available at http://www.familiesusa.org/resources/publications/reports/no-bargain-medicare-drug.html.

[10] Gagnon, M-A. and J. Lexchin (2008) 'The Cost of Pushing Pills: A New Estimate of Pharmaceutical Promotion Expenditures in the United States',

Accountability Office revealed that between the years 1997 and 2005, the total spending on direct-to-consumer advertising grew at twice the rate of R&D spending.[11]

Such findings provide compelling evidence for the argument that the research-based pharmaceutical industry has a systematic tendency to overstate the cost of drug development.[12] The potential magnitude of the overstatement remains unclear. The argument made here is highly important for one reason in particular. In patent scholarship, it is often said that the potential costs of R&D justifies the market exclusivity provided by the provision of a patent. In fact, the main *raison d'être* behind the patent system is not only to provide protection for the time, money and intellectual ability that has been invested, but also to encourage future R&D investment and the subsequent innovation that results from this investment. In this context, the high R&D costs require a number of trade-offs between patents and pharmaceutical innovation.

EXPLORING THE VERSATILE TRADE-OFF BETWEEN PATENTS AND PHARMACEUTICAL INNOVATION

There is a growing consensus that patents advance pharmaceutical innovation in a substantial way. For example, a great deal of empirical research appears to support this view. As noted in the previous chapter, innovation occurs differently within each industry, and each industry treats patents differently. Recent studies in the US, Europe and Japan, which assessed the means by which firms are able to make a return on their R&D investment, showed that patents are considered to be one of the major appropriability mechanisms in the pharmaceutical area.[13] Along similar lines, empirical analysis shows that pharmaceutical companies are the major users of the patent system. Furthermore, the net

---

available at http://www.plosmedicine.org/article/info:doi/10.1371/journal.pmed.0050001.

[11] 'Prescription Drugs: Improvements Needed in FDA's Oversight of Direct-to-Consumer Advertising', GAO-07-54, Washington, November 2006, available at www.gao.gov/new.items/d0754.pdf.

[12] Collier, supra note 6, p. 280.

[13] Cohen, W., R. Nelson and J. Walsh (2000) 'Protecting Their Intellectual Assets: Appropriability Conditions and Why US Manufacturing Firms Patent (Or Not)', NBER Working Paper, p. 1360; Kingston, W. (2009) 'Why Patents Need Reform, Some Suggestions for It' in C. Arup and W. van Caenegem (eds) *Intellectual Property Policy Reform: Fostering Innovation and Development*, Cheltenham, UK and Northampton, MA, USA, Edward Elgar, p. 12.

private returns from pharmaceutical patents tend to be significantly higher than that of other types of patents.[14] Even Lawrence Lessig, a prominent advocate of user and open-innovation, acknowledges that the pharmaceutical industry constitutes an exception to other industries, where the benefits derived from patents are often quite limited.[15] In a similar vein, Bessen and Meuer's empirical analysis on the benefits and costs of patents for public firms indicates that patents universally discourage innovation outside of pharmaceutical and chemical sectors.[16]

Indeed, patent exclusivity is accepted as a major incentive for the encouragement of innovation in the pharmaceutical industry. Hence, the patent system is stated to justify the costs and time associated with pharmaceuticals. In other words, the promise of monopoly protection for a limited time is a factor that dominates pharmaceutical R&D decision-making. Furthermore, economic analysis of the imitation costs in a number of industries has shown that patents significantly raise the costs incurred by non-patent holders seeking to use the idea or invent around the patent.[17] The range was estimated to be 40 per cent in the pharmaceutical sector, 30 per cent for major new chemical products and 25 per cent for typical chemical goods, while the proportion was only limited to 7–15 per cent in electronics.[18]

In sharp contrast to other fields of technology, it is arguable that patents have historically been quite effective in the pharmaceutical industry. For instance it is often argued that the distinction between the acts of invention and innovation enables maximum optimisation of patents for pharmaceuticals. Innovation in the pharmaceutical industry increasingly relies on costly and expensive R&D activities. The development of drugs requires not only significant expenditure on research but

---

[14] Moir, J.H. (2009) 'What are the Costs and Benefits of Patent Systems' in C. Arup and W. van Caenegem (eds) *Intellectual Property Policy Reform: Fostering Innovation and Development*, Cheltenham, UK and Northampton, MA, USA, Edward Elgar, p. 30.

[15] '... the strongest conclusion one can draw is that whatever benefit patents provide (except in industries such as pharmaceuticals), it is small', Lessig, L. (2001) *The Future of Ideas*, New York, Random House; Torrence, A.W. and B. Tomlinson (2009) 'Patents and the Regress of Useful Arts', *The Colombia Science and Technology Law Review*, V.10, p. 163.

[16] Bessen, J. and M. Meurer (2008) *Patent Failure*, Princeton, Princeton University Press, p. 142.

[17] Hippel, E. Von (1988) *The Sources of Innovation*, London, Oxford University Press. p. 52.

[18] Schacht, W. (2000) 'Federal R&D, Drug Discovery, and Pricing: Insights from the NIH-University-Industry Relationship', CRS Report p. 8.

also the transformation and commercialisation of those inventions into marketable commodities. Thus, the active agents in the innovation process are in fact, the large firms. Indeed, R&D, which is further aided by legal, administrative and marketing activities, has become a large-scale activity and a routine part of business operations in multinational pharmaceutical companies. In line with the Schumpeterian theory that large firms are more likely to keep the engine of technological innovation going, research-based pharmaceutical companies have become the dominant players in a variety of innovative areas in the sector. For Schumpeter, monopoly power favours innovation, because it is only through a monopoly that the innovator can appropriate enough of the returns of the innovation to justify the investment in R&D.[19] Schumpeter emphasised the routine activity of innovation, which necessarily gives rise to a temporary state of monopoly in favour of the innovator. However, 'monopoly offers no cushion to sleep on for companies'.[20] Therefore, it is necessary that pharmaceutical companies be in a position to assure a continuum of innovation from the laboratory to the marketplace.

Second, the notion of innovation in the pharmaceutical industry is increasingly associated with secrecy. In fact, much of the R&D in drug discovery and development is aimed at securing the relevant knowledge. The traditional proprietary approach in the pharmaceutical industry requires that the relevant knowledge, for example, pertaining to the therapeutically interesting molecules or the safety and efficiency of the drug candidate, to be kept secret. Patent protection provides for an accumulation of this knowledge.

Moreover, the ease of imitation is an issue of great concern in relation to pharmaceuticals. Once the knowledge is accumulated, a would-be generic imitator of a small-molecule drug is able to enter the market with an exact knock-off copy. Hence, the advanced process engineering level of generic companies has potential to erode the quasi-rents anticipated by a pharmaceutical innovator.[21]

Given the current *status quo* of the industry, a short-term, limited monopoly is often claimed to be necessary to encourage innovation in the pharmaceutical industry. According to Lemley and Burk, 'the prospect vision of patents maps closely onto invention in pharmaceutical industry'. In a scenario without patents, as the difference between the ratio of

---

[19]   Schumpeter, J. (1939) *A Theoretical, Historical and Statistical Analysis of the Capitalist Process*, Vol.1, New York, McGraw Hill, p. 105.

[20]   'A monopoly position is no cushion to sleep on. As it can be gained, so it can be retained only by alertness and energy', *Ibid.*, p. 102.

[21]   Scherer, supra note 2, pp. 27–8.

inventor cost and the ratio of imitator cost is quite large, it is usually claimed that innovation is likely to drop substantially.[22] It should be borne in mind that pharmaceutical innovation is not only about invention; drug discovery is the beginning of the process, not the end. In accordance with Schumpeterian theory, it is arguable that innovation in the pharmaceutical industry is a distinctly economic process and a matter of business activity. For instance, it is clear that much of the work occurs after the drug candidate has been identified. This work includes undertaking activities such as bulk manufacturing, market approval, advertising, marketing, sales promotion and so on. Hence, it is critical that patentees have control regarding downstream uses of inventions. In line with this, Burk et al. suggest that patents should stand alone, be broad, and confer almost total control over subsequent uses of the product.

Consequently, the pharmaceutical industry places a great deal of importance on the patent system. It is suggested that there are two likely reasons for this. First of all, the patents obtained by pharmaceutical companies are unusually strong when compared to the patents obtained by other industries. The subject matter of pharmaceutical inventions is usually a number of actual molecules, which have useful medicinal properties and its analogues. It is usually possible to refer to lists of recognised functional equivalents for each component of the molecule at issue rather than simply claiming each analogue. By way of illustration, for a molecule which has ten important component parts, a patent application may claim x plus ten recognised functional equivalents of x for each part. Therefore, it is clear that a pharmaceutical patent application can be made subject to millions of specific molecule claims without actually having to synthesise more than a few.[23]

One of the dilemmas that pharmaceutical patents typically create is that inventing around them is inevitably quite difficult. It is very unlikely that potential imitators will be able to work around the patent. Furthermore, the possibility of discovering another compound, which possesses the same therapeutic properties and does not infringe the original patent, is quite low.[24]

Hence, it is argued that the broad scope of patents in the pharmaceutical industry provides relatively more incentives for innovation and

---

[22] Burk, D.L. and M.A. Lemley (2003) 'Policy Levers in Patent Law', *Virginia Law Review*, Vol. 89, pp. 1574–77.

[23] Hippel supra note 17, p. 53.

[24] Malerba, F. and S. Brusoni (2007) *Perspectives on Innovation*, New York, Cambridge University Press, p. 11.

research into the development of new drugs.[25] It has been observed that the enactment of policies aimed at broadening the scope of patent protection tend to have significant positive effects on investment in R&D with regard to drug innovation.[26] However, broader patents may also constitute an obstacle to the development of spin-off innovations that are tangential to the original innovation. According to Merges and Nelson, patents play an essential role in appropriating returns from invention in the pharmaceutical industry, in cases where the invention is reasonably well defined and bounded. In contrast, in relation to broad patents, the boundaries of which are difficult to define, patents are arguably less useful. As Merges and Nelson point out, the provision of broad patents diminishes incentives for other competitors to stay in the innovation game.[27] Hence, it is arguable that the relationship between a tightly defined patent regime and a steady rate of innovation is not a linear one. Furthermore, it is suggested that neither increasing nor decreasing the level of patent protection has more than a minimal effect on encouraging innovation.[28]

In a seminal work, Cohen et al. categorise the pharmaceutical industry under the category of discrete product industries. Furthermore, the survey results revealed that patent blocking is one of the most persuasive factors in encouraging patent usage in discrete product industries. In addition, the majority of the industry is likely to use patents for blocking in order to create a patent fence for weaker patents. For instance, pharmaceutical companies often aim to build a patent fence around some patented core invention in order to impede the development of competing alternatives. Additionally, when compared to complex product industries, pharmaceutical companies are less likely to use patents in negotiations. The findings, also raise an important question concerning whether patents have been used by the pharmaceutical industry in ways that ultimately undermine the purpose of patent law.[29]

There has been much controversy in recent years about optimal patent duration. Economists have long discussed how long optimal patent life should be. However, the only conclusion that they can agree on is that it

---

[25]   Hippel conducted a wide survey among the patent attorneys for pharmaceutical firms and his discussion with them brought out the above-mentioned reasons for the situation. *See,* Burk and Lemley, supra note 22, p. 1730.

[26]   *Ibid,* p. 1733.

[27]   Merges, R. and R. Nelson (1990) 'On the Complex Economics of Patent Scope', *Columbia Law Review*, V.90, N.4, pp. 839–916.

[28]   Malerba, supra note 24, p. 17.

[29]   Cohen et al., supra note 13, p. 23.

is highly dependent upon the invention or class of inventions. Moreover, any effort to determine it a *priori* would in some cases be costly, and in most cases, simply impossible.[30] On the other hand, the pharmaceutical industry continues to argue that effective patent life is often lost due to the requirements of lengthy and costly clinical trials. Moreover, the regulatory approval process potentially affects patent life. As a result of these factors, the possibility of compensating R&D investment costs is reduced. Therefore, it is advocated that patents should be granted with an option to extend the term of protection. In their seminal work, Malerba and Orsoni explored the consequences of different patent durations. Malerba et al. took the standard patent term as 20 periods. When the protection was extended to 50 periods the findings indicated a substantial decrease in the number of surviving firms and consequently, less exploration. However, the market share of innovative firms and the level of concentration in each therapeutic category increased. Nonetheless, the overall concentration remained relatively constant. In fact, the findings of the study demonstrated that the number of therapeutic areas discovered decreased and the total quality remained practically unchanged. In some cases, the total quality level even decreased. This led them to the opinion that the provision of longer patent terms will lead to less exploration and less diversification for each firm. Undoubtedly, the analysis challenges the assumption that long-term monopolistic market conditions favour levels of pharmaceutical innovation. In other words, the provision of a long-term patent term gives rise to less exploration and is likely to reduce diversification. The principal reason for this is that the molecules discovered, but not developed by innovators, remain unexploited by the imitators for a long period of time.[31] The study demonstrated that there is an unambiguous relationship between the strength of patent protection and the rate of innovation. This confirms that innovators in a monopolistic position generally tend to concentrate on a small amount of therapeutic categories, where the prospective incomes tend to be higher. In this hypothetical scenario many pharmaceutical companies are likely to concentrate their efforts on the development of lifestyle drugs, which are usually aimed at high-income markets. Consequently, they will place less importance on the development of drugs to treat diseases of poverty, such as HIV/AIDS. This could eventually lead to fewer drugs being available for poorer populations, particularly in developing countries.

---

[30] Correa, C. (2006) 'Implications of Bilateral Free Trade Agreements on Access to Medicines', *Bulletin of the World Health Organisation*, V.84, N.5, p. 400.
[31] Malerba et.al., supra note 24, p. 23.

In addition, the findings show that firms would still continue to invest in R&D even with no patent protection at all. The reason for this is that the first mover advantage, that is, profits earned through the introduction of a new product, is found to be sufficient enough to maintain company profitability, and thus, R&D investment. In this scenario a lack of patent protection could lead to more exploratory activity, because the average number of therapeutic areas increases. The extension of the patent term[32] is highly likely to create diminishing returns in innovation effectiveness. The results indicate that patent term extensions have no effect at all above certain minimum levels of protection.[33]

Notwithstanding this argument in recent times the pharmaceutical companies have developed a multifaceted approach to gaining a competitive advantage. Companies typically draw on strategic patenting concepts, as well as the enforcement mechanisms in order to restrict competition for several years beyond the term of patent protection. These tactics range from the development of line extensions to evergreening through patent strategies, as well as next generation franchises and life-cycle management. Evergreening, also known as stockpiling, has become a major, high-stakes issue for pharmaceutical patents. In this way the pharmaceutical companies skilfully use patent law doctrines to secure evergreening in order to delay competitor's access to the patent or to extend the term of patent protection. Although it is not a formal concept that is derived from patent law, evergreening illustrates the myriad of ways by which patent holders try to exploit the law, as well as the regulatory processes, in order to prolong their patent exclusivities.[34] Evergreening simply refers to a system where a patent holder obtains multiple patents that cover different aspects of the same product over a period of many years. This strategy effectively extends the patent term of the product. The evergreen patents usually cover a wide-range of aspects of the drug such as active ingredient, formulations, methods of medical treatment, methods of manufacturing and chemical intermediates.[35] In practice, pharmaceutical companies typically apply for patents on new

---

[32]   The effects of changed regimes of appropriability crucially depend on demand conditions and other variables that contribute to determine profitability. Thus, it is assumed that market demand and other variables stay equal.

[33]   Malerba et. al, supra note 24, p. 24.

[34]   Faunce, T.A. and J. Lexchin (2007) '"Linkage" Pharmaceutical Evergreening in Canada and Australia', *New Zealand Health Policy*, V.4, I.8, pp. 1–11.

[35]   Thomas, J.R. (2009) 'Patent "Evergreening": Issues in Innovation and Competition', CRS, 13 November 2009.

delivery methods for the drugs, or on reduced dosage regimens, or even on new versions of the active compound. For instance, a company might try to patent a combination compound that has advantages, for example, fewer side effects over its parent compound.[36]

In essence, line extensions aim to switch the patent from a branded drug to its next generation, before the onslaught of generics. This tactic has become a crucial regulatory tactic for pharmaceutical companies. In applying this tactic, companies are able to secure a fresh monopolistic position through a set of new patent applications. Potentially this tactic could provide millions in extra income to their fiscal revenues.[37]

To cite a few examples, many drugs sold today are mixed drugs. Mixed drugs consist of both active and inactive parts. Generally speaking, when a company applies for a patent, the inactive part of the drug is disclosed as a result of the patent application. Usually, drug companies introduce a purer version of the drug, which consists of the inactive part, prior to generic competition launching. Companies do this to extend their monopolistic presence in the market. Another example of this kind of practice is the development of new versions of existing drugs. This is done by launching a new version of the drug, which includes an active metabolite. Following the administration of the older drug, the body, usually the liver, forms an active metabolite. This active metabolite exists within the new dosage and hence, it is usually launched as a new version of the existing drug. A well-known example of this kind of active metabolite is desloratadine. This drug has been marketed under the trademark of Clarinex by Schering-Plough since 2001, and has been typically used for the treatment of allergies. It is the active metabolite of loratadine, an antihistamine drug (marketed under the trademark of Lorastine by Schering-Plough in 1988). The relevant patents on loratadine expired in 2002. However, the patent on the new product is not due to expire until July 2019. Finally, the introduction of a known active ingredient, with an established efficiency and safety profile, or with a different pharmaceutical presentation, is another widely used strategy for the extension of market exclusivity. Paroxetine, for instance, is a widely used antidepressant developed by British pharmaceutical giant SmithKline Beecham. The company is known today as GlaxoSmithKline (GSK). The drug was originally marketed under the trade name of Paxil in 1992.

---

[36] Dutfield, G. (2003) *Intellectual Property Rights and the Life Science Industries*, Dartmouth, Ashgate, p. 109.

[37] Brown, H. (2005) 'Dealing with the Generic Threat', *PharmaFocus*, 14 September 2005, available at http://www.prophet.com/newsevents/news/story/20050914smith.html.

Within a very short period of time, paroxetine became a bestselling drug for the company and, following the September 11 attacks, the company increased its advertising campaign, especially in the US. Nevertheless, the patents on the drug were due to expire in 2003. However, in 2002, prior to market entry of generic versions, GSK introduced a new drug, Paxil CR, to the market. Essentially, Paxil CR contains the same active ingredient as the old Paxil, but it has a controlled release formulation. More importantly, it is patent protected until 2017.[38]

In an effort to maximise market exclusivity, the pharmaceutical companies also explore marketing strategies such as 'launching a patent prescription drug in an over-the-counter form prior to expiration of marketing exclusivity to build up an over-the-counter market position against future competition' or 'marketing campaigns to get consumers to switch to newer formulations ... of drug products from earlier formulations, for which patent protection has not yet, but is soon to, run out, thus undercutting market demand for generic versions of the older formulations'.[39]

In fact, there is a growing body of empirical research, especially regarding biotech patents, that involves DNA sequences that raises concerns about whether intellectual property rights (IPRs) are becoming fragmented. This problem is potentially damaging because it could lead to a situation where assembling the rights necessary to commercialise a new therapy or drug is prohibitively costly. Furthermore, it could contribute to a situation where some promising lines of research are abandoned prematurely.[40] This also raises an important question, that is, whether the granting of broad claims on patents, and biotech patents in particular, actually slows down the process of diffusion and circulation of knowledge.[41]

---

[38] *See,* Tomer, G. (2008) 'Prevailing against Cost-Leader Competitors in the Pharmaceutical Industry', *Journal of Generic Medicines,* V.5, pp. 305–14.

[39] Micheal Enzo Furrow, intellectual property attorney, observes that these strategies allow innovator firms to maximise their monopoly period. *See,* Thomas, supra note 35.

[40] Cohen, W.M. and S.A. Merrill (2003) *Patents in the Knowledge-Based Economy,* Washington, NRC, p. 2.

[41] Malerba et al., supra note 24, p. 12.

The strong incentives given by patents are intended to encourage new innovation. However, these incentives may also discourage further development of those initial innovations.[42] Correspondingly, it is possible that patent holders with broad claims may try to use those claims to hinder competitors. Patent holders might exercise their rights through licensing restrictions or through taking legal action against technologies on similar products. A well-known example of this can be seen in the case of Chiron's patent on the hepatitis C virus.[43] The aggressive enforcement of the Chiron patent on a cloned virus has held up extensive research on hepatitis C. Furthermore, it is considered to be a problem by a number of researchers who are currently working on an antiviral or a vaccine for hepatitis C.[44] Moreover, the patent-driven pharmaceutical industry utilises patents for a wide-range of other strategic purposes. As it turns out, pharmaceutical companies also employ techniques such as creating a broad zone of exclusion around a patent, or preventing other companies from exploiting their own patents, as a part of patent-cross licensing practice.[45]

Patent law also limits the scope of individual patents. This enables competition between different drugs in the same class as well as drugs in different classes that are targeted at the same underlying condition. In this way, patents are thought to help to create a vibrant market for innovation.[46] A further point worth considering is the successful utilisation of secondary pharmaceutical use claims that maximise patent lifecycles. This is acknowledged as another factor that strengthens pharmaceutical patents. Furthermore, the integration of patent term extensions, and the presence of data exclusivity provisions, increases the strength of pharmaceutical patents.

---

[42] Geroski, P.A. (2005) 'Intellectual Property Rights, Competition Policy and Innovation: Is There a Problem?', SCRIPTed, V.2, available at http://www.law.ed.ac.uk/ahrc/script-ed/vol2-4/geroski.asp, p. 425.

[43] Chiron Corporation collaborated with the Centres for Disease Control (CDC) in the discovery of the hepatitis C virus. The discovery led to a reliable blood test for the disease and sparked further efforts to develop a cure. Chiron then applied for a patent on the cloned virus but did not name the CDC. In 1990 the CDC gave Chiron full rights to the patent in return for a payment of $2.2 million.

[44] Maskus, K. (2006) 'Reforming US Patent Policy: Getting the Incentives Right', Council Special Report, N.19, p. 19.

[45] *See,* Dutfield, supra note 36, p. 109.

[46] Epstein, R. (2007) 'The Pharmaceutical Industry at Risk: How Excessive Government Regulation Stifles Innovation', *Clinical Pharmacology & Therapeutics*, V.82, N.2, 2007, p. 132.

The industry, theoretically, subordinates its patent-related interests to those of patients. To this extent, they argue that the lack of a limited period of exclusivity, as conferred by patent protection, will eventually lead to a shortage of cures for most diseases, and as a result, many patients would be unable to receive suitable medicines.[47] In reality, the evidence indicates that pharmaceutical companies favour the R&D of products and technologies that have high global demand. These products and technologies assure high profitability and are accompanied by the promise of a limited monopoly, as provided through patent protection or IPRs more broadly. Only a small amount of global R&D is focused on the needs of developing economies with low incomes and weak IPRs. This fact illustrates why the current system of pharmaceutical innovation largely ignores disease-afflicted poor populations in developing countries. In other words, innovation in the pharmaceutical sector usually relies on blockbuster R&D strategies that focus on the development of products in therapeutic areas with large potential markets. In these areas, failure is more likely to be caused by economic factors such as increased competition in the market. Moreover, having long recognised the market need for developing drugs for wealthy and healthy people, the pharmaceutical industry has begun to concentrate R&D efforts on a range of drugs that seek to improve the quality of people's lives. Confirming this fact, Henyr Gadsde, a head of Merck, stated in the 1950s that 'there are more well people than sick people. We should make products for people who are well'.[48]

Nevertheless, it is clear that changes to the patent system directly affect the industry. A well-known example of this is the enactment of the Bayh-Dole Act in the US. This act is intended to establish patent ownership as an incentive for private sector development and the commercialisation of federally funded R&D. Arguably it has positively affected innovation in the pharmaceutical industry. Many of the discoveries made by universities in the biomedical and pharmaceutical field have led to the creation of new drugs and therapies.[49] Although, it is

[47]   According to the European Federation of Pharmaceutical Industries and Associations 'without the limited period of exclusivity conferred by a patent on a product most new cures would not be created', and for PhRMA 'without patent protection, it is highly unlikely that a company would be rewarded for its invention – or, more importantly, that patients would receive many new medicines', *See,* Dutfield, supra note 36, p. 112.

[48]   Dutfield, supra note 36, p. 97.

[49]   Levenson, D. (2005) 'Consequences of the Bayh-Dole Act' available at http://www.uwm.edu/~ruediger/Imitation,%20Innovation%20and%20Threshold

regarded as having had a significant impact on US pharmaceutical research there is, however, increasing concern about the Bayh-Dole Act and its effect on the pharmaceutical industry. These concerns and issues will be critically examined under the chapter dealing with the US innovation system.

Furthermore, the continuous and multidimensional characteristics of innovation in the pharmaceutical industry produce difficulties for the development of new products or processes. In addition, the presence of uncertain regulatory environments, public mistrust and a highly volatile political climate also create difficulties for pharmaceutical companies.[50] It is often said that a strong IPR system is one of the key components of innovation. However, more is needed to build an environment based on sustained innovation in the pharmaceutical industry. Pharmaceutical innovation requires effective innovation policies. These policies should give priority to R&D and also include regulatory systems such as efficient tax systems, investment regulations, production incentives, trade policies, and competition rules.

HISTORY MATTERS: A SPOTLIGHT ON THE HISTORY OF PHARMACEUTICAL INNOVATION

An attempt to stimulate comprehensive debate about the relationship between pharmaceutical innovation and patents requires an evaluation of the existing structural features of the industry. The history of the pharmaceutical industry shows that there is an evolutionary process of adaptation to major technological and institutional shocks. In their seminal work, Malerba et al. examine the history of the industry in three major epochs. The first period is between the mid-19th to the mid-20th century. During this period only a minimal amount of new drug development occurred. Hence, the research conducted over this period was based on relatively primitive methods. The second epoch begins with the large-scale development of penicillin during World War II. The formalised in-house R&D programmes and relatively high rates of new drug launches characterise this period. The third epoch begins in the 1970s and it continues to the present day. This study included a research

---

%20Effects%20A%20Game%20Theoretic%20Approach%20Mohtadi%20Ruediger%202009.pdf.

[50]   Kaitin, K. (2008) 'Obstacles and Opportunities in New Drug Development', *Nature*, V.83, N.2, pp. 210–11.

methodology that drew on the advancements made in genetic engineering and biotechnology.

To a certain extent, the empirical analysis of the history of pharmaceutical innovation in this book follows the same patterns as Malerba et al. It essentially falls into three major epochs. These epochs are distinctive on the basis of key developments in the drug development process. Each epoch is aided by anecdotal success stories which highlight some of the practices that need to be considered during the drug development process. The first corresponds to a period between the late 19th century and World War I. This epoch is characterised by the German dyestuff industry's efforts to synthesise natural products and proactive patent strategies. The discovery, development and marketing of aspirin also illustrate the practice patterns during that period. The second epoch for the pharmaceutical industry starts with the penicillin revolution. The discovery of penicillin, or antibiotics more broadly, effectively pioneered the earliest drug screening techniques. Hence, this significantly contributed to the rise of the American pharmaceutical industry. The third epoch of pharmaceutical innovation, which continues to the present day, is characterised by the emergence of a wide range of antibiotics and screening efforts. Furthermore, this wave of pharmaceutical innovation includes the huge leap from random screening techniques to tailor-made drugs. Hence, the seeds of biotechnological or genomics revolution have been sown. It is possible that the fourth epoch, and perhaps a new golden age for the pharmaceutical industry, is just about to begin.

Epoch One: The Wonder Drug Aspirin and the German Dyestuff Industry

The roots of today's pharmaceutical industry go back to the late 19th century. Over the course of the 19th century, the dyestuff industry grew tremendously in Germany and German companies became world leaders in the synthetic dyestuff market. The successful attempts of the dyestuff industry in synthesising and testing dyestuff formulations prompted scientists in Bayer A.G. to test dyestuff formulations for medical effects in humans. Not long after, one of the drug candidates proved to be effective against fever and headaches. The candidate was based on synthesised salicylic acid – the active ingredient of willow bark.

In fact, the usage of willow bark for medicinal purposes has a long history that goes back to ancient Egypt. Willow bark had been widely used in ancient Egypt to reduce pain and fever. Furthermore, this practice continued throughout the centuries in Asia, China and Europe. During the last half of the 19th century, with the scientific revolution, efforts were made to synthesise plant parts into concentrated doses. French chemist Charles Frederic Gerhardt was the first to synthesise acetylsalicylic acid. Even though he produced good results the process took a substantial amount of time and produced severe side effects. Hence, he was unable to realise the potential of the formulation and decided to give up on the potential invention. Nevertheless, as an academic chemist he wrote an article about the synthesisation process of willow bark.

When two scientists in Bayer, Hoffman and Eicehengrun, learned about Gerdhardt's research, they immediately started work on the synthesisation process. Their hard work and dedication paid off in a very short time; the formulation was found to perform effectively without severe side effects. The process used was similar to the one Gerdhardt had discovered, but it now worked more efficiently. The drug candidate was called aspirin, a name that originated from *Spiraea,* the Latin abbreviation of plant genus. Subsequently, a new epoch started with the development of aspirin, which is widely accepted as the most remarkable drug the world has ever known.[51]

In undertaking an examination of the aspirin case, it is possible to observe underlying patterns of innovation behaviour in the pharmaceutical industry that exists to the present day. From the perspective of Schumpeterian theory, the discovery and commercialisation of aspirin presents anecdotal evidence that illustrates the distinction between invention and innovation. The Schumpeterian theory rests upon this distinction between invention and innovation. For Schumpeter, it was the inventor who produces ideas and the innovator who gets things done. He argued:

> It is in most cases only one man or a few men who see the new possibility and are able to cope with the resistances and difficulties with which action always meets outside of the ruts of established practice.[52]

In the context of Schumpeterian theory, invention is a technical idea that can either lead to new products, or that can be used to solve a current industrial problem. Innovation, on the other hand, refers to the process of introducing a new technology to the market. Hence, the case of Gerhardt is a good example of the Schumpeterian inventor. Gerhardt, in fact, was the first inventor of the wonder formula. He had the intellect to develop the formula, but not the will to deal with the resulting side effects. He

⁵¹ Lichterman, B. (2004) 'Aspirin: The Story of a Wonder Drug', *British Medical Journal*, V.329, p. 1408.
⁵² Schumpeter, J. (1947) 'The Creative Response in Economic History', *The Journal of Economic History*, V.7, N.2, p. 152.

was unable to realise the far-reaching potential of the formula and so did not commercialise it. Aspirin became the brand name for Bayer's drug. Thus, Bayer has been associated with the success of the drug as it can be described as the innovator under Schumpeterian theory. Therefore, it can be argued that the successful innovation of aspirin was a 'feat of will, not of intellect'.[53] The scientists in Bayer, especially Hoffman and Eichengrun, deserve to be given credit as the real innovators. They took the invention of Gerhardt and they worked on it passionately. Furthermore, even when the head of the pharmacology department of Bayer rejected the new substance, Eichengrun did not give up on aspirin. He first tried the drug on himself and he later arranged clinical trials in Berlin to demonstrate its efficiency.[54] He presents a very good example of Schumpeter's innovator. In Schumpeterian theory, he can be described as the one who saw the new possibilities that could result from the invention, and he was able to cope with the resistance and difficulties that he was faced with. This resistance is always felt when a pharmacist acts outside of the course of established practice of pharmacology. For Eichengrun, the efforts paid off; that little white pill known as aspirin became the most remarkable drug the world has ever seen.

Aspirin – a profitable product for the legal profession

The example of aspirin provides a good case for further analysis of how patents work in the pharmaceutical industry. Following the clinical trials, Bayer immediately made a patent application for the process of synthesising salicylic acid. At that time, the German Patent Act (*Patentgesetz*) provided patentability for methods of manufacturing chemical products, but not the products themselves. Chemical products were specifically excluded from patentability. In fact, the German Patent Act was constructed in an effort to serve the interest of the German dyestuff industry and the chemical industry. The dyestuff industry was highly active during the drafting process of this law. Furthermore, the German Chemical Association favoured patent protection for processes, but not products. In the petition submitted to the Reichstag, the German Parliament, it was stated 'a chemical product can be obtained by various methods and from different materials; the grant of a patent for the product itself would

---

[53]   'Successful innovation is as said before, a task *sui generis*. It is a feat not of intellect, but of will. It is a special case of the social phenomenon of leadership', Schumpeter, J. (1928) 'The Instability of Capitalism', *The Economic Journal*, V.38, N.151 p. 379.

[54]   Jeffreys, D. (2005) *The Remarkable Story of a Wonder Drug Aspirin*, New York, Bloomsbury Publishing.

prevent better processes discovered subsequently from being brought into effect in the interest of the public and of the inventors'.[55] Thus, the Reichstag took these industrial concerns into account and enacted the patent law in line with the industry's demands and rationalisation.

Hence, the process patent was the only viable option available for Bayer to protect its IPRs and ensure market exclusivity. Bayer attempted to file an application for a process patent. Nevertheless, a few weeks after the application, the German patent office rejected the application on the basis of lack of novelty. According the patent examiner, the process of synthesising acetylsalicylic acid was already in the state of the art. It was French chemist Charles Frederic Gerhardt who first synthesised acetyl-salicylic acid. Furthermore, German chemists Kraut et al.[56] had already published a scientific paper describing the manufacture of acetylsalicylic acid by heating salicylic acid with acetyl chloride and then re-crystallising the product from boiling water. Therefore, the patent office rejected Bayer's application on the basis that the discovery at issue was not the direct result of a new process.[57]

It should be noted that the patent examination in Germany was described as intensive and rigorous, when compared to any other country at that time. Germany adopted a rigorous examination process whereby patent examiners were required to conduct an extensive investigation into the prior art. The essential part of the examination was intended to determine the novelty of the relevant products or processes. It was also aimed at demarcating the scope of the claim. In addition, it was also possible for third parties to file opposition to the granting of the patent during the application process. As a result of this rigorous process, the German patent proved to be legally strong, once it was granted.[58] In this way, the decisions of the German patent office provided guidance to other patent offices in Europe. In this context, it was not a big shock for Bayer when the patent application also failed to meet the novelty

[55] Berecovitz-Rodriguez, A. (1991) 'Historical Trends in Protection of Technology in Developed Countries and Their Relevance for Developing Countries', Geneva, United Nations Conference on Trade and Development; Dutfield, supra note 36, p. 78.

[56] In 1869, Schröder, Prinzhorn and Kraut repeated both Gerhardt's synthesis and concluded that the reactions gave the compound of the acetylsalicylic acid.

[57] Jeffreys, supra note 54, p. 79.

[58] Murmann, J.P. (2003) *Knowledge and Competitive Advantage: The Co-evolution of Firms, Technology and National Institutions*, New York, Cambridge University Press, p. 87.

requirements of other patent regimes in Europe. At that time, most of the European countries provided patentability to chemical processes of manufacturing, but not products. Hence, the patent offices in countries such as France and Switzerland took the same view as the German patent office and rejected the patent application for the chemical process of manufacturing aspirin, on the basis of a lack of novelty. Nevertheless, Bayer did manage to secure a patent in two countries – Britain and the United States. Interestingly, these two countries were the largest target markets for the drug.

At that time, the patent examination process in Britain was not considered to be rigorous and intensive, when compared to patent examination in mainland Europe.[59] Thus, it had been fairly easy for Bayer to get a patent for aspirin in Britain. Furthermore, the British patent was of utmost importance for Bayer's worldwide marketing strategy. The British patent provided protection in Britain, and crucially, it also provided protection within the British Empire that covered a wide range of territories from India to Canada. Furthermore, it was widely regarded as a certificate of authenticity that demonstrated the value of goods. Hence, Bayer was able to rely on the protection of its patent rights as a way of controlling the profitable British market. When another German dyestuff company, Chemishe Fabrik von Heyden, started to import acetylsalicylic acid into the UK, Bayer filed an infringement case against its German rival. In practice, Chemishe Fabrik had been producing the unbranded version of acetylsalicylic acid in Germany and then exporting it to other European countries for a number of years. As stated above, the process was already in the state of art and thus, it was not protected by patents in Germany, nor in other European countries. The protection existed only in Britain and its territories.[60]

Consequently, in 1905 Bayer sued Chemishe Fabrik for infringement of the British patent of acetylsalicylic acid, which was sold under the name of aspirin. The respondent company denied the infringement and alleged that the patent was invalid. Chemishe Fabrik argued that there was nothing novel about the invention, due to the fact that the process of obtaining acetylsalicylic acid, by producing a chemical reaction between acetylsalicylic acid and acetyl chloride, existed within the state of art. On the other hand, the plaintiff company claimed that it had properly obtained a patent for acetylsalicylic acid as a new body or compound. Justice Joyce rejected the central claim of the plaintiff and held:

---

[59]   *Id.*
[60]   *See,* Jeffreys, supra note 54, pp. 84–8.

It would be a strange and marvellous thing, and to my mind much to be regretted, if after all that had been done and published with regard to acetylsalicylic acid before the date of this patent, an ingenious person, by merely putting forward a different, if you like a better mode of purification from that stated, and truly stated by Kraut to be feasible, could successfully claim as his invention and obtain a valid patent for the production of acetylsalicylic acid as a new body or compound. In my opinion, it was not a new body or compound and I hold the patent in question in this case to be invalid.[61]

The judge further noted that the patent specification contained no element of invention or discovery beyond what was common knowledge. Hence, the judge found that there was a lack of novelty and a lack of inventive step. Consequently, the court invalidated the patent.[62]

Nevertheless, Bayer's experience with the German patent system up to this date had been different. The company had developed the skills to enable the exploitation of loopholes in the patent regime. For this reason, the company was often able to claim patent exclusivity for products it had not invented by merely providing evidence to show that there was a slightly different way of producing it. Due to this phenomenon, with regard to their own inventions, German chemical companies were cautious about revealing their methodologies. In particular, the companies attempted to obscure the methodology behind an invention in order to hide the secrets of their trade. In doing so, the companies hoped to make it more difficult for competitors to copy their inventions. By way of illustration, Justice Joyce J. described Bayer's patent application as a remarkable document. In fact, none of the experienced counsel in the case had ever seen such an ambiguous patent application before. The judge further noted that the document was erroneous, or at the very least, misleading, and that it was '... by accident, error or design so framed as to obscure the subject as much as possible'.[63]

In the early years of the pharmaceutical industry, the German chemical industry was heavily oriented towards the export market. Companies sought to achieve a monopoly position within the world market. Hence, companies established many branches abroad and attempted to exploit international patent law. The companies were able to utilise the patent systems in countries that did not have a stringent patent application review system. In this way, the companies systematically patented

---

[61] Justice Joyce J. at Farbenfabriken vormals Friedrich Bayer & Company v Chemische Fabrik Von Heydon (1905) 22 RPC 501, p. 517.

[62] *Ibid*, p. 518.

[63] Joyce J., *Ibid*, p. 516.

everything that had been produced as part of their R&D activities. The companies filed patent applications in all possible areas of organic chemistry. This clearly had the potential to inhibit future research efforts.[64] This aggressive attempt to patent a huge amount of research was undertaken by the German companies, particularly in Britain, and it raised significant concerns regarding the efficiency of the patent regime. The granting of a large number of German patents had the effect of blocking many potentially lucrative R&D possibilities in the country. At this time, the German chemical companies were lobbying hard for an innovation-friendly patent system in Germany, while also using patent law strategically in Britain in order to stifle local innovation.[65]

Arguably, this situation is similar to what happened in the early years of the US software industry. When software-related patents were introduced for the first time in the US, many firms patented as many inventions as possible, so as to create patent portfolios. In a similar way, German companies patented everything that came out of their R&D labs, and thus, they created huge patent portfolios. These portfolios provided them with effective bargaining chips for possible future court battles. In line with this, in the US industry, the granting of software patents created barriers to market entry for new entrants due to the fact that new entrants were forced to license some of the patent protected inventions.

As a result of the German companies' actions, it became evident that the British patent system was in need of serious reform in order to rehabilitate the local chemical industry. Hence, at this time there were a number of attempts to modify the law in the interests of the local industry. For instance, in 1902, the patent law was amended in order to enable revocation in the case of non-working inventions. However, the amendment was flawed and it failed to resolve the issue in practice. In other words, the amendment did not offer any immediate benefits to British firms in relation to encouraging competition in the British market. In addition, the German companies continued to flood the country with non-working blocking patents. German companies also enjoyed the economies of scale that existed within the British market, where the average cost per unit decreased with the level of increased production just as the fixed costs were shared over an increased number of goods.[66]

---

[64]   Murmann, supra note 58, p. 92.
[65]   Dutfield, supra note 36, pp. 83–4.
[66]   Economies of scale give big companies access to a larger market by allowing them to operate with greater geographical reach. For the more traditional (small to medium) companies, however, size does have its limits. After a point, an increase in size (output) actually causes an increase in production costs.

Hence, the German companies were able to reduce their prices in order to undercut the domestic competitors, while still making a tidy profit. Thus, British companies were concerned that German companies were dominating the domestic market. Furthermore, it appeared that at this time British patent law created greater incentives for the German companies than for the local ones. This in turn raised concerns regarding the purpose of the patent regime in Britain. The industry argued:

> English brains created the colour industry, English brains developed it, and English legislative folly has been the principle source of its decline.[67]

In reality, as observed by Justice Joyce in the aspirin case,[68] the German patent applications were drafted using obscure language in order to avoid dissemination of the inventive processes. It is arguable that, at this time, the German companies were in the pursuit of a world-monopoly in the organic chemical field. Furthermore, the patent system in Britain served that aim very well.

Moreover, the aspirin case shed new light on the understanding of the relationship between patents and local innovation. It is suggested that the Bayer case led to the indirect reform of British patent laws.[69] As such, and influenced to a certain extent by Justice Joyce's observations in the aspirin case, David Lloyd George, the then Minister of Trade, stated:

> Big foreign syndicates have one very effective way of destroying British industry. They first of all apply for patents on a very considerable scale. They suggest every possible combination, for instance, in chemicals, which human ingenuity can possibly think of. These combinations the syndicates have not tried themselves. There are not in operation, say, in Germany or elsewhere, but the syndicates put them in their patents in obscure and vague terms so as to cover any possible invention that may be discovered afterwards in this country.[70]

This is called diseconomies of scale. *See,* Definition of Economies of Scale, Investopedia, available at http://www.investopedia.com/terms/e/economiesof scale.asp.

[67] Ivan Levinstein, owner of the largest British dye firm, commented on British patent laws in *Nature* (1903): *See,* Murmann, supra note 58, p. 91.

[68] It was 'erroneous and misleading ... by accident, error or design so framed as to obscure the subject as much as possible' Justice Joyce (1905) 22 RPC 501.

[69] Jeffreys, supra note 54, p. 88.

[70] David Lloyd George reiterated Chamberlain's view in 1907 when discussing the prospective revision of British patent law: *See,* Borkin, J. and C.A. Welsh

In 1907, a new act entitled 'The Act to Consolidate the Enactments Relating to Patents for Inventions and the Registration of Designs and Certain Enactments Relating to Trademarks' was introduced. The terms of this act included strengthened revocation provisions. These provisions were enacted in order to put strong pressure on the German synthetic dyestuff manufacturers to work their patents in Britain. The act effectively encouraged the main German dyestuff companies to set up factories in Britain to manufacture their patented dyes. Despite the British government's strategic approach to the development and regulation of its domestic chemical industry,[71] it is arguable that the German industry's control of patents and know-how made it almost impossible for Britain to build and operate the chemical plants that were required for the war effort during World War I.[72]

On the other hand, until the World War I, the German chemical industry controlled the entire scientific world to a large extent. Arguably, it was the German patent system that provided both a shield and a spear to the industry.[73] According to Murmann, 'the interface between the German chemical industry and the government was well-developed in the last quarter of the nineteenth century, allowing such important collective policy initiatives as the passage of a patent law to be especially tailored to the needs of the chemical industry'.[74] In this context, Borkin and Welsh observed that 'the methodical but almost frenetic determination which inspired German research did not observe any scruples in borrowing inventions from other countries'.[75]

An analysis of William Henry Perkins's, later Sir William and best known as the inventor of the first aniline dye, experience with the German patent system provides an understanding of how the patent system worked in Germany:

(1943) *Germany's Master Plan: The Story of the Industrial Offensive*, London, John Long.

[71]   Dutfield, supra note 36, pp. 84–5.

[72]   Borkin and Welsh, supra note 70, the chapter on *I.G. – The Vials of Wrath*.

[73]   Borkin and Welsh, supra note 70.

[74]   Murmann, J.P. and R. Landau (1998) 'On the Making of Competitive Advantage: The Development of the Chemical Industries in Britain and Germany since 1850' in A. Arora, R. Landau and N. Rosenberg (eds) *Chemicals and Long-Term Economic Growth: Insights from the Chemical Industry*, New York, John Wiley & Sons, Inc, pp. 27–70; *See also,* Dutfield, supra note 36, p. 82.

[75]   Borkin and Welsh, supra note 70.

He went so far as to say that, for years before he left the business, he and other English chemists had entirely abandoned attempts to patent their discoveries in Berlin. He had found, by sad experience, that whenever he sent over an application for a patent on a new dyestuff, or new chemical compound of importance, the German Patent Office would at once call in, for consultation, the leading German chemists who were interested in that line of work. He would get request after request for more and more detailed information about every part of the process; and then, when they had got from him every bit of information that they could, they would grant the patent to some one of his German competitors.[76]

Clearly, the German patent regime favoured the local industry by creating incentives to exploit every possible chemical route to the development of a particular dye product. In contrast to the situation in Britain and the US, the lack of patent protection for chemical products prompted the creation of true research laboratories whose only function was to search for new dyes. Thus, the German patent regime was of crucial importance to the German industry in relation to its building-up of domestic skills and research capacities. Given the ideal patent environment up to this date, the German dye industry had the ability to dominate the world market. For Murmann, the industry would not have been able to develop a virtual world monopoly that was capable of being maintained over a long period of time, had this ideal patent environment not existed.[77] In other words, it is suggested that German patents, in the hands of the German industry, proved to be a branch of German arms following the enactment of the Patent Act in 1877.[78]

Following World War I, the German companies faced strong pressure from the US government. The wartime shortage of medicines coupled with the dependency on German industries, presented a compelling rationale for the US goal of maintaining a self-sufficient local pharmaceutical industry. The US government realised the importance of developing wide ranging industrial capabilities in drug manufacturing in order to counterbalance the influence of German companies that dominated the market. With the enactment of the Trading with the Enemy Act,[79] which authorised the use of economic sanctions against foreign nationals and companies, all the German chemical patents were sold to the Chemical Foundation, which represented the US chemicals sector. Although most

---

[76] *Id.*
[77] Murmann, supra note 58, p. 91.
[78] Borkin and Welsh, supra note 70.
[79] Trading With the Enemy Act of 1917, 6 October 1917, Ch 106, 40 Stat. 411.

of the German patents were written in obscure language, as stated above, so as not to disclose the inventions, the US industry still benefited from this trade-off to a certain extent. More importantly, the US government finally adopted a more mercantilist approach to its industry, an approach that was similar to that of the German government, in prioritising and implementing policies that were specifically aimed at promoting the development of local industry.[80]

Back in Europe, the worldwide success of aspirin, the first synthetic compound, prompted further research into the possibilities of using dyestuff variants as medicines. In a period of less than a half-century, the German dye industry discovered a new class of so-called sulpha drugs, which proved to be effective against bacterial infections such as spinal meningitis, various forms of pneumonia and so on, and which provided a first line of defence. The encouraging results allowed the dyestuff industry to concentrate on developing key skills in organic chemistry. Nevertheless, taking the leap from traditional dyestuff research to organic chemistry was not easy, and thus, it posed significant challenges for the industry. It required a long-term vision aimed at dominating the market through encouraging innovation. In fact, a few large firms soon dominated the market because the industry was highly capital intensive, that is, it involved a level of cost that was beyond the means of most small firms. By the beginning of the twentieth century, there were only six leading companies in the market, in both Germany and the world: BASF, Bayer, Hoechst, Agfa, Cassella and Kalle A.G.[81] Furthermore, the German dye industry had established strong links with major German research institutes that undertook research into areas of organic chemistry and related medical fields. The strength of the German university system in the field of organic chemistry, according to Murmann, also assisted German industry in developing a better understanding of the formation of dye molecules. It was particularly important for the industry to understand how these molecules bonded with fabrics. It was also necessary to provide essential training for chemists who populated the firms' R&D labs.[82] The university system helped to enable the industry in these areas. These efforts provided the industry with an increased ability to synthesise

---

[80]   Dutfield, supra note 36, p. 101.

[81]   In 1925, the main German chemical industry established I.G. Farben, which immediately became a dominant player in various types of chemical products as well as pharmaceuticals. At the end of World War II, Hoechst and Bayer were the only surviving companies from I.G. Farben. *See,* Dutfield, supra note 36, pp. 99–100.

[82]   *See,* Murmann, supra note 58.

molecules and analyse chemicals, and consequently, aided to develop the current understanding of microorganisms, which lays the foundation for more modern pharmaceutical research.

Epoch Two: Penicillin – A Breakthrough in the History of Pharmaceutical Innovation

The discovery of penicillin is frequently referred to as one of the most important breakthroughs in the history of pharmaceutical innovation. In fact, penicillin became the first widely used antibiotic agent that was capable of providing a defence against bacterial infections. Undoubtedly, the discovery and development of penicillin started the antibiotic revolution. This period of scientific breakthrough revolutionised the treatment of bacterial infections and, in so doing, changed the course of medical history. Thus, the story of penicillin contains important lessons for pharmaceutical innovation today, and in particular, the importance of recognising the distinction between invention and innovation.

In the final decades of the nineteenth century, scientists discovered that bacteria were the cause of many of illnesses. This theory is known as germ theory. It is widely attributed to Pasteur, who is acknowledged as the father of microorganism research. Indeed, Pasteur, Koch[83] and Ehrlich[84] were the first to identify the particular microbes that caused several major diseases, and they went on to contribute to the development of highly effective vaccines.[85]

For instance, Ehrlich and his colleagues synthesised and tested more than 600 molecules for therapeutic effects against syphilis, a widespread and essentially incurable disease. In an effort to optimise the biological activity of a lead compound through systematic chemical modifications, the scientists discovered the process for isolating salvarsan, the very first organic anti-syphilitic drug. The discovery of this process is widely

---

[83]   Robert Koch is widely regarded as one of the founders of microbiology. He searched for the causes of many diseases. *See,* Robert Koch developed many microbiological techniques, available at http://www.microbiologytext.com/index.php?module=Book&func=displayarticle&art_id=26.

[84]   Paul Ehrlich received the Nobel Prize in 1908 for his work in immunology. He was also the founder of modern chemotherapy and the discoverer of salvarsan, the first specific and effective cure for syphilis. *See,* 'From Nobel Prize to Courthouse Battle: Paul Ehrlich's "Wonder Drug" for Syphilis Won Him Acclaim but also Led Critics to Hound Him', *The Washington Post,* 27 July 1999, available at http://www.encyclopedia.com/doc/1P2-615079.html.

[85]   Dutfield, supra note 36, p. 90.

acknowledged as a great advancement from the use of inorganic compounds. This discovery essentially created the basis for nearly all modern pharmaceutical research.[86] The identification and characterisation of bacterial toxins as the primary cause of disease pioneered the discovery of penicillin.[87] The discovery of general-purpose chemotherapeutic agents, known as the sulphonamides, prompted the antibiotic revolution that started in the era of chemotherapy.[88]

The discovery of penicillin was coincidental. Nonetheless, the story of its discovery was compelling. Alexander Fleming, from St Mary's Hospital, London, returned from holiday to find some mould growing in one of his discarded staphylococcus culture plates. This enabled him to discover the anti-bacterial action of a specimen of mould. He found that the mould had drifted onto and killed the bacteria that he was culturing in a petri dish.[89] Although his efforts to stabilise penicillin failed, he and his assistants managed to produce it in a very weak form. The very first version of penicillin could inhibit the growth of other microbes from a swab. Thus, it could facilitate the flourish of influenza B. Furthermore, penicillin was able to signal the presence of influenza. This was an important milestone in terms of diagnosing the disease. Furthermore, the discovery gave impetus to the process of developing a vaccine against influenza B. Given the fact that there were several problems in relation to replicating the experiment successfully, coupled with penicillin's lack of effectiveness at treating influenza, Fleming decided to stop the research project.[90] He did, however, write an influential scientific article regarding the discovery of penicillin and its effects.

Almost a decade later, two scientists, Howard Florey and Ernst Chain, from the University of Oxford, took Fleming's invention a step further. Florey and Chain managed to isolate the bacteria-killing substance found in the mould – penicillin. Fleming's paper prompted Chain's research into penicillin. By working on the problems that defeated Fleming, Chain stabilised and purified the active substance. Furthermore, the controlled experiments produced a number of positive results in relation to mice

[86]   Scherer, supra note 2, p. 6.
[87]   Dutfield, supra note 36, p. 90.
[88]   Prontosil emerged in 1935 out of Domagk's work, also on dyestuffs, in the great German chemical conglomerate of I.G. Farben: *See* Kingston, W. (2003) 'Antibiotics, Invention and Innovation' in W. Kingston (ed.) *Innovation: The Creative Impulse in Human Progress*, Washington, The Leonard R. Sugerman Press Inc., p. 73.
[89]   Scherer, supra note 2, p. 6.
[90]   Kingston, supra note 88, p. 75.

with bacterial infections. A full-scale test on a few human cases also proved to be successful. While the initial experiments were successful, Florey and Chain faced the dilemma of carrying out full-scale clinical trials. Furthermore, it was necessary to produce a large amount of penicillin in order meet the wartime demand in Britain.

Indeed, when Florey and Chain advanced their research on penicillin, Britain was already in the midst of World War II. Nevertheless, the solution to the practical problems faced by Florey and Chain did not lie in Britain. The British drug industry was unable to carry out the production of penicillin in bulk. The industry was already facing problems concerning wartime shortages for the existing range of drugs. Furthermore, the British industry generally took a conservative attitude regarding experimental medicines, and hence, it was reluctant to invest in new inventions.[91]

However, Florey's enthusiasm transformed the speculative experiment of penicillin into a research programme. The reason for this was that Florey was not only a good scientist but he was also an innovator and entrepreneur. Thus, when he failed to persuade any of the British companies to produce penicillin, he did not give up and go back to his lab, as many other scientists would have done. He went to America and visited a number of the pharmaceutical companies to explain the invention of penicillin. Initially, he managed gain the support of the Committee on Medical Research of the United States Office of Scientific Research and Development. It was at this stage that the US drug industry, including the leading firms such as Merck, Squibb and Pfizer, decided to devote funds to a massive research and production effort that focused on industrial manufacturing of penicillin.[92]

The story of penicillin illustrates the key interaction involved in innovation. Furthermore, it serves as anecdotal evidence in favour of Schumpeterian theory. Kingston, for instance, argues that the contrast between what was done by Fleming and what was done by Florey clearly illustrates Schumpeterian theory, and in particular, it shows the clear-cut line that exists between inventor and innovator. Fleming discovered penicillin. However he was unable to realise the potential of his invention. Due to research problems, he was unable to take his discovery any further. Like many other scientists, he was committed to science. He wrote a paper on the discovery of penicillin and its potential usage. In

---

[91] *See, Ibid*, p. 79; Palombi, L. (2009) *Gene Cartels, Biotech Patents in the Age of Free Trade*, Cheltenham, UK and Northampton, MA, USA, Edward Edgar.

[92] *See,* Kingston, supra note 88, pp. 70–130.

this context, Fleming presents a very good model of the Schumpeterian inventor.[93] Florey, however, was the Schumpeterian innovator of penicillin. Florey believed in penicillin and he explored the industrial potential of the invention. He did this to ensure a high level of production of penicillin so that the invention could meet its therapeutic potential. In fact, when the American medical profession took a conservative approach towards penicillin, he directly intervened. He went to a battlefield in North Africa and advocated the healing potential of penicillin. He showed the doctors how to successfully treat wounds with penicillin. If it had not been for Florey's enthusiasm and his persuasive powers, penicillin would not have been widely available during World War II.

For Kingston, Florey is an innovator because he set goals for himself and he took all necessary steps to achieve them.[94] The Schumpeterian definition of an innovator focuses on the entrepreneur who is able to see the potential of the invention and who is capable of coping with the inevitable resistance that innovators face when they attempt to move outside established practice. Florey was totally committed to the penicillin project. The resultant difficulties that occurred regarding the development of the drug did not prevent him from advocating the production of penicillin. His colleagues at Oxford described him as 'not a profound visionary, like Copernicus or Galileo or Faraday; he was not an outstanding experimental innovator like Pasteur or Koch or Ehrlich; he was not a towering scientific intellect like Newton or Darwin or Einstein. But he had one supreme virtue: he knew exactly what had to be done next, and he got it done'.[95] Once again, this description proves to be remarkably accurate with respect to Schumpeter's innovator, that is, the person who 'seeks out difficulties, changes in order to change, and delights in

---

[93]   ' Fleming ... once he had written his scientific paper describing the use of penicillin for identifying influenza, decided not to try to take it any further and went on to other things. He was a very model of the inventor as described by Schumpeter.' Kingston, supra note 88, p. 86.

[94]   '"fire and energy" was precisely what characterized Florey's performance. ... The scientific aims with which the original study had started out, necessarily became secondary in importance to the achievement of penicillin's therapeutic potential. Both in setting these goals for himself, and in achieving them, Florey showed the personal commitment to a project that is so characteristic of innovators. *See,* Kingston, supra note 88, p. 86.

[95]   Harris, H. (1999) 'Howard Florey and the Development of Penicillin', Notes and Records of the Royal Society of London, V.53, N.2., p. 252.

ventures'.[96] Therefore, in the story of penicillin, it was Florey who ended up getting things done and thus, he was able to turn Fleming's invention into 'an untried technological possibility'.[97]

Apart from providing anecdotal evidence of Schumpeterian invention and innovation theory, the penicillin story reveals a number of important real-life lessons that have relevance for pharmaceutical innovation today.

Above all, the foremost lesson that can be drawn from the history of penicillin is acknowledgement of the advantage of 'standing on the shoulders of giants'. In 1945, Fleming, Chain and Florey received the Nobel Prize for Physiology or Medicine from King Gustav V of Sweden, in recognition of the fact that they had made one of the most important and valuable contributions to the development of modern medicine. In his banquet speech, Fleming highlighted the role of teamwork as crucial to the success of penicillin. He emphasised 'team work may inhibit the primary initiation of something quite new but once a clue has been obtained team work may be absolutely necessary to bring the discovery to full advantage'.[98] Florey, similarly, expressed his gratitude to all the scientists who were somehow involved in the project or supported it. He then concluded:

> Let us all fervently hope that what can be achieved in the way of friendship on the personal plane among scientists may soon be translated to wider spheres so that the great technical achievements of mankind can indeed be used for its benefit.[99]

In fact, penicillin was the greatest invention of the last century. It has been described as a 'splendid example of different scientific methods co-operating for a great common purpose'.[100] Florey and Chain owed a tremendous debt to Fleming's initial invention. In the meantime, there

---

[96] Schumpeter, J. (1934) *The Theory of Economic Development: An Inquiry into Profits, Capital, Credit, Interest and the Business Cycle*, Cambridge, Harvard University Press, pp. 93–4.

[97] Schumpeter, J. (1942) *Capitalism, Socialism, and Democracy*, New York, Harper Brothers Publishers, p. 132.

[98] Sir Alexander Fleming, The Nobel Prize in Physiology or Medicine 1945, The Banquet Speech, 10 December 1945, available at http://nobelprize.org/nobel_prizes/medicine/laureates/1945/fleming-speech.html.

[99] Sir Howard Florey, The Banquet Speech, The Nobel Prize in Physiology or Medicine 1945, 10 December, 1945, available at http://nobelprize.org/nobel_prizes/medicine/laureates/1945/florey-speech.html.

[100] The Nobel Prize in Physiology or Medicine Presentation Speech by Professor G. Liljestrand, member of the Staff of Professors of the Royal Caroline Institute on 10 December 1945.

was no possibility that Fleming could have received the Nobel Prize in Medicine without the efforts of Chain, Florey or the Oxford team.[101] Hence, Florey and Chain stood on the shoulders of Fleming and in so doing; they were able to reach new heights. Florey was the real innovator of penicillin because he consistently believed that a successful outcome could be achieved only through the collaboration of several individuals. Thus, it can be said that, working under the undisputed leadership of Florey, the scientific enthusiasm of the Oxford team made a significant contribution to science and humanity.

It is an interesting irony, and it is probably exceptional in the history of pharmaceutical innovation, that neither Fleming nor Florey tried to patent penicillin. Indeed, the antibiotic revolution was a result of cumulative research. There were no patents on the processes or the product of penicillin. Fleming never attempted to patent penicillin because he believed that it could have the potential to be used in drug discovery research.[102] Florey had long arguments with Chain over whether to patent the process for the production of penicillin. Chain had studied and worked in Germany and thus, he adopted the German approach to patents. Recalling the German chemical companies' tradition of patenting every type of pharmaceutical process, Chain felt puzzled that Florey had a negative attitude towards patents. However, Florey truly believed that any kind of patent application would have violated the academic ethos of the time.[103] Notwithstanding this fact, it should be noted that it is difficult to say whether any attempt to patent penicillin could ever have been successful, given the publication of Fleming's article on penicillin.[104]

Chain was not the only person who was puzzled that neither Fleming, nor Florey, was willing to patent penicillin. Almost a century after the discovery of penicillin, the pharmaceutical and biotechnology industry

---

[101]   Florey gathered a team of scientists in Oxford who individually assisted the development of penicillin. The team included Edward Abraham, Charles Fletcher, A.D. Gardner, Norman Heatley, Margaret Jennings and Lady Florey.

[102]   *See,* Macfarlane, G. (1984) *Alexander Fleming: The Man and the Myth,* Oxford, Oxford University Press.

[103]   'When Chain appealed his case to other colleagues, he was accused of 'money grubbing'. *See,* Bishop, M.J. (2003) *How to Win the Nobel Prize: An Unexpected Life in Science,* Cambridge, MA, Harvard University Press, p. 129.

[104]   According to Kingston, even it escaped being ruled to be 'a product found in nature' and if Fleming's 1929 scientific Paper had not destroyed patentable novelty by releasing the information into the public domain, later disclosures such as Chain and Florey's paper, and those to the US pharmaceutical firms by Florey and Heatley on their tour there, would almost certainly have precluded the grant of a valid patent; *See,* Kingston, supra note 88, p. 103.

described the decision not to patent penicillin as a perfect example of a lost opportunity. The conventional wisdom of the industry states that penicillin didn't become commonly available until 1941 due to the fact that Fleming did not patent it in 1928 when it was first discovered. Nevertheless, the history tells a different story. Florey was able to assure penicillin production in the US in exchange for the patent rights. It was Andrew Moyer, an American government scientist, who first patented the method of penicillin production, in 1948, not Fleming or the Oxford team. It has often been noted that it took several years to develop and produce penicillin because there were no patents and thus, no incentives for any pharmaceutical company to invest in penicillin.[105] Nonetheless, the reality is different from what is commonly argued. The historical facts that occurred, namely the wartime conditions at the time, and the limitations on pharmaceutical production that existed in Britain, were arguably the main reasons why penicillin had to be taken to the US for production. In a hypothetical scenario, which envisages Fleming patenting penicillin when he discovered it, it remains unknown as to how much longer it would have taken before the mass production of penicillin was possible. Clearly, penicillin was a result of a process of cumulative research and the development of the drug was made possible only through the collaboration of several individuals. In other words, if there had been patent restrictions on penicillin, it is likely that there would not have been any input from either Chain or Florey. Without Chain or Florey, there would have been no penicillin, at least for the period of patent protection. Arguably, this would have, led to there being no available penicillin during World War II. Undoubtedly, this scenario would be highly undesirable, given the fact that penicillin was widely used during World War II and saved many lives.

Since World War II the technology for producing penicillin has been subjected to numerous patents. 'The American monopolisation of a great British discovery'[106] led the American pharmaceutical companies to be

---

[105] 'Because there was no patent, there was no incentive for any company to determine what penicillin did, and it lay undeveloped for many, many years. Eventually a company secured a patent on a method of manufacturing penicillin and it was finally developed as a drug. It would have been perfectly appropriate to patent penicillin if a company could have isolated it, purified it, identified its structure, and determined its value to human health.' *See,* Feisee, L. (2001) 'Anything under the Sun Made by Man', Biotechnology Industry Organization, Director for Federal Government Relations and Intellectual Property, available at http://www.bio.org/speeches/speeches/041101.asp.

[106] Kingston, supra note 88, p. 88.

the economic winners of the patent race. They subsequently extended their patents to the other potent antibiotics such as streptomycin, aureomycin, chlormeycetin and so on.[107] The antibiotic revolution contributed to patent policy liberalisation in the US. The replacement of flash of genius requirement by the inventive step requirement or non-obviousness test improved the ability of pharmaceutical companies to utilise the patent system for antibiotic inventions. Thus, it was now the turn of the American pharmaceutical industry to conquer the world market. The increasing rate of scientific advancement in antibiotics, coupled with strong patent protection and aggressive marketing tactics, enabled American companies to grow into pharmaceutical world powers.[108]

There are number of lessons in relation to discovery, invention, innovation and patents, that can be drawn from exploring the story of penicillin. In his seminal work on antibiotics, invention and innovation, Kingston argues that there are real-life lessons for pharmaceutical innovation within the penicillin story. He notes, for example, the fact that government intervention contributed to the innovation of penicillin. Kingston further argues that penicillin could not have been innovated on a large-scale basis without the intervention of US government agencies. In this context, it is arguable that the particular arrangements that were in place at the time allowed the free transfer of information between different pharmaceutical firms. This in turn enhanced the supply of penicillin during wartime.[109] In fact, if these agencies had not been capable of operating efficiently, it is likely that penicillin supplies would have been exhausted long before the end of the war. Moreover, the institutional structure surrounding the industry shifted significantly at this time. There was a great deal of public support for drug discovery and development. Public support had been quite modest before the war, but during the war it increased to an exceptional level. This undoubtedly helped to set the stage for a period of great prosperity.[110]

Another important point to consider in the story of penicillin is the existence of university-industry collaboration. As mentioned earlier, as a result of the conservative attitude of the British pharmaceutical companies towards scientific research being undertaken in academic laboratories, Florey brought his research to the US for British industry; the idea of developing a viable drug from the biological production of penicillin

---

[107]   Palombi, supra note 91, p. 110.
[108]   *Id.*
[109]   Kingston, supra note 88, pp. 114–15.
[110]   Malerba et.al., supra note 24, p. 5.

was unrealistic and utopian.[111] As noted above, it was initially the German chemical industry that established strong links with both academia and research labs. Furthermore, the long record of collaboration between various institutions and industries in the penicillin case demonstrates very clearly that a close relationship between industry and academia is essential for successful pharmaceutical R&D. Merck & Co. Inc., for example, was one of the first companies which appreciated the critical role that university research played in the R&D process. When Florey did a tour of US pharmaceutical companies, Merck was the only firm that gave encouragement to his idea of producing large quantities of penicillin. For Kingston, the reason for this was that Merck understood the importance of university research and the company had already recruited researchers in order to work on Fleming's papers. Hence, Merck was the only firm ready to commit itself to penicillin production.[112] Moreover, Merck provided funding for the screening programme initiated by Selman Walksman that undertook tests on soil samples in anticipation of discovering antibacterial qualities. The screening efforts of Walksman and his team eventually led to the discovery of streptomycin, a new antibiotic effective against tuberculosis. In addition, the team undertook systematic screenings of substances occurring in nature.[113] Finally, the US Patent Office decision to grant a patent for streptomycin to Merck has proven to be a landmark decision.[114] The decision[115] changed the structure of the industry dramatically and pioneered competition among American pharmaceutical companies through product development.[116]

Undoubtedly, the discovery of penicillin has kick-started the antibiotic revolution in pharmaceutical innovation. As a result, antibiotics came into

---

[111] Palombi, supra note 91, p. 114.

[112] Kingston, supra note 88, pp. 115–16.

[113] Scherer, supra note 2, p. 7.

[114] For Kingston, as the discovery of streptomycin was effectively under the control of Merck, the research on it was intended to lead to patents. The patent office appeared to have held that the modifications carried out to purify and stabilise it amounted to the production of 'a new composition of matter' as required by the Patent Act. *See,* Kingston, supra note 88, pp. 104–5.

[115] The court held that the modifications carried out to purify and stabilise streptomycin amounted to the production of 'a new composition of matter' as required by the Patent Act, and approved the issue of patent to Merck. *See, Id.*

[116] *Ibid.,* p. 105; CTIETI, (1983) *The Competitive Status of the US Pharmaceutical Industry: The Influences of Technology in Determining International Industrial Competitive Advantage*, Washington, National Academy Press, p. 9.

widespread production and are now used all around the world. Furthermore, it has dramatically changed the behaviour of the pharmaceutical industry. The pharmaceutical companies have built upon the lessons learned from the development of aspirin, penicillin and streptomycin and have often used organic molecule synthesising, a process inherited from aspirin. Furthermore, companies often undertake screenings of naturally occurring substances, a process inherited from penicillin in order to develop new and more powerful lines of antibiotics.[117]

Epoch Three: From Serendipity to Tailor-Made Drugs

During the period between 1950 and 1960, the American pharmaceutical industry was committed to excellence in in-house R&D. In consequence, American companies emerged as leaders in the world pharmaceutical market. In large part, this success was down to the launch of penicillin and streptomycin. In addition, new technological opportunities for drug development had emerged. As a result, the pharmaceutical industry assigned a greater priority to the screening of natural products for therapeutic use. In particular, the industry made advances in the areas of extraction and purification. Many of the drugs developed within this period followed the same patterns, which were based upon the discovery of substances found in nature.[118]

By the 1970s, the number of substances that were being prepared, extracted, or isolated for medical research reached 130 000. New molecules and compounds were discovered through random screening and a large number of compounds were tested. Major serendipitous discoveries occurred at this time. Multiple drug screening efforts, which were aimed at discovering the mechanism of actions of the drugs, were a major part of pharmaceutical innovation.[119] More importantly, screening efforts were undertaken to identify better compounds quickly and efficiently. These efforts led to the development of extensive libraries of molecules. The existence of these libraries was vital to subsequent drug development efforts.[120]

The 1950s and 1960s were truly the golden age of the pharmaceutical industry. For instance, a number of important breakthroughs, such as the discovery of beta-blockers, took place during this period. Rational drug

[117]   Scherer, supra note 2, pp. 7–8.
[118]   Dutfield, supra note 36, p. 91.
[119]   Malerba et. al, supra note 24, p. 5.
[120]   Scherer, supra note 99, p. 8.

design replaced the phenomenon of the accidental discovery. Nevertheless, starting from the early 1970s, studies started to report a substantial decline in drug innovation. For example, a study undertaken during the period between 1969 and 1989, showed that the number of new chemical entities launched per year dropped significantly, from 90 to 40. Furthermore, these results ultimately revealed that modified versions of existing drugs, often called me-too drugs, were becoming highly prevalent in the market.[121]

In their 1973 seminal work, Taylor and Silberston developed an extensive analysis of the pharmaceutical industry. The study findings raise an important question about the potential serious consequences of failing to keep up the momentum of discovery. According to the authors, the prospects for future progress in less tractable areas of science were reduced due to the fact that the larger portion of R&D investment was being made in the more tractable areas of drug research. Importantly, during the course of their survey, it was revealed that the end of the first chemotherapeutic revolution was almost in sight. As a result a much greater level of R&D expenditure would be required in future to produce advances comparable with those of past.[122]

The process of drug discovery and development was conducted not only by the industry but also by research hospitals and academic institutions. This led to a focus towards creating candidate drugs. Thus, university research arguably had a positive and significant impact on medical research. Furthermore, in the US, the close links between industry and university research provided for better utilisation of publicly funded research. Typically, the information about the structure of a drug receptor, or one of its natural ligands, is used to identity drug candidates. In the late 1990s, armed with such information, drug companies began to use powerful computer programs to search through databases containing the structures of many different compounds. This type of computer-aided drug design allowed researchers to select compounds that were most likely to interact with the receptor, and these were then tested in laboratories.[123] Nevertheless, as the pharmaceutical companies made

---

[121]   Dutfield, supra note 36, p. 96.
[122]   Taylor, C.T. and A.Z. Silberston (1973) *The Economic Impact of Patent System: A Study of the British Experience*, Cambridge, Cambridge University Press, pp. 364–5.
[123]   Twyman, R. (2002) 'Rational Drug Design: Using Structural Information about Drug Targets or Their Natural Ligands as a Basis for the Design of Effective Drugs', The Human Genome Project, Wellcome Trust, available at http://genome.wellcome.ac.uk/doc_WTD020912.html.

advances in drug development, the number of newly discovered chemical entities dropped with each year that went by. Today, new molecules or compounds capture only a small part of pharmaceutical innovation activities. In fact, today, the industry increasingly relies on methods of inventing around existing molecules, such as the introduction of new combinations or new drug delivery models.[124] In this context, much innovation is focused on me-too drugs. The term 'me-too' is usually used when referring to products that are structurally very similar to known drugs.[125] There has been much controversy over me-too drugs. The pharmaceutical industry has been under fire in relation to investment in the development of me-too drugs, rather than bringing forward new drug candidates. Indeed, according to statistics from the Food and Drug Administration (FDA), between the years of 1989 and 2000, 65 per cent of the new drugs that were approved for sale in the US contained active ingredients found in existing products. Interestingly, 54 per cent of these new drugs 'differed from the marketed product in dosage form, route of administration, or were combined with another active ingredient' and further to this, 11 per cent 'were identical to products already available on the US market'.[126]

Over the period between the late 1970s and the early 1980s, it was widely believed that no new pharmaceutical company would be able to enter the market due to the impossibility of competing with the industry's giants.[127] Research based pharmaceutical companies' capacities in relation to random screening methods were built up through internal organisation processes and the development of tacit skills. Building up the necessary skills and research capacities required huge investment. Furthermore, these skills and capacities were difficult to imitate once established and, thus, they became barriers to market entry for new companies.[128] Nevertheless, in recent years, the advancements in science and in technology have driven industrial change in pharmaceutical companies. The development of new drug research techniques has been constant. There have even been a number of radical new approaches adopted by companies. For instance, modern genetic methods began to be used for the identification and synthesisation of therapeutic modules. In addition, gene sequences have been described and identified by scientists.

---

[124]   Malerba et.al, supra note 24, p. 6.
[125]   Medical Dictionary Definitions, available at http://www.medterms.com/script/main/art.asp?articlekey=33748.
[126]   Dutfield, supra note 36, p. 96.
[127]   Gassmann et al., supra note 4, p. 33.
[128]   Malerba et al., supra note 24, p. 6.

For example, the usage of high-speed DNA-sequencing techniques enabled the identification of specific proteins that underlie disease mechanisms. In this way, pharmaceutical innovation became more associated with the area of biotechnology. Founded in 1976 in the US, Genentech[129] was the first successful biotechnology start-up. Since its inception, it has served as a model for most of the university spin-offs, which have had the aim of applying scientific discoveries to commercial drug development.[130]

In essence, innovation in the industry today is based to a great extent on organic chemistry, biochemistry and chemical engineering. These developments in biotechnology, however, have led to advances in many new areas such as chemical engineering, molecular genetics, protein chemistry and enzymology. These areas have now become part of pharmaceutical innovation.[131] For instance, the biotechnological revolution led the emergence of biopharmaceutical drugs, which are based on proteins. These protein-based drugs are derived directly from living organisms such as human blood and plasma, proteins, and monoclonal antibodies.[132] Biotech drugs are becoming increasingly significant in the market and sales of these drugs are growing faster than sales of synthetic compounds.[133] For example, biotech drugs accounted for an average of 18.2 per cent of all products launched over the period between 1996 and 2000. As such, by the end of 2000, there were 76 biotech drugs that hit the market. At the same time, 369 more biotech drugs were in human clinical testing with an aim of 200 disease targets.[134]

There is little doubt that the biotechnological revolution changed the structure of the market. As a result of the revolution, a dense network of collaborative relationships emerged between university start-up firms and the larger pharmaceutical companies. For instance, a number of spin-off

---

[129] It is widely considered as the founder of the biotechnology industry and was created by Herbert Boyer (one of the scientists who developed the recombinant DNA technique) and Robert Swanson, a venture capitalist. It uses human genetic information to discover, develop, manufacture and commercialise medicines to treat patients with serious or life-threatening medical conditions. In 2009, it was acquired by the Roche Group. For more information *see*: http://www.gene.com/gene/index.jsp.

[130] Malerba et al., supra note 24, p. 8.

[131] Gassmann et al., supra note 4, p. 33.

[132] Dove, A. (2000) 'Betting on Biogenerics', *Nature Biotechnology*, V.19, p. 117.

[133] Twenty per cent to 30 per cent, compared with 6 per cent to 8 per cent for synthetic compounds annually.

[134] Gassmann et al. supra note 4, p. 33.

companies became the main suppliers of technology and R&D services, whereas the established pharmaceutical companies assumed the role of capital and complementary assets provider. It became evident that pharmaceutical innovation requires not only the integration of different disciplines, but also techniques, and experimental procedures and routines. The reason for this is that the relevant knowledge is fragmented and dispersed. Nonetheless, the rate of technological change is still very high. Thus, it remains unlikely that a single institution could internally develop all the necessary ingredients for bringing new products to the marketplace.[135]

Furthermore, the remarkable advancements in large-scale DNA sequencing of genetic endowments coupled with the presence of individuals willing to administer the drugs, led to the emergence of pharmagenomics. Pharmagenomics research aims to identify the human genetic basis. This genetic basis identifies individual variability in drug response.[136] Rather than the traditional one-dose-fits all approach, it became necessary to take a novel approach towards the areas of customised medicine and tailor-made drugs. There is now wide optimism about the future of pharmaceutical innovation. The breakthrough advances in science and technology have enabled computer-aided structurally based drug design, low-cost molecular manipulation as well as screening, DNA screening and recombinant genetics. Such improvements in drug discovery and development present major opportunities for the pharmaceutical industry. The attitude of the industry further supports the view that a new golden era is about to begin for pharmaceutical innovation.[137]

THE LOCAL PHARMACEUTICAL INDUSTRY IN DEVELOPING COUNTRIES

Generic drugs are often the only medicines that developing country nations are able to access and afford. The availability of a wide-range of generic drugs is of utmost importance for poor people within developing countries as part of their fight against poverty. Thus, developing countries typically excluded patent protection in relation to pharmaceuticals. They therefore offered little protection for patents and regard it as an effective policy for public health and access to medicines. According to the 1988

---

[135]   Malerba et. al, supra note 24, p. 9.
[136]   *See,* Mancinelli, L., M. Cronin and W. Sadée (2000) 'Pharmacogenomics: The Promise of Personalized Medicine', *PharmSci*, V.2, E.1, 2000.
[137]   Scherer, supra note 2, p. 12.

study of the World Intellectual Property Organisation (WIPO), among the 98 members of the Paris Convention, 49 excluded pharmaceutical products from protection and 22 excluded chemical products.[138] Hence, over the last 25 years, pharmaceutical companies from developing countries, including but not limited to India, China, Brazil, Egypt, Turkey and South Africa have developed into giants in generic medicines.

To cite few examples, the rise of the generic industry in India began in the 1970s with the adoption of the Indian Patent Act, which reduced the scope of patentability for food, chemicals and pharmaceuticals to processes only. It is widely accepted that this lack of patent protection, particularly for pharmaceutical products, was a key to the growth of the generic industry in India.[139] Indian companies also expanded their business to include generic export markets overseas. As a result of the existing patent regime, the Indian local pharmaceutical industry emerged as competitive suppliers in the world generic market. In doing this, the industry moved from being an industry dependent on imports to an industry capable of generating increasing export surpluses.

The instrumental use of a weak IPRs regime in building up local capabilities gradually became a phenomenon observable within developing countries. The trend began in India and spread to many other developing countries including Brazil, Argentina, Mexico, Taiwan and Egypt.[140] The presence of relatively weak patent laws in these countries ultimately had a significant impact on the countries' health and development policies.

Brazil, for instance, as a part of national economic development strategy in the post-war era, established a strong state-owned generic pharmaceutical industry. This industry was ultimately privatised in the 1960s and 1970s. As an integral part of a development strategy, and in an effort to achieve sustainable local production, the Industrial Property Act of 1971 abolished patents for pharmaceutical products and chemicals in order to allow the local industry to absorb and assimilate existing

---

[138] WIPO, 'Existence, Scope and Form of Generally Internationally Accepted and Applied Standards Norms for the Protection of Intellectual Property', WO/INF/29 September 1988, Issued as GATT Document Number MTN.GNG/NG11/W/24/Rev.1.

[139] Kumar, N. (2003) 'Intellectual Property Rights, Technology and Economic Development: Experience of Asian Countries', RIS Discussion Paper No.25/2003, p. 27.

[140] Walker, S. (2001) 'The TRIPS Agreement, Sustainable Development and the Public Interest', IUCN Environmental Law Centre, Discussion Paper, 2001, p. 23.

knowledge and technology and, thus, enhance its productivity. In the meantime, the governments in developing countries took a large role in the development of local pharmaceutical capacity and centralised drug purchases. By the 1980s, Brazil was one of the global powerhouses in the area of generic drugs, an industry worth $2 billion. Furthermore, Brazil was the largest exporter of generic drugs in Latin America.[141]

On the other hand, Turkey inherited its first patent law from the Ottoman Empire, which was a translated version of the French Patent Law (1844). This law excluded pharmaceutical compounds, as well as many other kinds of medicinal products from patent protection. Nevertheless, the law provided patent protection for pharmaceutical processes. In the 1960s, the country started to suffer from heavy foreign exchange losses. Essential medicines were being purchased at prices several times higher than they would otherwise have been under normal circumstances. Medicines were expensive and unaffordable for a large proportion of the population. Thus, in May 1961, the Constitutional Assembly abolished process patents due to the perceived problem of the monopoly positions exercised by the patent holders.[142] Since the healthcare system was funded entirely from the tax base, the government emerged as the largest buyer of drugs in Turkey. Hence, the Turkish government was primarily focused on making locally manufactured generic drugs cheaper than branded drugs. Moreover, having the largest generic drug manufacturing capacity in the Middle East and Mediterranean region, Turkish generic companies penetrated established export markets in neighbouring countries.

In other words, the lack of patent protection for pharmaceuticals in developing countries enabled the local generic companies to copy drugs and manufacture them without being held liable for infringement of patents. Within a short period of time, these companies emerged as strong competitors of 'Big Pharma'[143] nationally, regionally and internationally.

---

[141]   Nunn, A. (2009) *The Politics and History of AIDS Treatment in Brazil*, New York, Springer, pp. 75–6.

[142]   *See,* Turkish Official Gazette, 12 May 1961, for the justification of constitutional assembly.

[143]   The term 'Big Pharma' is ambiguous; it generally refers to large multinational pharmaceutical companies representing more than two fifths of the pharmaceutical market. 'Big Pharma' had a total revenue of $251 billion and R&D spending of $44.5 billion in 2006. Multi-nationality, or the decree of internationalisation, is widely accepted as another important feature of 'Big Pharma'. *See,* Held, S. et al. (2009) 'Impact of "Big Pharma" Organizational Structure on R&D Productivity', *Schriften Zur Gesundheitsokonomie.*

Indian companies, for instance, dominated the huge markets for drugs in low-income countries in Africa and Asia. The Brazilian generic industry became the largest exporter in Latin America. The South African national strategy for the fight against HIV/AIDS aimed to increase access and affordability of essential medicines. This strategy included expanding into the generic market, as exemplified by other African countries, in order to treat the HIV/AIDS crisis.

It is clear that the growth of the generic drug industry in developing countries during the 1980s became one of the most significant factors that ultimately laid the foundations of today's global patent regime. The extensive manufacturing capacity of generic companies and the wide availability of generic medicines in developing countries compelled multinationals to cut prices dramatically. Facing the threat of generic competition in developing countries and significant trade deficits, originator companies began to lobby the US government and Congress to take action against developing countries with a weak IPRs regime. Subsequently, in an effort to establish links between trade and intellectual property, the US trade policy changed direction dramatically during the 1980s. This adjustment of US foreign trade policy eventually led to a demand for a fundamental change in world trade policy. This, in turn, was followed by a call for worldwide IPRs protection from other developed countries, particularly in relation to innovative pharmaceuticals. In order to keep pace with the forces of economic globalisation, it is arguable that the developing countries did not have any option but to become parties to the resultant agreement, the Agreement on Trade Related Aspects of Intellectual property Rights (TRIPS).

TOWARDS THE END OF THE BEGINNING:[144] THE TRIPS AGREEMENT

The tension that had arisen between multinational pharmaceutical companies, developed countries and developing countries regarding globalisation and IPRs protection in developing countries resulted in the TRIPS Agreement. This agreement became the first multilateral treaty solely dedicated to intellectual property. TRIPS, taking effect on 1 January 1995, was introduced during the final part of the Uruguay Round of the WTO negotiations. The introduction of TRIPS has proven to be a critical

---

[144] 'Now this is not the end. It is not even the beginning of the end. But it is, perhaps, the end of the beginning', Winston Churchill.

turning point in the history of intellectual property. There is little doubt that a new era for IP was initiated with the introduction of IPRs in the international trading system.

Thus, TRIPS stands as a powerful symbol of the globalisation of IPRs. It covers a wide range of IP issues, including provisions on the domestic enforcement of IPRs and as well as a procedure for achieving binding dispute settlements. TRIPS has a unique character, which stems from the fact that it establishes the minimum standards for IPRs for all WTO members.

There is currently a fundamental legal and political challenge for developing countries in relation to IPRs and innovation. This challenge must be overcome before developing countries can deploy efficient national innovation policies. Over the last decade, there have been a number of heated discussions and debates revolving around the subject of TRIPS. These debates have usually centred on the implementation of TRIPS at a domestic level, as well as its potential impact on innovation and the subsequent costs of compliance. For developing countries, it is important to consider both the positive and negative outcomes of IPRs in the post-TRIPS environment.

The TRIPS Agreement is part of a package. In other words, certain concessions had to be made in order to receive certain trade benefits. The negotiations were based on incomplete information and, as a result, it was regarded as an imperfect bargain for the developing countries.[145] The combination of hardball diplomacy coupled with a lack of appreciation on the part of the developing countries regarding the possible future impact of the undertakings, enabled the developed countries to win the battle and achieve the first global governance regime for IPRs as part of the new WTO system.[146]

It is possible to view the TRIPS Agreement as unique because of the way it was negotiated. There was a key part strategy to get the right mix of issues on the table, even if they were previously unrelated, in order for these issues to be linked for bargaining purposes. This was known as linkage-bargain diplomacy. Thus, the issue of intellectual property was

---

[145]   For TRIPS Negotiation Narrative, *See* Gervais, D. (2007) *Intellectual Property Trade and Development: Strategies to Optimize Economic Development in a TRIPS-Plus Era*, New York, Oxford University Press.

[146]   May, C. and S. Sell (2006) *Intellectual Property Rights: A Critical History*, London, Lynne Reiner, p. 158.

negotiated across sectors[147] or to put it quite simply; IPRs were traded in negotiations for deals on fruits or textiles.

TRIPS may be described as a constitution-like agreement because it reaches into the nation–state, giving rights to individuals.[148] It contains more than mere wishes. According to legal scholars, the TRIPS method of dictating rules to countries, whether developed, developing or least-developed, regarding what they must do and when and how they must do it, is unprecedented in multinational treaties. As a result, there has been widespread discussion on whether this will have far-reaching effects on national legal systems to an extent that goes far beyond the realms of intellectual property.[149]

The agreement establishes a balance between rights and obligations. The principles of TRIPS are detailed with an explicit reference to 'the promotion of technological innovation and to the transfer and dissemin-ation of technology, to the mutual advantage of producers and users of technological knowledge'.[150] This represents a compromise between developed and developing countries. From the perspective of the devel-oped countries, it reflects the prevailing justification for the granting of IPRs in relation to technological fields and, as such, is a tool for the promotion of innovation. On the other hand, it also reveals the concerns of the developing countries regarding the transfer and dissemination of technology.

Throughout the TRIPS negotiations, the developed countries regarded a strong IPRs regime as the main promoter of innovation, from which all the regions of the world benefit. Nonetheless, developing countries have tried to voice their concerns over this matter, using the counter argument that tighter IPRs strengthens the monopoly power of large pharmaceutical companies that are based in industrial countries, to the detriment of the less developed countries.[151] Thus, during the negotiations patent rights were a central part of the discussions. A key issue was providing patent protection for pharmaceuticals. Developing countries historically viewed

---

[147]   Ryan, M.P. (1998) *Knowledge Diplomacy: Global Competition and Politics of Intellectual Property*, Washington, Brookings, p. 92.

[148]   Charnovitz, S. (2001) 'The WTO and the Rights of the Individual', *Intereconomics*, V.38, p. 98.

[149]   Mossinghoff, G. (2000) 'National Obligations under Intellectual Property Treaties: The Beginning of a True International Regime', 9 *Federal Circuit Bar Journal*, V.4, p. 603.

[150]   *See*, Article 7, TRIPS Agreement.

[151]   Helpman, E. (1993) 'Innovation, Imitation and Intellectual Property Rights', *Econometrica*, V.61, N.6, 1993, p. 1248.

patent law differently to developed countries and they typically excluded pharmaceuticals from patent protection.

However, after a number of long and tough discussions between both sets of parties, agreement was reached. TRIPS granted patent protection to any invention whether it was a product or process, in all fields of the technology, without any discrimination. In addition to patentability of pharmaceuticals, further protection in relation to undisclosed information and trade secrets was also confirmed.

TRIPS remains an effective compromise between developed and developing countries over the scope of IPRs protection. It tries to balance the needs and desires of all the members in order to harmonise the world IPRs regime, and particularly the patent systems. However, doubt still remains regarding whether conflict has surpassed over compromise, even though the world may not be ready for a globally harmonised patent system.

Arguably, when the developing countries signed up to TRIPS, they gave away more IPRs concessions than they received in return. For instance, the TRIPS assumptions regarding technological self-sufficiency of developing countries have proven to be inaccurate.[152] In this context, under the TRIPS patent regime, the local pharmaceutical companies from developing countries appeared most likely to suffer from a technological gap. They had potentially been forced to undergo structural adjustments in order to assure their long-term survival in the market.

Thus, the implementation of TRIPS led to a wide-ranging debate regarding the positive and negative sides of introducing strong IPRs regimes into developing countries. These concerns have historically played an inordinate role in shaping changes to the political landscape since the enactment of TRIPS.

Consequently, the harmonisation of IPRs under TRIPS was a painful process for those countries that were not in a position to absorb the deadweight losses that resulted from the global protection of IPRs.[153] This gave rise to serious problems. In other words, the strategy of TRIPS represented an unprecedented experiment that effectively accelerated the

---

[152]   Reichman, J. and R. Dreyfuss (2007) 'Harmonization without Consensus Critical Reflections on Drafting a Substantive Patent Law Treaty', *Duke Law Journal*, V.57, p. 97.

[153]   Opderbeck, D. (2005) 'Patents, Essential Medicines and the Innovation Game', *Vanderbilt Law Review*, V.58, p. 507.

introduction of higher IPRs standards into countries that would not ordinarily be expected to adopt these standards.[154]

The ambition of TRIPS was high. The agreement was presented to developing countries as an instrument for securing a long-term interest towards the goals of sustainable development and innovation. However, not long after the signature of TRIPS its controversial provisions gave rise to discussions that focused on the costs and side effects of introducing IPRs into developing countries. To a great extent, the patent regime has been linked to rising healthcare costs and problems regarding access to medicine. Many developing countries are faced with public health problems. These countries have experienced difficulties related to the increasing prices of medicines. It became evident that patents substantially affected the price, access and generic entry into the market of drugs. As a result, TRIPS has come under fierce criticism.

In this context, it is important to discuss the unsuccessful legal challenge that was taken by the multinational pharmaceutical companies against the South African government. It is widely accepted that the multinational pharmaceutical companies emerged from TRIPS as one of the biggest winners.[155] Given the relatively powerful position of the multinational pharmaceutical companies, it was no surprise when the companies sued the government of South Africa. The companies claimed that the Medicines and Related Substances Control Bill, that allowed compulsory licences and parallel imports, infringed both TRIPS and the South African Constitution. This case turned into a public relations disaster for the pharmaceutical companies. Following a significant amount of pressure from both the public and a number of non-governmental organisations (NGOs), the pharmaceutical companies dropped the case in 2001. This is widely believed to have been a significant event in the history of IPRs.

The emergence of patent issues in relation to increasing public health expenditures and access to medicine coupled with the raised level of public awareness following the South African case, eventually led to the introduction of the Doha Declaration. This document aimed to establish a fair balance between the need for access to medicine and the need to protect IPRs. The Doha Declaration was a strong political statement. Furthermore, it demonstrated that when a group of countries does not feel

---

[154]   Maskus, K.E. (2000) *Intellectual Property Rights in the Global Economy*, Washington, Institute for International Economics, p. 144.

[155]   Reichmann, J.H. (2009) 'Compulsory Licensing of Patented Pharmaceutical Inventions: Evaluating the Options', Comment, *Pharmaceutical Regulations*, V.37, I.2, p. 247.

that a treaty has given them a fair deal, they could continue the political fight at a later date.[156]

The pharmaceutical companies lost face in the eyes of the public in the South African case. Hence, this is widely recognised as the lost battle. The Doha Declaration was another battle lost by 'Big Pharma' to the developing countries. However, analysis of the wider picture shows that the war was not completely lost. The three leading IPR-based industries in the US were not entirely satisfied with the terms of TRIPS or the compromises given to the developing countries as part of the Doha Declaration. TRIPS set certain minimum standards. However, the industries wanted more. Thus, the term TRIPS-plus emerged. It was decided that the globally visible WTO negotiations, coupled with the growing public awareness of the negative sides to IPRs, meant that a forum shift was necessary in relation to IPRs negotiations. A one-to-one system of free trade agreement (FTA) negotiations was envisaged. These negotiations were held behind closed doors.

The TRIPS-plus provisions have the potential to influence the future of IPRs normatively at the international level. These provisions mandate an increased level of protection. They also argue in favour of stricter terms of enforcement. This includes inflexible limits regarding the scope of existing flexibilities in relation to TRIPS and other multinational instruments. Thus, the extensive title of TRIPS-plus has started to be widely used in reference to provisions that either exceed the requirements of TRIPS or eliminate the flexibilities underpinning TRIPS.

It is important to state that a collateral problem had arisen due to the extra-legal pressures, which were applied to developing countries to induce them to decline the system of TRIPS flexibilities, and to fall in line with the ill-suited TRIPS-plus solutions.[157] The high number of FTAs, or bilateral investment treaties, shows that TRIPS is being increasingly marginalised, although its passing has not been officially pronounced yet.[158] Since 1994, the US has signed more than 15 free trade agreements (FTAs) with both developed and developing countries including Jordan, Morocco, Peru, Chile, Australia and Singapore and so on. These agreements introduce standards that go beyond the requirements of the TRIPS Agreement. It appears that the TRIPS Agreement was just the beginning of a long-term strategy for developed countries that places a

---

[156]   Gervais, supra note 145.
[157]   *See*, Sell, S. (2002) *Private Power, Public Law: The Globalization of Intellectual Property Rights*, Cambridge, Cambridge University Press.
[158]   El-Said, M. (2007) 'Editorial: Free Trade, Intellectual Property and TRIPS-Plus World', *Liverpool Law Review*, V.28, p. 8.

high emphasis on the success of multinational companies. From this point of view, much work still remains to be done in order to eliminate the TRIPS flexibilities completely.

The United States is currently negotiating a regional, Asia-Pacific trade agreement, known as the Trans-Pacific Partnership (TPP) with 12 countries in the Asia-Pacific region including Vietnam, Malaysia, Brunei Darussalam, Singapore, Australia, New Zealand, Peru, Chile, Canada, Mexico and Japan. The TPP aims to shape a high-standard, broad-based regional pact in Asia-Pacific, which would contribute to the pursuit of the Free Trade Area of the Asia Pacific (FTAAP).

The proposals tabled by the United States Trade Representative (USTR) for the intellectual property chapter of the TPP introduces significant 'FTA-plus' intellectual property standards, which appear to be more restrictive than the ones in other FTAs signed by the US. These standards serve the best interest of pharmaceutical companies by expanding pharmaceutical patenting and creating new drug monopolies, eliminating safeguards against undeserved patents and favouring big pharmaceutical companies in national courts. The US proposals to the TPP imposes several further limitations that would prolong drug monopolies, eliminate local competitors, increase drug prices, and inhibit the development of national pharmaceutical industries in the Asia-Pacific region.

The increasing use of TRIPS-plus provisions illustrates that the status quo of developing countries must change in order for these countries to continue to develop and prosper. As developing countries begin to wake up from the pipe-dream that the enactment of strong IPRs standards will necessarily bring benefits for development, sustainability and economic growth, the focus must be given to the establishment of a clear equilibrium between the public interest and IP.

For instance, it is clear that the sole introduction of TRIPS, that is, the compatible norms of IPRs into the legal system of a developing country, will not in itself generate massive developmental gains. In fact, it may indeed entail substantial welfare costs. This phenomenon has been observed in many countries, which have changed their IPRs laws in response to bilateral pressure.[159] For the countries below a certain threshold of development, the global IPRs regime introduced by TRIPS is

---

[159]   In response to US pressure under authority of its Special 301 trade law, many developing countries reformed their intellectual property right laws even before TRIPS was signed.

unlikely to contribute to increased growth and prosperity.[160] Yet, some countries still argue positively about the merits of intellectual property.[161]

Catching up in the post-TRIPS era is more costly than ever. Historical analysis of the catching-up process in industrial countries reveals that they enjoyed great freedom to choose appropriate institutions and flexibility regarding the IPRs system. More importantly, a strong IPRs system, as imposed upon developing countries, did not exist anywhere in the world.[162] In fact, IPRs regime in those countries co-evolved with the economy and has been modified over the stages of economic development in response to changing needs of the day.[163]

Nonetheless, the good policies of yesterday are not necessarily the good polices of today. Developed countries are trying to prevent developing countries from using the bad catching-up policies, which they pursued to climb up the ladder.[164] In today's world, there is little doubt that the implementation process of TRIPS engages governments and business elites at a fundamental level. This is a debate about a particular economic development strategy, which poses both economic and political threats to the established relationships of business and governments.[165] In order to optimise the potential benefits within today's trade regime, to stimulate innovation and creativity, TRIPS is needed. However, simply ratifying TRIPS will not be enough. TRIPS, therefore, has to be used appropriately within a system of governance.

Building up the necessary institutional and economic capacities to regulate the use of IPRs does not happen overnight.[166] Under TRIPS and TRIPS-plus, developing countries are expected to take self-restrictive

---

[160]   Park, G. and J.C. Ginarte (1997) 'Intellectual Property Rights and Economic Growth', *Contemporary Economic Policy*, The World Bank, V.15, pp. 51–61; *See,* Kumar, supra note 139, p. 14.
[161]   Sell, S. (1995) 'Intellectual Property Protection and Antitrust in the Developing World: Crisis, Coercion and Choice', *International Organization* V.59, p. 332.
[162]   Khan, Z. (2005) *The Democratization of Invention: Patents and Copyrights in American Economic Development, 1790–1920*, New York, Cambridge University Press, p. 289.
[163]   Odagiri, H., A. Goto and A. Sunami (2010) 'Introduction' in H. Odagiri, A. Goto, A. Sunami and R. Nelson (eds) *Intellectual Property Rights, Development and Catch-up*, New York, Oxford University Press, p. 12.
[164]   Chang, H.J. (2002) *Kicking Away the Ladder – Development Strategy in Historical Perspective*, London, Anthem Press, pp. 126–56.
[165]   Ryan, supra note 147, p. 144.
[166]   Drahos, P. (2005) 'An Alternative Framework Fort: The Global Regulation of Intellectual Property Rights', CKGD, Working Paper, p. 17.

actions with the focus on each country's local economic and social circumstances. IPRs regimes should be tailored to consider each country's domestic technical capacities. There is no one-fits-all approach or even a standard recipe for the implementation of TRIPS. Countries are different, regions are different and further to this, legal cultures are different. Each case should be considered on its own merits. It is therefore essential to gain a better understanding of TRIPS. It is often argued that it is important to use established flexibilities extensively as these will provide a starting point for the development of a number of policy tools that are embedded in the national innovation strategy.[167]

Looking Forward

The TRIPS Agreement is widely regarded by developing countries as an unfair deal. Even now, 19 years after the emergence of the agreement, there are still ongoing discussions focusing on the question of whether the agreement is unbalanced. In fact, it is arguable that today's international IP regime, which is based on TRIPS, was enacted as a response to the call of the strong, and unfortunately, the voices of the weak largely went unheard during negotiations. As Chang puts it, that is how the world works; the strong developed countries call the shots and the weak, developing countries have little choice but to follow orders.[168]

Developing countries have long been concerned about the agreement and its consequences. However, it is not in the interest of developing countries to dwell on the past. They now have to accept that TRIPS is the legal framework for global IPRs. Nonetheless, IPRs should not be overrated, as they constitute only one component of the innovation system. The upshot is to consider IPRs as part of a portfolio of instruments where other elements also need to be strengthened. Of particular importance in this respect is redesigning the IPRs regime to increase its benefits and reduce its costs, which is most likely to boost economic efficiency and increase the pace of innovation.[169]

Hence, in the course of a wider strategy, developing countries may consider taking a holistic approach, focusing on growth prospects through innovation policies. The key lesson for developing countries is that a country can develop a national IPRs strategy that works within the

---

[167] Correa, C. (2010) *Designing Intellectual Property Policies in Developing Countries*, Kuala Lumpur, TWN; Gervais, supra note 145.

[168] Chang, supra note 164, p. 135.

[169] Stiglitz, J. (2008) 'Economic Foundations of Intellectual Property', *Duke Law Journal*, V. 57, p. 1724.

TRIPS framework, and matches the nature of its innovation strategy and local realities. In fact, according to Kuan, while recognising the need to adopt international patent standards, countries might still have the option of adopting 'a more sophisticated framework in which there are degrees of differentiation in outcomes and standards by content and time, to cater to the specific needs of each technological industry and nation'.[170]

In this context, Helpman argued that the absorptive capacity of developing countries largely depends on each country's unique resource base. This necessarily includes the availability of a sufficiently skilled labour force as well as a suitable level of organisational know-how.[171] Maskus identifies the various activities that must be carried out in order to increase absorptive capacity. These activities include the closing down of companies that undertake infringing activities and the placing of market-power pricing. This often occurs with regard to sensitive areas such as the pharmaceutical industry. Considering the hampering effect in strengthening the IPRs regime on the basis of economic development, he also highlights the high cost of innovation and the increase of potential abuses.[172] Nevertheless, in most of the developing countries, there is little doubt that the profits from free riding and piracy outweigh any IPRs.[173] According to Gervais, a balance may be struck by achieving an optimal degree of protection, which appropriately protects and rewards creativity and ingenuity, and thus, provides an incentive to continue creating, while not deterring the creativity and inventiveness of others.[174]

One should note that the real engagement, exploitation and contribution of local innovation and expression depend upon an effective implementation of TRIPS, and the enforcement of these provisions within national political economies.[175] TRIPS stands out as an influential initiative of international law and organisation. However, neither the specific laws of IPRs, nor the judicial reforms necessary for their effective enforcement, will be easily implemented into the legal systems of developing countries.[176]

---

[170]   Kuan, S.: 'The Impact of the International Patent System on Developing Countries', Assemblies of the Member States of WIPO, Thirty-Ninth Series of Meetings, Geneva, 22 September to 1 October 2003.

[171]   Helpman, supra note 151, p. 1276.

[172]   *See,* Maskus, supra note 154, pp. 157–68.

[173]   Sell, supra note 157, 2002 p. 332.

[174]   Gervais, supra note 145, p. 50.

[175]   Ryan, supra note 147, p. 156.

[176]   *Ibid*, p. 158.

A great deal of latitude depends upon the political willingness of countries to set their IPRs policy in accordance with their own national needs and priorities. Thus, one of the key aims of this book is to identify whether TRIPS can effectively be used to build up IPRs capabilities and formulate sound policies to get the most out of the system. For developing countries, the main challenge is to transform the IPRs regime from a rent transfer mechanism into an effective instrument in order to drive local innovation.[177] IPRs are just one of the broader set of measures that are required to increase levels of R&D, knowledge development and economic growth. Innovation is the outcome of knowledge production and is an intensive dynamic process. A successful, national system of innovation must have many component elements other than IPRs. Therefore, developing countries should overlook the negative aspects to introducing, or increasing the strength of, IPRs protection and enforcement. Developing countries should plan for longer-term economic benefits, utilising the framework of national innovation policies.

The TRIPS Agreement was not the end. It was not even the beginning of the end. But it was, perhaps, the end of the beginning. In the long term, there cannot be a lot of optimism about the future of a half-hearted IPRs system. It is generally accepted that the next ten years will bring a new multilateral free trade agreement like the TPP and Transatlantic Investment Partnership (TTIP) that strengthen the IPRs regime of TRIPS and thus, establishes new international norms. Hence, the developing countries do not have much time to catch up. There is a crucial need for the development of proper institutions and effective policies that can facilitate the transfer and development of technology and promote innovation in developing countries.

The TRIPS Agreement changed the nature of the development game. The new game has its own set of rules but this does not necessarily mean that the winner-takes-it-all. One may hypothesises that the way to becoming a winner in this game starts with learning the rules and identifying a winning strategy. Once developing countries truly understand what makes the more developed states so successful, they too can develop their own strategy and achieve success.

The underlying issues are complex. In relation to patents, and IPRs more broadly, much remains to be done in order to encourage technological learning and local innovation. Nevertheless, it may be hypothesised that once developing countries improve their understanding of the

---

[177] *See,* Sherwood, R. (1997) 'The TRIPS Agreement: Implications for Developing Countries', *The Journal of Law and Technology,* V.37, p. 493.

TRIPS regime and IPRs as a crucial component of a national innovation system, they can look forward and start benefiting from the global IPRs regime.

4. Looking at the big picture: national innovation system

Since the introduction of the Agreement on the Trade Related Aspects of Intellectual property Rights (TRIPS), the intellectual property (IP) landscape has changed dramatically. Eventually, intellectual property rights (IPRs) came to be linked with innovation. It is widely accepted that IPRs are economic assets that are necessary to develop world-class standards of innovation and creativity. Thus, they should be considered as forming part of a broader set of measures that are designed to optimise the development and utilisation of knowledge.[1]

While many scholars and international organisations approach IPRs simply from a legal angle, it is important to open up debate about IPRs as an essential component of innovation by integrating legal, political, technological and socio-economic considerations. The debates are still ongoing between countries, politicians, non-governmental organisations (NGOs) and academics on TRIPS and innovation. Nevertheless, one thing is clear – TRIPS still remains in place. Given the recent trend of free trade agreements (FTAs), we would be lucky if TRIPS continues to remain in place.

A better understanding of the nature of TRIPS, and its components, can help to raise awareness of the need for a comprehensive innovation policy. Hence, it is important to outline the issues surrounding the concept of IPRs and innovation.

INTELLECTUAL PROPERTY RIGHTS: A PREREQUISITE FOR INNOVATION?

The systematic promotion of innovation has arguably resulted in innovation becoming a part of the development agenda. Innovation, particularly in developing countries, increasingly takes both legal and economic

---

[1] Gervais, D. (2007) *Intellectual Property Trade and Development: Strategies to Optimize Economic Development in a TRIPS-Plus Era*, New York, Oxford University Press, p. 4.

scholars into account. A large and growing body of literature has explored the subject. However, no solid conceptual framework has yet been demonstrated. It has been stressed that innovation and economic growth, and therefore development, are somehow linked to each other. Innovation, in fact, has the potential to drive a country's long-term economic performance. The innovation process in developing countries is usually described as imitative, adaptive and incremental in nature. Of particular importance in this respect is the correlation between innovation, imitation and intellectual property.

It is widely acknowledged that the on-going project for establishing a strong IPRs regime worldwide, as envisaged by TRIPS, is adversely affecting the technological activities of companies in developing countries, by choking the knowledge spillovers.[2] Hence, the role of IPRs in the innovation process is crucial for designing effective innovation strategies in developing countries. According to theoretical research, the optimal level and impact of IPRs in the innovation process could be variable as a result of the processes of economic development. As in the case of developing countries, adoption of the developed world's standards of protection could result in the level of protection exceeding the optimal level. Hence, the implementation of today's IPRs regime relies largely on the size of the potential market as well as the nature of local R&D within the country.[3] Thus, the successful exploitation of IPRs in the innovation system and the corresponding maximisation of levels of economic growth require a comprehensive knowledge of optimisation strategy.[4]

Depending on the characteristics of a country and provided that R&D in the country is highly productive; it is possible that stronger IPRs protection could have positive effects in relation to developing economies. This is likely to result in significant cost reductions depending on the overall market share of the product. On the other hand, in countries with little or no R&D activities, strengthening IPRs protection may lead

---

    [2]   Kumar, N. (2003) 'Intellectual Property Rights, Technology and Economic Development: Experience of Asian Countries', RIS Discussion Paper No.25/2003, p. 2.
    [3]   Park, G.W. (2008) 'Intellectual Property Rights and International Innovation' in K. Maskus (ed.) *Intellectual Property Growth and Trade*, Amsterdam, Elsevier, V.2, p. 298.
    [4]   Gervais, supra note 1, p. 46.

to welfare reductions. This is because patent holders would typically engage in monopoly pricing which would distort consumer choice.[5]

In recent years, there has been an increasing amount of empirical research on the subject of innovation and the optimal use of IPRs. These studies are diverse. However, some general findings do emerge. Recently, Park carried out a number of selective surveys of the theoretical and empirical literature on the relationship between IPRs and international innovation from an economist's perspective. He attempted to discover whether developing countries are able to derive any benefits through, for example, an increased level of technology transfers. Among the theoretical models he surveyed, Eicher and Penalosa's model is useful for drawing some overall lessons about the impact of IPRs on innovation in developing countries.[6]

In 2006 Eicher et al. constructed a model within which a critical market size is required before IPRs can positively influence innovation. Thus, they introduced the concept of threshold effects as a component of the development dimension of IPRs. For markets that exist below the threshold size, no significant relationship between patents and innovation was found. In contrast, for the markets above the threshold size, a high degree of innovation was feasible, if patent rights were strong and enforceable. Further to this, IPRs would typically become strong if research activity is vibrant enough to create vested interests within such a system. Two sectors were introduced in the model. The first sector was involved in imitation while the second was involved in the performance of R&D. The model demonstrated that in order to go from the low-level equilibrium to the higher level, a minimum market size is required. On the one hand, in the case of weak patents, the returns from investment in R&D are low. Thus, few funds are available to invest in institution building and in further innovation. On the other hand, in the case of a sufficient level of IPR protection, returns on R&D investment are high. Hence, a sustainable level of funds is available for institutions and innovation. According to Park, the model of Eicher et al. clearly demonstrates that the impact of IPRs on innovation is variable depending on the level of economic development.[7] In the context of this wider

---

[5] *See,* UNIDO, (2006) 'The Role of Intellectual Property Rights in Technology Transfer and Economic Growth: Theory and Evidence', Vienna, Working Paper.

[6] Eicher, T. and C. Penosola (2006) 'Endogenous Strength of Intellectual Property Rights: Implications for Economic Development and Growth', Economics Working Paper, University of Washington.: *See,* Park, note 3, p. 298.

[7] Park, supra note 3, p. 298.

debate it has been suggested that IPRs might offer major benefits to developing countries and provide a greater degree of technology transfer through a number of different channels. Nevertheless, the empirical evidence indicates that socio-economic factors, such as a country's imitative ability and its level of development, play a major role in such a process.[8]

In this regard sequences of innovation may provide the context for further discussions. Innovation process involves three sequences. First, a country imitates foreign technology. This is known as the imitation phase, which itself requires some level of technical skills. Second, a country modifies foreign technology in order to suit its domestic needs and markets. This is known as the local innovation phase. Finally, a country starts to produce innovations, either as new products or processes, or as products based on improvements of existing ones. These products are globally competitive and hence, this is known as the global innovation phase.[9]

Quantitative studies indicate that the strength of a patent regime is strongly connected to the level of development of a country. It is empirically demonstrated that the global minimum standards for patent protection, as introduced by TRIPS, are not likely to contribute to increased growth in countries that exist below a certain threshold in developmental terms.[10] Moreover, Thompson and Rushing, using panel data collected from 55 developed and developing countries over the period between 1970 and 1985, found that a system of strong IPRs, coupled with effective enforcement policies, results in more rapid economic growth in countries with an initial level of GDP that is greater than or equal to $3400. These results further support the argument that the cost of strengthening the IPRs regime and thus, granting an increase in monopoly power to the developed countries, comes at the expense of developing countries. The empirical results also confirm the assertion that patent protection is necessary to encourage entrepreneurs to start off the chain of events that eventually leads to economic expansion.[11] Thompson and Rushing further demonstrate that there is a positive association

[8]   UNIDO, supra note 5.

[9]   Gervais, supra note 1, p. 46.

[10]   Park, G. and J.C. Ginarte (1997) 'Intellectual Property Rights and Economic Growth', *Contemporary Economic Policy*, The World Bank, V.15, pp. 51–61; *See,* Kumar, supra note 2, p. 14.

[11]   Thompson, M. and F. Rushing (1999) 'An Empirical Analysis of the Impact of Patent Protection on Economic Growth', *Journal of Economic Development* V.24, I.1 pp. 61–79.

between high levels of patent protection and improvements in total factor productivity, and hence, levels of growth, in wealthy or developed countries.[12]

In fact, Chen and Puttitanun's theoretical model[13] suggests that there is a U-shaped relationship between the optimal strength of IPRs and rates of economic development. This strengthens the empirical foundation of these arguments. According to the study, in less developed economies, which are in the imitation phase according to former theory, governments are more likely to choose low levels of IPR protection, because the quality of local innovation is low and to encourage local imitation facilitates in the copying and diffusion of high-quality foreign innovations. However, in more developed economies, that is, countries which are in the last phase of local innovation, or in the global innovation phase, the quality of local innovation is higher.[14] Thus governments choose stronger IPRs protection in order to provide stronger incentives for research and innovation.[15] The theoretical model is tested empirically by evaluating separate systems of equations that measure rates of IPRs protection in relation to rates of innovation. The model is based on panel data that was collected from 64 developing countries over the period 1975 to 2000. The empirical results demonstrate that there is a U-shaped relationship between IPRs protection and a country's level of development. Furthermore, IPRs protection has been proven to have a stronger impact on innovation in countries with a higher level of development.[16]

The non-linear relationship between levels of IPRs protection and levels of development suggests that as economies move from low- to middle-income status, they develop greater abilities to imitate new technologies. Hence, the strength of patent protection tends to shift towards lower standards.[17] Besides, any assumption that there is direct line between IPRs and innovation bypasses the real-life experiences of

---

[12] *Ibid.*, pp. 67–76.
[13] Chen, Y. and T. Puttitanun (2005) 'Intellectual Property Rights and Innovation in Developing Countries', *Journal of Development Economics*, V.78, I.2, pp. 474–93.
[14] *Id.*
[15] Park, supra note 3, p. 298.
[16] UNIDO, supra note 5, p. 19.
[17] Maskus, K., M. Penubati (1995) 'How Trade-Related are Intellectual Property Rights?', *Journal of International Economics*, V.39, pp. 227–48.

developed countries. This can be observed from the absence of meaning-ful IPRs protection throughout the pre-TRIPS period.[18] The empirical evidence has shown that successful industrialised countries completed their transformation from 'developing' to 'developed' within a relatively weak patent system. However, it must be noted that the absence of a strong patent system did not hamper the industrialisation of countries such as Germany, Switzerland and Japan. The weak IP regime allowed a certain amount of free riding. This was significant for the industrial-isation of a number of countries.[19] As Chang puts it, when they were themselves developing countries, the developed countries' IPRs regimes were deficient by the standards that are demanded of today's developing countries. He elaborates that the policies that the developed countries typically used in the past are precisely the same as the policies that the developing countries were utilising, pre-TRIPS, and which they are now prevented from using by TRIPS.[20]

A well-known example of this is the German dye industry. The German firms became strong competitors in the worldwide dye market in the absence of an effective patent regime in the early twentieth century. In his comparative study of the dye industries of Germany and Britain, Murmann concluded that, had the German patent law arrived earlier, fewer firms would have entered into the industry. As a result, only the most efficient firms would have survived, as was the case in Britain.[21]

Indeed, it has been long suggested that a country's choice of patent laws has often been influenced by the nature of the country's tech-nologies. By way of illustration, the Swiss chemicals industry was initially sceptical about the introduction of a patent system because this would constitute a barrier to technology transfer from abroad. Hence, the Swiss patent law provided for a specific exclusion in relation to a certain category of inventions, that is, the category of dyeing and chemical processes. Thus, the law excluded any invention that could not be

---

[18] Maskus, K.E. (2000) *Intellectual Property Rights in the Global Economy*, Washington, Institute for International Economics, pp. 169–70.

[19] Granstrand, O. (2006) 'Intellectual Property Rights for Governance in and of Innovation Systems' in B. Andersen (ed.) *Intellectual Property Rights, Innovation, Governance and the Institutional Environment*, Cheltenham, UK and Northampton, MA, USA, Edward Elgar, p. 284.

[20] Chang, H.J. (2002) *Kicking Away the Ladder – Development Strategy in Historical Perspective*, London, Anthem Press, p. 128.

[21] Murmann, J.P. (2003) *Knowledge and Competitive Advantage: The Co-evolution of Firms, Technology and National Institutions*, New York, Cambridge University Press, p. 29.

presented by a model or physical replica.[22] Nonetheless, the Swiss patent law did not satisfy the German chemical industry. Hence, the German industry lobbied for the extension of patent protection to chemicals. During the German-Swiss tariff negotiations of 1904, the German government requested that the Swiss patent law be amended. However, the Swiss government initially resisted before eventually declaring that unless Swiss patent law was changed by the end of 1907, Germany had authorisation to raise duties in relation to the importation of coal-tar dyestuffs from Switzerland. Consequently, the patent law was amended in June 1907. However, on request of the Basle chemical industry, chemical processes were excluded from patentability.[23] Swiss law did not grant patentability to these inventions until 1954. Nevertheless, the patent-less period[24] did not appear to hamper the rate of pharmaceutical innovation in Switzerland.

In today's world, it is arguable that the stronger countries have the power to call the shots. As a result, the weaker countries tend only to follow the actions of the stronger countries. Thus, it is said that many developing countries have been forced to adopt the IPRs policies of the stronger, developed countries.[25]

In the post-TRIPS era, catching up with the developed countries is more complex and costly than ever for the developing countries. Today, most developing countries are characterised by strong import growth and in particular, a relatively high rate of technology-intensive import growth rather than the presence of strong local innovation clusters. Thus, the global shift to higher-value-added activities creates a fundamental challenge for developing economies. However, a review of history reveals that the industrialised countries generally enjoyed greater freedom to choose the appropriate institutions for the protection of IPRs than the majority of developing countries do today. During the period when the current group of developed countries were developing, a strong IPRs

---

[22] Moser, P. (2005) 'How do Patent Laws Influence Innovation? Evidence from Nineteenth-Century World Fairs', NBER, Working Paper 9909, available at http://www.nber.org/papers/w9909, p. 35.

[23] Penrose, E.T. (1951) *The Economics of the International Patent System*, Baltimore, The John Hopkins Press, p. 16.

[24] Lee, B. and D. Vivas: 'Intellectual Property Rights: Challenges for Development ICTSD/UNAIDS', Non-attributed Report, 17 June 2004, Sao Paolo, Brazil, available at www.iprsonline.org/unctadictsd/dialogue/2004-06.../ 2004-06-17_report.pdf, (22.09.2010).

[25] Chang, supra note 20, pp. 131–2.

system did not exist anywhere in the world.[26] In other words, the IPRs regime in developed countries co-evolved with the economy of the country. Thus, the IPRs regime could be modified during each stage of economic development, in response to changing needs.[27] The next chapter, though country case studies, will demonstrate how the US and Japan, in particular, have historically taken advantage of the IPRs system to bolster their economic and technological development.

Nonetheless, it is arguable that the following analogy provides an accurate description of the attitude of the developed countries: they are attempting to kick away the ladder which they themselves used to climb. It must be reiterated that in order to be successful, a country must be able to adapt its policy focus to changing economic and political circumstances.[28]

Therefore, the successful implementation of a patent regime in the innovation system of a country inevitably requires taking account of the interplay between economics and the technical dynamics of the country.[29] For instance, the recent economic study of Mohtadi and Ruediger proved the existence and importance of threshold effects and further demonstrated that in a poor economic environment, an economy is characterised by the absence of stable economic institutions, by a low human capital stock, or by a weak financial system, meaning the fixed cost of innovation may be so high that it could actually prevent a firm from being successfully able to innovate.[30] The study also reported that the introduction of IPRs into a poor economic environment, which exists under a certain threshold, would not necessarily improve the situation. The existing threshold can be calculated by assessing the availability of human capital, the quality of institutions and the development of the financial markets. The current level of this threshold usually affects the decision of a firm to either innovate or imitate. Thus, economic analysis

[26]   Khan, Z. (2005) *The Democratization of Invention: Patents and Copyrights in American Economic Development, 1790–1920*, New York, Cambridge University Press, p. 289.
[27]   Odagiri, H., A. Goto and A. Sunami (2010) 'Introduction' in H. Odagiri, A. Goto, A. Sunami and R. Nelson (eds) *Intellectual Property Rights, Development and Catch-up*, New York, Oxford University Press, p. 12.
[28]   Chang, supra note 20, pp. 126–56.
[29]   Granstrand, supra note 19, pp. 284–5.
[30]   Mohtadi, H. and S. Ruediger (2009) 'Imitation, Innovation and Threshold Effects: A Game Theoretic Approach', available at, http://www.uwm.edu/~ruediger/Imitation,%20Innovation%20and%20Threshold%20Effects%20A%20Game%20Theoretic%20Approach%20Mohtadi%20Ruediger%202009.pdf.

has clearly demonstrated that in the absence of sound economic conditions, an imitating firm would not have an incentive, even with the introduction of IPRs, to begin to innovate.[31]

The development of scientific and technological infrastructure and the building up of local capacities are the keys to a successful system in which IPRs are expected to stimulate innovation. As stated above, empirical studies have reported that the introduction of IPRs into a poor economic environment will not necessarily improve the situation.

Furthermore, the model developed by Chen et al. reveals that a simple adaption of the developed worlds' IPRs standards would be inefficient for promoting innovation in developing countries. It is clear that more is needed and it is vital to consider the threshold effects, as well as issues surrounding the larger market and larger research sector that are required for an IPRs regime to provide real incentives for increasing R&D expenditures. As Park has observed:

> Strengthening IP rights from an initially low level to a somewhat higher level may not suffice to provide necessary incentives or the wherewithal to provide a legal infrastructure to support research and innovation (such as research facilities, a court system, IPR administration, specialised professionals, or a market for licensing).[32]

According to Khan, the major lesson that should be derived from the economic history of the US is that the entire IPRs system was correlated in tandem with the level of development and in light of the overall institutional environment. In other words, the IPRs system was developed in line with the needs and interests of the wider economy. Likewise, Stiglitz elaborates that IPRs should be seen as merely part of a portfolio of instruments. In other words, many other elements of this portfolio are also required. He confirms the importance of IPRs but he ascertains that the level of this importance has been exaggerated, because this constitutes only one component of the innovation system. Of particular importance in this respect is redesigning the IPRs regime in order to increase its benefits and reduce its costs. This project would be most likely to boost levels of economic efficiency and increase the pace of innovation.[33]

[31] *Id*, p. 5.
[32] Park, supra note 3, p. 312.
[33] Stiglitz, J. (2008) 'Economic Foundations of Intellectual Property', *Duke Law Journal*, V.57, p. 1724.

In this context, if the debate is to be moved forward, a better understanding of IPRs norms in developing countries is needed. TRIPS was the centrepiece of a global effort to promote the enforcement of IP laws,[34] which sets minimum standards of IPRs at a common denominator level for all member countries. The correct implementation of TRIPS requires a combination of careful analysis of the suitable IP policy relevant to a country or region as well as maximum enhancement of the TRIPS flexibilities. Thus, one may argue that in order to establish a linkage between IPRs and innovation, developing countries should integrate TRIPS in a broader sense, seeing TRIPS as a whole package. The simple adoption of the IPRs norms into the legal system, without paying due attention to the distinctive characteristics of each country, and the relevant flexibilities, would probably not help innovation and economic vitality.

THE CONCEPT OF AN INNOVATION SYSTEM

From the standpoint of development, the IPRs regime is often viewed as a critical component of the innovation process.[35] A system of innovation generally describes the vital economic, social, political, organisational and institutional factors that have the potential to influence the development and diffusion of innovation.[36]

Lundvall first coined the term innovation system in 1985 to describe the interplay between firms and institutions involved in knowledge production. Under this definition, independent organisations constituted a system of innovation that focused on relationships. Adam Smith, the celebrated eighteenth-century economist, identified the role of both experience-based and science-based learning as the basis for stimulating innovation. This, in turn, signified the importance of a vertical division of labour for the wealth of nations. The idea of the system of innovation also goes back to Friedrich List's conception of the 'National System of Political Economy'. In this system, the role of innovation was clearly recognised as vital for the future of all nations:

---

[34]   Roberts, C. and S. McCoy (2000) 'TRIPS around the World: Enforcement Goes Global in 2000', *Legal Times*, April 10, p. 46.

[35]   Gervais, supra note 1; Maskus, supra note 18.

[36]   Edquist, C. (2005) 'System of Innovation: Perspectives and Challenges' in J. Fagerberg, D. Mowery and R. Nelson (eds) *The Oxford Handbook of Innovation*, New York, Oxford University Press, p. 182.

The present state of the nations is the result of the accumulation of all discoveries, inventions, improvements, perfections and exertions of all generations which have lived before us: they form the intellectual capital of the present human race and every separate nation is productive only in the proportion in which it has known how to appropriate those attainments of former generations and to increase them by its own acquirements.[37]

Hence, List acknowledges the interdependence of tangible and intangible investment at the national level. He further points out the necessary link between industry and the institutions of science and education. Furthermore, he also identifies the fact of interdependence between the importation of foreign technology and the provision of domestic technology. He advised nations not only to acquire the achievements of other more advanced nations, but to also improve on these achievements by making their own efforts.[38]

The use of the term innovation system by Lundvall was aimed at making people aware that a level of interplay also took place between basic research (producers), applied research (users), universities (knowledge producers) and industry (knowledge users). This shift in perspective is attached to supply and demand, which plays a crucial role with respect to the growth of the innovation process.[39]

Modern innovation theory typically analyses the level of interaction that occurs between the various actors that are usually involved in the innovation process. It also examines the interplay between different institutions. Modern theory reformulates this data into a single policy framework instead of distinguishing between the inter-related fields.[40] Furthermore, modern theory is specifically aimed at highlighting the 'cultural landscape of the institutions that engage in scientific research, accumulate and disseminate knowledge, educate employees, develop technology, and create and distribute innovative products and processes; in this category also belong appropriate regulatory regimes (standards,

---

[37]   List, F. (1904) 'The National System of Political Economy' in Freeman, C. (1995) 'The "National Innovation System of Innovation" in Historical Perspective', *Cambridge Journal of Economics*, V.19, p. 6.

[38]   *Ibid.*

[39]   Lundvall, B. (2002) *Innovation, Growth and Social Cohesion*, Cheltenham, UK and Northampton, MA, USA, Edward Elgar, p. 43.

[40]   Caracostas, P. (2007) 'The Policy-Shaper's Anxiety at the Innovation Kick: How Far Do Innovation Theories Really Help in the World of Policy?' in F. Malerba and S. Brusoni (eds) *Perspectives on Innovation*, New York, Cambridge University Press, p. 465.

norms, laws) as well as government investments in appropriate infrastructures'[41] which constitute the research and innovation system of a society. The generation of innovation depends upon the encouragement of new initiatives in order to bring new ideas to the implementation stage. For Kuhlman, the innovation system represents all the diverse sectors of society that attempt to reach into other areas via the education system or through entrepreneurial innovation.[42] In line with this thinking, there is a strong connection between the learning and innovation processes. This connection is regarded within the context of an institutional setting, as the 'common habits, routines, established practices, rules or laws that regulate the relations and interactions between individuals and groups'.[43] Hence, it is widely recognised that 'no innovation system is identical to another, just as no society is identical to another'.[44]

In a narrow sense, a greater focus can be placed on the interplay between universities, research departments, and overall technological policy. The relevant institutional conditions may be patent laws or other mechanisms related to the enforcement of IPRs. This kind of system can be seen by observing the economic structure of the US economy, which mainly depends upon huge corporations operating on the basis of science and research.

Nevertheless, several case studies have found that a significant number of major inventions have historically been discovered by smaller firms.[45] In particular, for certain industries, such as the software industry, where the fixed-costs of invention are low and the level of commercialisation is short-term scaled, it is clear that small companies and individuals[46] dominate the market. Additionally, Katz and Shapiro found that industry leaders have often made major innovations in markets where patent

---

[41]   Kuhlman, S. (2003) 'Evaluation of Research and Innovation Policies: A Discussion of Trends with Examples from Germany', *International Journal of Technology Management* V.26. N.2–4, pp. 131–49.

[42]   *Id.*

[43]   Edquist, supra note 36, p. 183; Mytelka, L.K. (2006) 'Pathways and Policies to (Bio) Pharmaceutical Innovation Systems in Developing Counties', *Industry and Innovation*, V.13, I.4, p. 420.

[44]   Kuhlman, supra note 41.

[45]   Nelson, P. (2002) 'Relationships between Market Structure and Innovation', Presentation to Economists Incorporated, 20 February 2002.

[46]   'The archetypal software invention is made by two people working in a garage'. Burk and Lemley illustrate their argument with Hewlett and Packard, and Jobs and Wozniak – the inventors of the first personal computers and later the Macintosh computers. *See,* Burk, D.L. and M.A. Lemley (2003) 'Policy Levers in Patent Law', *Virginia Law Review*, Vol.89.

protection is most strong. However, if imitation is easy for companies, industry followers or entrants will not usually make major discoveries.[47]

Furthermore, Lundvall emphasised that innovation has always taken place in small and medium-based firms that have a low level of R&D investment. Thus, he proclaims that these companies clearly have the ability to continually implement new technologies in order to make production more efficient.[48] This level of dynamism reveals the crucial importance of small companies for developing countries and small economies.

National Innovation System

Over the years, the 'national innovation system' (NIS) concept was applied in many countries in relation to modern innovation research and as a result, the theory enjoyed significant recognition from policymakers in industrialised economies. The theory offered an alternative approach to explaining economic growth and eventually became a common analytical tool for international organisations such as the European Union (EU), the United Nations Conference on Trade and Development (UNCTAD), and the Organisation for Economic Co-operation and Development (OECD).

Freeman was apparently the first to use the concept of national system of innovation as an essential element of economic analysis.[49] The concept refers to the collection of organisations, institutions, policies, and linkages that affect creation, development, commercialisation and diffusion of new technology within an economy.[50] It encompasses the connections between the actors involved in innovation as a key to improving a country's technological performance. To a certain extent, providing an assessment of the way actors relate to each other within the economy is vital for determining the innovative performance of a country.[51]

---

[47]   Katz, M. and C. Shapiro (1987) 'R&D Rivalry with Licensing and Imitation', *The American Economic Review*, V.77, N.3, p. 419.

[48]   Lundvall, B. (2002) *Innovation, Growth and Social Cohesion*, Cheltenham, UK and Northampton, MA, USA, Edward Elgar, p. 45.

[49]   Freeman refers particularly to List (1841), supra note 37, pp. 7–8.

[50]   Nelson, R. and N. Rosenberg (1993) 'Technical Innovation and National Systems' in R. Nelson (ed.), *National Innovation Systems*, New York, Oxford University Press, pp. 4–5.

[51]   OECD, (1997) National Innovation Systems, available at www.oecd.org/dataoecd/35/56/2101733.pdf, p. 9.

Lundvall's idea of a system of innovation refers to the institutions that typically intervene during the learning process. These institutions include universities, specialised research organisations, science based industries and other professional units engaged in the production of tangible goods. Lundvall's definition refers to the innovation as 'the outcome of user-producer interactions'.[52]

Freeman primarily draws attention to the potential for institutions to provide a new impetus for technical and economic change. Taking stock of the accumulated evidence and the experience of the German dyestuff industry, Freeman has noted the importance of in-house industrial R&D departments. The German dyestuff industry was the first to introduce an in-house R&D department in the 1850s. The reason for this was in order to put the business of research for new products and development of new chemical processes on a regular, systematic and professional basis.[53] As a result of this approach, Germany became a major industrial power, possessing the dominant chemical and pharmaceutical industries in the last quarter of the nineteenth century. The German government invested in education and training, supported the provision of in-house research, and encouraged collaborations between industry and university. Furthermore, the government supported industry with its trade policies.[54]

The enormous success of the German chemical industry initiated a change in industrial behaviour. For instance, it directly led to the growth of government laboratories, research institutes and university research bodies. The German industry was the first science-based industry that allowed a lab-created invention to be quickly transformed into a commercial product. It should be noted that the industry also built up its technological capacities and completed its transformation into a world leading industry in the absence of a domestic patent system. The absence of patents did not hamper the industry. On the contrary, it provided for a certain amount of free riding on foreign technologies. This led to the improvement of methods to produce cheap magenta, which led to further developments that eventually transformed the industry into a strong competitor in the world market. Indeed, the German government granted

---

[52]   'If the cultural environment of a user is very different from that of the producer, it will be costly to establish a channel of information and to develop common codes. Not only will different national languages impair the communications, differences in culture will be reflected in different interpretations of identical signals', Lundvall, supra note 48, p. 47.

[53]   Freeman, supra note 37, p. 8.

[54]   Dutfield, G. (2003) *Intellectual Property Rights and the Life Science Industries*, Dartmouth, Ashgate, p. 75.

patents for chemical products only when the companies were prepared to shift from the position of being imitators of dyes to being innovators of new products.[55]

The German experience clearly demonstrates the strong correlation between government policies and the R&D priorities of the industry. It provides evidence that flexibility is important in relation to the overall design of the national innovation policy. Hence, it is suggested that the effectiveness of a national innovation policy is highly dependent upon the translation of policy instruments into policy mixes. These policy mixes must be capable of offering complementary and mutually reinforcing support.[56]

In light of this, it is clear that every developing country wishing to succeed in a global knowledge-based economy must develop a national innovation system that is properly 'constituted by elements which interact in the production, diffusion and use of new and economically useful, knowledge'.[57] Thus, Gervais argues that development policies should be aimed at achieving objectives other than merely obtaining new imports. Although obtaining imports may be useful, it would not be efficient for the reason that building up domestic IP generating activities is vital. This can be achieved in part through FDI, technology transfer and acquisition.[58]

The concept of the National Innovation System (NIS) is a recent phenomenon for developing countries. It emerged as a significant economic and political issue in the latter half of the 1980s. Nonetheless, it is now widely acknowledged that a well-designed innovation system is vital for economic development and the provision of social improvements in developing countries. At present, the world is moving in the direction of a knowledge-based economy, which is directly based upon the production, distribution, and use of knowledge and information.[59] As a result, there is a greater reliance on the areas of knowledge and technology.

---

[55]   *See,* Moe, E. (2000) *Governance, Growth and Global Leadership: The Role of the State in Technological Progress,* Aldershot, Ashgate Publishing, pp. 143–6.

[56]   UNECE (2007) 'Creating a conducive environment for higher competitiveness and effective national innovation systems; Lessons learned from the experiences of UNECE countries', Geneva, New York, p. 92.

[57]   Gervais, supra note 1, p. 45.

[58]   *Ibid.,* p. 53.

[59]   The term 'knowledge-based economy' results from a fuller recognition of the role of knowledge and technology in economic growth. Knowledge, as embodied in human beings (as 'human capital') and technology, has always been central to economic development. *See,* OECD, (1996) The Knowledge Based

Recent descriptions of NIS policies address technological innovation. These policies involve not only R&D policies, but also assessments of the actual workings of the marketplace. These initiatives also accord with the earlier observations, which showed that the innovation process involves not only economic factors, but also institutional, organisational, social and political factors.[60] According to the OECD, the fluidity of knowledge flows among enterprises, universities and research institutions is crucial for the smooth operation of innovation systems. In this context, tacit knowledge, or know-how, is exchanged through informal channels. On the other hand, codified knowledge, or information that is codified in publications, patents and other sources are deemed to be correlated with the mechanisms aimed at enhancing knowledge flows in joint industry research. Examples of these joint projects can be seen with the development of public/private sector partnerships, technology diffusion and movement of personnel.[61] Moreover, the innovative performance of a country depends to a large extent on an assessment of how the actors relate to each other. According to the OECD, these are all elements of a collective system of knowledge creation and use.[62]

Furthermore, IPRs play a crucial role in encouraging economic development. A NIS contributes to the growth of the technology sector and the resulting dissemination of knowledge. In order to achieve optimal knowledge economy conditions, countries, and specifically, the developing countries, are required to create effective innovation strategies, aimed at prioritising technology transfer and information flow. Nonetheless, the setting of these priorities depends to a large extent on the effective management and exploitation of different types of IPRs.

Thus, it is of crucial importance that IPRs be appreciated as one of the important components of a successful national innovation system. Nevertheless, each component of NIS must be evaluated within its political, economic, social and cultural context. In line with this, it is important to not place undue emphasis on a single component of NIS, whether it is IPRs or government incentives, or university–industry linkage. To do so

Economy, OCDE/GD(96)102, available at www.oecd.org/dataoecd/51/8/1913021.pdf.

60 Edquis, J.B. and B.A. Lundvall (2010) 'Economic Development and the National System of Innovation Approach', Paper presented at the first Globelics Conference, available at: http://www.globelicsacademy.net/pdf/BengtAkeLundvall_2.pdf, p. 6.

61 OECD, (1997) National Innovation Systems, Paris, accessed 22 September 2010 at www.oecd.org/dataoecd/35/56/2101733.pdf.

62 OECD, (1993) Report on National Innovation Systems.

would simply not be enough to bring about success in terms of innovation output. In reality, the post-TRIPS experiences of developing countries have shown that IPRs alone will not be sufficient to create economic growth. It is important to step out of the frame and see the whole picture, not just the legal aspects surrounding IPRs. Gervais has stated that 'intellectual property is but one train in a comprehensive knowledge and innovation policy, and the trains of surrounding norms must also make it to the station if the objective is to be attained'.[63]

Developing countries, and the weaker developing countries in particular, have long been told to bear in mind that without the necessary 'complementary essentials in place that entail a critical level of skills, information, capital and markets',[64] an IPRs regime is unlikely to support development and economic growth. Hence, according to UNCTAD, for instance, implementation of broad-based science, technology and innovation policy initiatives, aimed at promoting and facilitating capacity building for the enhanced absorption of new technologies at the enterprise level, is a prerequisite for developing countries.[65]

In the context of this wider debate, one may suggest that countries must tailor their particular approach to each specific context. Furthermore, the innovation system can be strengthened within a comprehensive and coherent set of policy initiatives. These initiatives include, but are not limited to, further structural reform of enterprises, liberalisation of trade and investment, promotion of financial and innovation systems in order to commercialise new technologies, expansion of educational opportunities to build up human capital resources and specification of rules for maintaining effective competition in developing country markets.[66]

As such, apart from assuring political stability and economic growth, initiatives can embed the IPRs regime within a broader view of social policies and hence, link the initiatives to capacity building initiatives that collectively seek to promote local innovation. The relevant initiatives that would typically support effective exploitation of IPRs include providing for socio-economic measures. These measures are typically drawn from the standpoint of the innovation system. This includes introducing policies enhancing domestic capabilities, serving local needs and

---

[63] Gervais, supra note 1, p. 46.
[64] UNCTAD LDC Report Highlights: LDC report series, N.2, December 2007, p. 4.
[65] *Ibid.*, p. 4.
[66] Maskus, K., S. Dougherty and A. Mertha (2005) 'Intellectual Property Rights and Economic Development in China' in C. Fink and K. Maskus (eds) *Intellectual Property and Development*, Oxford, Oxford University Press, p. 304.

demands, building up human capital resources, establishing strong links between university and industry, and restructuring public institutions.

Setting priorities and enhancing domestic innovation capabilities

According to Odagiri et al., in order to achieve rapid technological progress in developing countries, large-scale improvement of the capacity to absorb and use new technologies is required. Catching up is the first step that eventually leads to innovation and development. This term describes a multi-dimensional phenomenon. It includes 'the process in which a late-developing country narrows its gap in income (as one may specify by the word "economic catch up") and in technological capability (equally "technological catch up") vis-à-vis a leading country'.[67]

For Fagerberg and Godinho, successful catch up policies have not only focused on the adoption of existing techniques in relation to established industries, but also on innovation, and in particular, the organisational kind of innovation.[68] If a country aims to upgrade from imitation to local innovation phase, the country must be able to assimilate the knowledge and innovative activities of the developed countries into its own system. Catching up is a historical and institutional process as well as an evolutionary tradition. Thus, it is a prerequisite that the contextual and institutional factors present in each country are assessed. In a hypothetical scenario, that is, where two countries import the same set of technologies, it is likely that the countries would not be able to achieve the same catch up speed. Catching up involves learning the engineering know-how and also requires the organisation, co-ordination and management of related activities under a very different set of institutions. Thus, for Odagiri et al., the country is able to develop its own social capability levels considering local realities, that is, in relation to the position of the legal, economic and scientific institutions in the country.[69]

During the catching up process, it is necessary that countries adapt the imported technologies to their own local needs. Following this, countries should concentrate on local capacity building as part of the next sequence. Furthermore, there is a common misconception that catching up is simply about copying or reverse-engineering. However, it is important to take account of strategic priorities as well as the domestic realities of the adopting countries. This process necessarily requires

---

[67]   Odagiri et al., supra note 27, pp. 2–3.

[68]   Fagerberg, J., and M. Godinho (2005) 'Innovation and Catching-up' in J. Fagerberg, D. Mowery and R. Nelson (eds) *The Oxford Handbook of Innovation*, New York, Oxford University Press, p. 515.

[69]   Odagiri et al., supra note 27, pp. 4–5.

making creative modifications in order to tailor foreign practice in line with national conditions. The adaptation of foreign technologies on a country's own terms will often lead to an increase in the use of industrial capabilities. Facilitating advancements in relation to existing technologies typically allows a smoother transition towards innovation and development. For Stiglitz, increasing the pace of development often depends upon attaining the right combination of global and local knowledge. The scientific knowledge that exists in industrialised countries typically involves substantial elements of adaptation and thus, can be said to combine both global and local knowledge. Thus, Stiglitz recommends that developing countries make efforts to complement the adaption of foreign technologies with the expansion of local knowledge.[70]

Lundvall has asserted that there is no way of designing an effective innovation policy without first analysing the domestic innovation system and therefore identifying the mechanisms that produce and reproduce knowledge and competence.[71] For instance, in Europe the creation of free innovation zones has been proposed as an alternative to the traditional Brussels-oriented innovation policies.[72] The main idea behind free innovation zones lies within the 'start small and build on successes' approach. The system is essentially based upon the local realities of Europe. In this scenario, the policymakers are expected to designate a sector with a promising future. In choosing this sector, it is necessary that Europe already has the relevant built-in technological capabilities. It is necessary that policymakers consider creating a stable and flexible legal environment in order to stimulate innovation. This effort involves review and reform of the existing legislation. Thus, the envisaged system would further include a mechanism to promote patent protection in relation to the specific inventions that are to be developed in the free zone. It would also include tax incentives for investors and businesses in order to promote collaboration with researchers in the zone.[73]

---

[70] Stiglitz, J. (1999) 'Knowledge as a Global Public Good', available at http:// www.worldbank.org/knowledge/chiefecon/index2.htm.
[71] Lundvall, B. and S. Borras (2005) 'Science, Technology and Innovation Policy' in J. Fagerberg, D. Mowery and R. Nelson (eds) *The Oxford Handbook of Innovation*, New York, Oxford University Press, p. 624.
[72] 'In Brussels the technocrats in are thinking big: big budgets, big directives, big political fights that may, in the end, accomplish nothing.' The Science/Business Roundtable Innovation Report, (2006) 'Innovation: The Demand Side, New Ways to Create Markets and Jobs in Europe', available at www.sciencebusiness.net/documents/demandside.pdf.
[73] *See, Ibid*, p. 18.

This initiative in Europe could potentially provide guidance to developing countries. It could help developing countries to develop innovative strategies aimed at enhancing domestic innovation capabilities. However, it should be noted that before designing innovation strategies for the future, it is required that each developing country set its own priorities and enhance its own domestic innovative capabilities. It is important to carefully observe the components of innovation in each developing country and to take account of the prospective results of the flow of innovation. In this area, these factors are key to enabling domestic innovation[74] because the knowledge-based global economy requires an ability to innovate by improving on the worldwide state of art and/or making adjustments to existing products and processes in relation to local and regional preferences. Thus, economic theory requires that prospective innovation policies be designed in order to balance the level of incentives required to encourage investment in innovative activity with the promotion of technology transfer itself.[75]

Serving local needs and demands

According to Lundvall, the institutionalisation of policy fields in developing countries must be aimed at contributing to increased levels of local innovation. In this context, the fundamental aim of innovation policy must be framed by the process of reviewing and redesigning the various linkages that exist between the different parts of the national system.[76]

It goes without saying that innovation strategies must aim to serve local needs and local demands in developing countries. A common failing of development policy is to concentrate solely on markets in developed countries in relation to exports, while avoiding local needs and the related developing domestic market. The developing markets and specific local needs of developing nations differ from the respective markets and needs of developed nations. Innovation is a dynamic process and innovation levels often respond to the changing needs of the market. Hence, one may hypothesise that investing in R&D and innovation in a manner that properly supplies the demand of developing markets is necessary within a long-term success strategy for economic growth and development. As Trajtenberg has observed:

---

[74]   Trajtenberg M. (2005) 'Innovation Policy for Development: An Overview', STE Program Working Paper, STE-WP-34-200, p. 16.

[75]   Gervais, supra note 1, pp. 54–5.

[76]   Lundvall, supra note 71, p. 615.

... there is no such thing as just one way of going about R&D and innovation; namely, plugging into the global network of high-tech, in order to supply the demand emanating mostly from developed countries. Rather, there are vast areas of economic activity where innovation is needed to serve local needs and local demand, whereby 'local' may mean a large fraction of the world population.[77]

Thus, economic theory asserts that enabling competition between rivals encourages firms to find ways to lower costs, improve quality, develop better products and/or focus their products towards different markets. This may be illustrated by examining the example of the US automobile industry during the 1970s. When the Japanese automobile firms Nissan and Toyota penetrated the large US market, these companies were regarded as little fishes in a very competitive pond. Their only option to escape competition was to make better and cheaper cars. The leading US firms were not interested in small cars, where profits were low. Thus, the Japanese companies concentrated their efforts and innovative activities solely on small cars. Eventually, the Japanese companies became the market leaders in the small car market.[78]

In a similar vein, Trajtenberg[79] has drawn attention to the relative lack of innovation in the pharmaceutical industry in relation to neglected diseases.[80] Today, the pharmaceutical industry spends billions of dollars developing drugs to cure Western illnesses but the industry spends comparatively little on research into healing the diseases that kill millions of people in the developing world. According to the World Health Organization (WHO), nearly one billion patients suffer from a neglected infectious disease.[81] Nevertheless, the number of drugs developed for these diseases is limited – it accounts for only 1 per cent of the drugs that were placed on the market.[82]

Thus, the developing world needs pharmaceutical innovation that satisfies the priority health care needs of the rest of the population. In

[77] Trajtenberg, supra note 74, p. 16.
[78] Baker, J.B. (2007) 'Beyond Schumpeter vs. Arrow: How Antitrust Fosters Innovation', AAI Working Paper 07–04, p. 11.
[79] Trajtenberg, supra note 74, pp. 16–17.
[80] Diseases that seriously disable, or or are a threat to life for those living in developing countries where treatment options are inadequate.
[81] Chan, M. (2007) Keynote address delivered at the Prince Mahidol Award Conference, available at http://www.who.int/neglected_diseases/dgspeech2/en/index.html.
[82] European Parliament Report on Major and Neglected Diseases in Developing Countries, Committee on Development.

other words, Trajtenberg argues that the pharmaceutical industries in developing countries should not act as an effective subsidy to the existing industries in developed countries by concentrating solely on profit-driven blockbuster drugs.[83] The local industries in developing countries should maximise their opportunities to build up their capacities to undertake R&D on treatments for those diseases which particularly affect the developing world.[84] A well-defined strategy would concentrate on pharmaceutical innovation for local needs. Furthermore, this strategy is likely to provide a return on investment over the long term and thus, bring economic growth.

According to Mytelka, creating optimal incentives for innovation is critical because simply pumping up the supply side in the context of human capital, that is, the provision of researchers, would not be suffice to encourage innovative research. It is therefore important to distinguish between the supply and demand sides of industry. Policies aimed at inducing R&D, which is specifically focused on domestic healthcare problems could be assessed on the supply side. On the other hand, the demand side could be focused on matching local demand in the health care system with local innovation.[85]

Therefore, in addition to concentrating on the promotion and support of formal R&D in those technologically advanced sectors, developing countries should also consider the collective impact of small and informal innovations in traditional sectors. One should emphasise that the participation of these existing sectors to the innovation process will not only provide localisation of innovation but also growth and sustainability.[86]

Linkage of the university system to local industry
Universities and publicly funded research organisations are widely acknowledged as potential contributors to dealing with local health care challenges, especially for developing countries.[87] In the context of this wider debate, Aubert points out the dislocation of the university system in relation to local realities, particularly in relation to the labour market, in developing countries. This potentially constitutes a significant barrier in relation to the innovation climate in developing countries.[88] The

[83] Trajtenberg, supra note 74, pp. 16–17.
[84] Aubert, J.E. (2004) *Promoting Innovation in Developing Countries: A Conceptual Framework*, Washington DC, World Bank Institute, p. 25.
[85] Mytelka, supra note 43, p. 425.
[86] Trajtenberg, supra note 74, p. 6.
[87] Mytelka, supra note 43, p. 417.
[88] Aubert, supra note 84, p. 10.

universities in developed countries have a long history of development successes and have played a major role in developing human and institutional capacities as well as generating new technologies. Since the 1970s, governments have launched numerous initiatives by linking university research to industrial innovation. In addition, governments have further sought to spur local economic development based on university research. One initiative is the creation of science parks within university campuses that provide support for business incubators as well as the provision of public seed capital funds and other such bridging institutions.[89] Hence, Nelson highlights the importance of the university system as a critical institutional feature for innovation. He states that:

> One important feature distinguishing countries that were sustaining competitive and innovative firms was education and training systems that provide these firms with a flow of people with the requisite knowledge and skills. For industries in which university-trained engineers and scientists were needed, this does not simply mean that the universities provide training in these fields but also that they consciously train their students with an eye to industry needs.[90]

According to Nelson, providing an examination of university research in the US and Germany illustrates this point very clearly. In his collection of studies on national innovation systems, it was suggested that the US and Germany surged ahead of other countries at the turn of last century in the science-based industries due to the fact that the university systems were much more responsive to the training needs of the industries.[91] Moreover, it is widely acknowledged that Japanese universities played an essential role in Japan's early industrialisation processes by assisting the local industry to upgrade its technological capacities – which eventually gave the industry a competitive advantage.[92]

The link between the university system and industrial innovation has been widely investigated. It is accepted that technological change in relation to important segments of the economy has been based significantly upon

[89] Mowery, D. and B. Sampat (2005) 'Universities in National Innovation Systems' in J. Fagerberg, D. Mowery and R. Nelson (eds) *The Oxford Handbook of Innovation*, New York, Oxford University Press, p. 209.
[90] Nelson and Rosenberg, supra note 50, p. 511.
[91] *Ibid.,* p. 511.
[92] Odagiri et al., supra note 27, p. 415.

academic research.[93] A number of studies[94] have also revealed that university research tends to lead to more significant advances in industrial innovation in the areas of biotechnology and pharmaceuticals than in other sectors. It is also reported that university research results in more pharmaceutical R&D projects.[95]

Thus it can be said that academic research lays the groundwork for scientific innovation. It tends to deal with new theoretical and empirical findings as well as new types of instrumentation that are crucial for scientific innovation. Nevertheless, it provides only the tools and starting points for this process. It does not necessarily provide the specific invention itself.[96] Therefore, the linear model of innovation (see Figure 4.1) may serve as a basis for understanding the contribution of academic research to the areas of science and technology in relation to the economy. This model of innovation is structured around three stages: basic research, applied R&D (contributing to production) and the diffusion stage. The basic research phase starts the innovation process, it is then developed as applied research and eventually continues with the development process, which leads to product creation and diffusion.[97]

Figure 4.1   The linear model of innovation

This model was widely used during the industrialisation process that followed World War II. In understanding that 'science invents, industry

---

    93   Mansfield, E. (1995) 'Academic Research Underlying Industrial Innovations: Sources, Characteristics and Financing', *The Review of Economics and Statics*, V.77, N.1, p. 55; *See also*, Jaffe, A. (1989) 'Real Effects of Academic Research', *The American Economic Review*, V.79, pp. 957–70; Nelson, R. (1986) 'Institutions Supporting Technical Advance in Industry', *The American Economic Review*, V.76, p. 186–9; and Hippel, E. Von (1988) *The Sources of Innovation*, London, Oxford University Press.
    94   *See,* Mansfield (1991), Levin et. al, Cohen for the details of these studies.
    95   Mowery, supra note 89, p. 222.
    96   Mansfield, supra note 93, p. 56.
    97   Godin, B. (2006) 'The Linear Model of Innovation: The Historical Construction of an Analytical Framework', *Science, Technology & Human Values*, V.31, p. 639.

adapts and society conforms',[98] the model played an influential role in policy debates regarding the science and technology areas of industry. In the US, for instance, the linear model of innovation was used to justify the allocation of public funds to R&D activities. Thus, the US government extensively funded scientific and engineering research at universities and the R&D activities of companies.

Universities were described as being at the normative base of the linear model of innovation. In other words, universities exist at a unique locus point of scientific research. The theoretical foundations of the model consistently drew upon the notion that government should fund basic research.[99] Nevertheless, the linear model of innovation has not escaped criticism. In recent years, it has been subject to fierce and continual debate. It has been argued that the model underrates the complexity and variegated nature of innovation. Thus, much modern research on innovation focuses on the systematic and interactive nature of innovation as well as the co-operative relationships that exist between the actors. Non-linear innovation theory regards innovation as a collective process involving not only firms and universities, but also other agents and institutions that necessarily interact with each other. For the purposes of this study, it suffices to say that basic research, or more broadly scientific research, still constitutes the fundamental, but certainly not the unique, source of technological advancement, and thus of economic growth.[100] Particularly in the context of life sciences, basic research is a fundamental component and in most cases a pre-condition, for product development. This is because the drug discovery and development process involves 'trial and error and experimentation without a clear priori understanding of how and why the drugs should work'.[101] Thus, scientific research is a key component of technological advancement in the area of life sciences. This assessment leads to the conclusion that public support for basic scientific research must remain a core component of government policy.

---

[98] One of the slogans of the 1933 Chicago Worlds' Fair; Gulbrandsen, M. 'The Role of Basic Research in Innovation' available at www.cas.uio.no/Publications/Seminar/Confluence_Gulbrandsen.pdf.

[99] 'Bush suggested the creation of a National Research Foundation that would publicly support basic research on a regular basis.' *See,* Godin, supra note 97, p. 660.

[100] *See,* Balconi, M., B. Stefano and L. Orsenigo (2008) 'In Defence of the Linear Model: An Essay', KITeS, Working Paper 216, available at ftp://ftp.unibocconi.it/pub/RePEc/cri/papers/WP216BalconiBrusoniOrsenigo.pdf, p. 32.

[101] *Ibid,* p. 24.

Thus, modern innovation theory rests upon an examination of the interactive process of innovation. Universities are collaborators within this interactive process. Knowledge-based innovation systems increasingly rely on the triple helix model of innovation capturing multiple reciprocal relations at different points.[102] This model strictly avoids the myth of linear innovation and introduces a spiral model of innovation where the institutional spheres overlap, collaborate and co-operate with each other (see Figure 4.2).

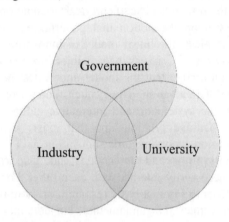

Figure 4.2   Triple helix model of innovation

For Gervais, publicly funded R&D is an essential component for enabling the assimilation and diffusion of foreign technologies during peak periods when the technological capacities of a country tend to be highly dependent on foreign technology.[103] Thus, a careful assessment of the university system is critical for efficient priority setting. This requires a good understanding of the consequences of academic research and of government policies that seek to accelerate the transfer of research results from university laboratories to industrial firms. Therefore, initiatives that are aimed at enhancing returns from university research investment must acknowledge the importance of university research. The importance of

[102]   *See,* Etzkowitz, H.: 'The Triple Helix of University – Industry – Government Implications for Policy and Evaluation', Working Paper 2002–11, Science Policy Institute.

[103]   *See,* Gervais, supra note 1, p. 58.

universities in this area can be easily quantified by examining the relevant output levels.[104]

Indeed, one may suggest that providing for extensive funding in the area of applied research, as well as increasing investments in relation to experimentation and diffusion activities are ultimately essential requirements for developing countries. In recognition of this fact, greater attention must be drawn to the particular educational and institutional capacity building needs of each developing country. It is arguable that the establishment of strong links between universities and companies in developing countries will motivate the industry to participate in further innovative activities. Therefore, given the importance of university research to innovation, it is suggested that developing countries must enhance their educational and institutional capacities.

What governments can do is to bring in policies that are aimed at encouraging the formation of regional economic clusters, as well as spin-off companies that are founded upon university research. One example of such a cluster is seen with the Silicon Valley model. Mowery emphasises the importance of implementing policies that are aimed at stimulating university patenting and licensing activities. An example of such a policy is the Bayh-Dole type legislation which is widely acknowledged as an important policy instrument in the context of linking university research to industrial innovation.[105] It has been long suggested that universities must be equipped with the necessary business skills and organisational flexibilities in order to successfully innovate. In Europe, for instance, the creation of market-friendly and industry-friendly universities is encouraged within the framework of the future of EU innovation policy. It is clear that the policymakers in Europe have observed that the innovation process should not be considered to be complementary to existing structures, or driven solely by the technology transfer office. Policymakers have highlighted the constant need for an outward-facing, business-friendly, professional and systematic approach, which first and foremost requires root and branch reform at the university level within Europe.[106]

In the context of this wider debate, the US experience in general, and the implementation of the Bayh-Dole Act in particular, should be taken into account. The following chapters will expand this issue further. Nevertheless, suffice it to say that certain safeguards should also be

---

[104] *See,* Mowery, supra note 89, pp. 209–39.
[105] *Ibid,* pp. 222–3.
[106] Lundvall, supra note 71, pp. 624–6.

considered by developing countries. Developing countries should not blindly adopt the US model as this may lead them to expect a far greater return than they are ever likely to receive.[107]

Restructuring public sector organisations and institutions

It is widely acknowledged that the public sector organisations gradually erode the implications of effective innovation strategies in developing countries. There are numerous public sector organisations in developing countries that exist for the promotion of enterprise development, but the support system of these organisations is relatively beleaguered.[108] The relevant structures and institutions that exist within developing countries need to be improved.[109] The fundamental distinction between innovation policies lies between initiatives that are aimed at promoting innovation within the institutional context, and initiatives aimed at changing the institutional and organisational context in order to promote innovation, which includes reforms of public institutions, universities, education, labour markets, capital markets, and so on.[110] Empirical evidence gathered from innovation case studies conducted in India, Cuba, Iran, Taiwan, Egypt and Nigeria has shown that the sheer number of organisations such as universities, research institutes and private companies, is far less important than the actual practice of organisations with respect to learning, linkage formation and investment.[111]

It should be noted that it is not easy to establish new, efficient institutions and organisations for the promotion of innovation. Even where it is possible, the organisations often lack flexibility and can easily become politicised. On the other hand, undertaking a move from technology user to knowledge producer and innovator does not seem possible without reforming the traditional public sector organisations of a country. It is also necessary to recalibrate the habits, practices and mindsets of economic agents, and in particular, to reform the practices related to learning, linkages, long-term investment and innovation.[112]

Indeed, creating an institutional climate capable of contributing to innovation in developing countries requires the presence of independent

---

[107]   So, D.A. et al. (2008) 'Is Bayh-Dole Good for Developing Countries? Lessons from the US Experience', *PLOS Biology*, V.6, I.10, p. 2082.
[108]   *See,* Aubert, supra note 84.
[109]   Lundvall, supra note 71, p. 626.
[110]   *Ibid.*, p. 613.
[111]   Mytelka, supra note 43, p. 420.
[112]   *Ibid*, p. 418.

organisations that take a business-oriented approach.[113] Moreover, the promotion of interaction between government departments, members of the business community, trade unions, and knowledge-based organisations may well be necessary to develop socially relevant and clear innovation policies. Indeed, Lundvall argues that in order to achieve a truly innovative policy turn, all public organisations must be involved in this process.[114] As far as policy restructuring is concerned, the process must also involve an explicit consideration of learning by government. Thus, the adoption of an approach based upon learning rather than planning is a necessary condition for the successful enhancement of the innovation process.[115]

In addition, IP institutions, such as patent and trademark offices, necessarily play a crucial role. IP institutions are required to provide efficient support for innovation thereby enabling the collection of fruits of the innovation process. In this respect, the international IPRs regime can help to provide economic growth and sustainability.[116] These offices should be funded considering the importance of their technical and educational role in the innovation cycle. It follows that the efficiency of the market for ideas often depends upon the efficiency of the local IP institutions in educating local users about IPRs. In this way, the international IP system can be used to develop a vibrant local IP community by bringing users of the system and IP service firms together.[117]

A growing body of empirical research appears to support the view that IPRs can be adapted quickly over time to suit the needs of each territory. However, the findings of Weinhold and Reichert indicate that, in practice, the necessary changes actually occur very slowly. As a result, it is possible to state that the IPRs regime must be embedded within the larger society. Furthermore, it can be discussed in relation to greater institutional quality issues such as the rule of law and the independence of the judiciary.[118]

---

[113]   Aubert, supra note 84, p. 18.
[114]   Lundvall, supra note 71, p. 614.
[115]   Teubal, M. (1996) 'R&D and Technology Policy in NICs as Learning Processes', *World Development* V.24, I.3, p. 456.
[116]   Gervais, supra note 1, p. 60.
[117]   Andersen, B. (2006) 'If "Intellectual Property Rights" is the Answer, What is the Question? Revisiting the Patent Controversies' in Andersen, B. (ed.) *Intellectual Property Rights, Innovation, Governance and the Institutional Environment*, Cheltenham, UK and Northampton, MA, USA, Edward Elgar, p. 132.
[118]   Weinhold, D. and U. Reichert (2009) 'Innovation, Inequality and Intellectual Property Rights', *World Development*, V.37, I.5, pp. 895–6.

Government funding of innovation activities

Today, developing countries are effectively the new players of the old innovation game. In general, innovation strategies involve firms working together with other actors, such as government departments, official innovation support units, business incubation centres, research institutions and others.[119] Within developmental innovation policy, the use of targeted incentives and subsidies can encourage economic activity in relation to the creation and acquisition of new knowledge, the building up of human capital and the attraction of foreign investment.[120] Thus, it is recommended that developing countries create a concrete developmental environment that is supportive of innovation and entrepreneurship.

Incubation has proven to be a diversified and integrated service for entrepreneurial ventures. It contributes to national innovation rates and economic growth levels. In this context, it may be hypothesised that business incubators constitute an important instrument for the development of an economy. This can be achieved through the support of entrepreneurship and innovation. They serve as a consultant organisation for knowledge resources and policy co-ordination for both enterprises and innovation systems.[121]

Thus, business incubation demands investment – it requires funds for incubating common property innovations for which individual demand in the short term may not be possible. Hence, public investments should aim to establish an environment favourable to business creation and private sector R&D. This support can be established with the use of integrated packages that apply to all levels. These packages can apply at the micro level for enterprise upgrading, and at macro level for the building of a broad climate conducive to innovation.

Foreign Direct Investment

Foreign Direct Investment (FDI) may also be considered for developing countries. It provides a way for stimulating change and bringing in new technologies to a country. It should be noted that a simple increase of

---

[119]   Tsai, F-S. L.H.Y. Hsieh, S-C. Fang, and J.L Lin (2009) 'The Co-evolution of Business Incubation and National Innovation Systems in Taiwan', *Technological Forecasting and Social Change*, V.76, I. 5, pp. 629–43.

[120]   Lewis, J. (2008) 'Intellectual Property Protection: Promoting Innovation in a Global Information Economy', A Report of the CSIS Technology and Public Policy Program, p. 48.

[121]   Tsai et al., *supra* note 119, p. 50.

FDI flows alone does not necessarily bring about innovation.[122] There is a common belief that having FDI in a country will automatically create a coherent and comprehensive innovation policy for that country. However, Gervais persuasively argues that FDI should not be considered as an innovation strategy because it is not necessarily a precursor of innovation – it is more akin to an instrument of economic development.[123]

However, FDI and innovation are positively correlated. As Fu has suggested, a developing country can enjoy the contribution of FDI in four ways. First, FDI generates more sophisticated technology. R&D generated by foreign firms and R&D labs tends to increase the innovation outputs in the host country. Second, FDI facilitates knowledge transfer through the supply chain from foreign to local firms. Thus, spillovers that emanate from foreign innovation activities may have positive effects in relation to innovation performance within the region. Third, FDI may positively affect local innovation capacity through the competition effect. Finally, FDI may contribute to regional innovation capabilities by introducing advanced practices in innovation management, thereby providing for greater efficiency in the innovation process.[124]

Furthermore, the explicit usage of FDI-related spillover may be utilised for technological advancement. The absorptive capacity of the host country must be acknowledged when formulating a catching up strategy.[125] Innovation is an evolutionary and accumulative process. Due to this process, only the countries with the capability to identify, assimilate and develop the necessary knowledge will have the ability to benefit from the advanced technology that is embedded in FDI.[126] Narula argues that the lower the technological gap between the local and foreign industry, the higher the absorptive capacity of the former is. Thus, the higher the expected benefits will be in terms of technology transfer to the local

---

[122] China's case is a bit of special, it relatively depends on exceptional circumstances of the country.

[123] Gervais, supra note 1, p. 31.

[124] Fu, X. (2008) 'Foreign Direct Investment, Absorptive Capacity and Regional Innovation Capabilities: Evidence from China', OECD Global Forum on Investment, 27–28 March 2008, available at http://www.oecd.org/dataoecd/44/23/40306798.pdf, (23.09.2010), pp. 5–8.

[125] Narula, R. and A. Zanfei (2005) 'Globalization of Innovation: The Role of Multinational Enterprises' in J. Fagerberg, D. Mowery and R. Nelson (eds) *The Oxford Handbook of Innovation*, Oxford, Oxford University Press, p. 339.

[126] Fu, supra note 124, p. 4.

industry. It is clear that the ability to absorb and utilise foreign technology is required as a necessary condition for innovation spillover to take place.[127]

In this regard, the OECD has suggested that FDI contributes to both factor productivity and income growth in host countries. Furthermore, this growth is beyond what domestic investment would normally trigger.[128] In order to create the right climate for FDI, good governance support is required on the part of the host country. The absorption capacity of an economy, the availability of a skilled labour force with up-to-date skills, and the flexibility to adapt to new technologies and new management styles are the main assets that a developing country must possess in order to attract FDI.[129] Finally, Maskus comments that as a part of the regulatory system, the protection and enforcement of IPRs is fundamentally vital. However, this factor is no more vital than the relevant tax regime, investment regulations, production incentives, trade policies, and competition rules.[130]

Nonetheless, it is worth noting that the importance of the correlation between FDI and the IPRs regime is not universally supported by available data. It is arguable that in IPRs-sensitive areas, FDI is discouraged when IPRs protection is weak. Across all sectors, low IPRs protection encourages foreign firms to focus on distribution rather than local production.[131]

Further to this, Javorcik has observed that US firms are much more concerned about IPRs protection in a host country when they consider manufacturing FDI than when they plan investments in sales and distribution outlets. Moreover, economic analysis tends to demonstrate that weak IPR protection has a strong deterring effect on FDI. This is particularly clear in relation to the four technology-intensive sectors: drugs, cosmetics and health care products, chemicals, machinery and equipment and electrical equipment.[132] The lack of, or inadequacy of, IPRs rights may also create uncertainties regarding the possible returns

---

[127]   Narula et al., supra note 125, p. 339.
[128]   OECD, *Foreign Direct Investment for Development, Maximising Benefits, Minimising Costs*, Paris, 2002, p. 9.
[129]   Aubert, supra note 84, p. 23.
[130]   Maskus, K. (2000) 'Intellectual Property and Foreign Direct Investment', Centre International Economic Studies, Working Paper No.22.
[131]   Gervais, supra note 1, p. 32.
[132]   Javorcik, B.S. (1999) 'Composition of Foreign Direct Investment and Protection of Intellectual Property Rights in Transition Economies' available at http://ssrn.com/abstract=180128 or DOI: 10.2139/ssrn.180128.

on FDI. This is a particular problem for R&D intensive industries and for firms possessing innovative technologies.

Because competition for FDI is fierce, many countries are strengthening their IPRs regimes. However, for the countries that have nothing more to offer other than a strong IPRs regime, FDI remains a wishdream. A strong IPRs regime alone is not sufficient to attract FDI inwardly. This is proven by the fact that FDI is not present within the Sub-Saharan African countries at the same level as it is in China, Brazil and other high-growth, large-market developing economies that actually have weak IPRs regimes.[133]

As an UNCTAD study on Incentives and Foreign Direct Investment states:

> When governments compete to attract FDI, there will be a tendency to overbid in the sense that every bidder may offer more than the wedge. The effects can be both distorting and inequitable because the costs of incentives are ultimately borne by the public and hence, represent transfers from the local community to the ultimate owner of a foreign investment.[134]

In such a fiercely competitive market for FDI, it becomes harder for countries to derive advantages by merely strengthening their IPRs regimes. Furthermore, it is well known that it has been the poorest countries that have become poorer still as a result of the enactment of TRIPS.

To conclude, the current economic analysis suggests an important role for IPRs in providing incentives for inward FDI. Nevertheless, other factors such as the relevant trade regime and the relevant tax and competition laws[135] may also play a determinant role in attracting FDI. The following chapters will highlight some of these factors in more detail.

CONCLUDING REMARKS

Both legal and economic research summarised in this chapter strongly emphasises that the IPRs framework is the key component of national

---

[133]   Maskus, K. (1998) 'The Role of Intellectual Property Rights in Encouraging Foreign Direct Investment and Technology Transfer', *Duke Journal of Comparative, International Law*, V.9, p. 109.

[134]   UNCTAD/DTCI, (1996) Incentives and Foreign Direct Investment, Current Studies, Series A, No. 30, UN Publications, Geneva.

[135]   Gervais, supra note 1, p. 33.

innovation systems. A review of the literature indicates that the enactment of an IPRs regime is, therefore, necessary in order to induce local
innovation. Nevertheless, innovation is not about IPRs alone. Innovation
has many other components. Thus, it may be hypothesised that there is a
constant need for developing countries to develop a broad understanding
of complex concepts such as innovation and development and to also
understand how to formulate and implement effective innovation policies.

Developing countries have genuine and diverse characteristics in terms
of development, economy, culture, and so on. There is no standard one
size fits all strategy that can be successfully adopted by each developing
country. Thus, the application of national innovation systems differs
across countries, but the basic elements generally remain the same. Thus,
it is argued here that through case study analysis the role and significance
of IPRs in a successful innovation strategy can be taken in conjunction
with the potential role that utilisation of TRIPS flexibilities could play in
an effective catch up strategy. Hence, by acquiring a better knowledge
and understanding of the TRIPS regime, and in particular by examining
the existing TRIPS flexibilities, developing countries may be more easily
able to identify the gaps between innovation and intellectual property. As
a result these countries will be better able to find ways to fill these gaps.

In fact, developing a solid understanding of innovation policies largely
depends upon the utilisation of the technological and organisational
possibilities that are available today at the national level. A careful
examination of the important components of successful innovation systems throughout the world appears to be vital. In so doing, each country
will then be able to tailor its own policy schemes in consideration of its
own 'national peculiarities in all walks of development economics and
regions'.[136]

---

[136]   Aubert, supra note 84, p. 25.

5. Innovation country case studies

It is important to identify and present the most relevant indicators for innovation and to explain how these indicators can be interpreted and used in policy design. In order to embody a deep knowledge of innovation and generate a number of theoretical propositions for explaining the potential outcomes a case study method may be adopted. The experiences of the United States (US), Japan, South Korea and Israel may well provide an analysis of contemporary issues with regard to innovation and an explanation of how these issues have been addressed in each of those countries.

In this chapter, the case study of each of these countries will set the context and assess both past and current experiences. In doing so, the study will define the relevant issues, analyse the various models or strategies, describe the current approaches and identify any obstacles and criticisms.

As an early developing country, the US case study concentrates on the relevant legal framework within its national innovation system (NIS). The second case study, on the Japanese innovation system, gives an overview of Japanese experience in this area. It illustrates the changing role of the intellectual property rights (IPRs) system throughout the development process of the country. The third case study discusses the experience of Korea as a relatively late catching-up country. The study reveals the characteristics of the Korean national innovation system as well as the patent regime. It provides anecdotal evidence of how industrialisation and overall technological capacity building within the pharmaceutical industry was pursued in Korea under a relatively strengthened patent regime. The final case study focuses on the unique experience of Israel. It gives an account of innovation practices in the country. Specific focus will be given as part of this study to an examination of the whole set of strategies that have been adopted for the protection of IPRs. At the same time the study will look at how IPRs were utilised to promote the capacity building of local pharmaceutical industry.

NATIONAL INNOVATION SYSTEM OF THE UNITED STATES

The US is the world's innovation leader. It has achieved this position through a commitment to basic research, a world-class workforce and the provision of a climate that rewards innovation. Previous studies have determined the characteristics of the US's national system. The factors that have been identified within the US system include the abundance of cheap and accessible materials, energy and land, taken in conjunction with successive waves of immigration. These factors, which are highly specific to the US, make the system quite unlike the national systems in Europe.[1] In this context, economists have long recognised that technological advancement and the availability of enhanced human capital are the principal engines of the US innovation system.[2]

Furthermore, the NIS of the US refers to the institutions that perform research and development (R&D) as well as the level and sources of funding for such R&D. Part of the system also includes government policies, such as the federal antitrust policy, the enforcement of intellectual property (IP) laws, and the enactment of a regulatory policy that prioritises technological development. As part of this process, the US government provides funds for the training of scientists and engineers and also encourages technology adoption.[3]

Thus, the US system mainly focuses on the related functions of producing and applying new knowledge. This knowledge is primarily classed as technical knowledge. The system therefore encompasses many important activities. Most of these activities are carried forward by private-sector entities operating under the influence of the market. The system is self-organised rather than being designed. During the early 1980s, there were policy discussions on whether to set up a centralised innovation agency and pick 'would-be winners'. The proponents of this policy were inspired by the success of the Japanese system and pushed

---

[1]   Freeman, C. (1995) 'The "National Innovation System of Innovation" in *Historical Perspective'*, *Cambridge Journal of Economics*, V.19, p. 9.

[2]   Menell, P. (2003) 'Intellectual Property: General Theories', Levine's WP Archive (618897000000000707); Scherer, M. and D. Ross (1990) *Industrial Market Structure and Economic Performance,* 3rd edn, Boston, Houghton Mifflin..

[3]   Mowery, D. (2001) 'The United States National Innovation System after the Cold War' in P. Laredo and P. Mustar (eds) *Research and Innovation Policies in the New Global Economy*, Cheltenham, UK and Northampton, MA, USA, Edward Elgar, p. 17.

hard for a centralised industrial policy. However, the policymakers in the US were resistant and opposed the idea of 'would-be winners'. The US system remained decentralised and the markets picked the winners relying on global American leadership in scientific and engineering research.[4] The network of institutions and linkages has largely arisen through a myriad of actions undertaken by the system's constituent agents. Unlike other national innovation systems, the operation of the American system never involved a regime of strict proportionality. Neither does it involve a requirement of constant return to scale.[5]

In the US, the presence of highly mobile employees, networked firms, venture capital, university excellence and university spin-off firms are the major factors that contribute to increased scientific and technological development. The cultural openness of US universities creates a fertile environment that fosters intellectual development, high achievement and overall integrity. The importance of these factors is evidenced by the ever-increasing levels of university inventions within the US.[6] The high level of innovation in the US can also be correlated to the presence of a strong IP regime. Yet, a striking feature of the transformation of US policy towards strong IPRs began with the strengthening of the patent regime.

The US Patent Regime

In contrast to the position in Europe at the time, during the industrialisation process in the US, patents were potentially accessible and available to a broad spectrum of the population. Patents were not complex and costly as they were in Europe. Specifically, there was a wide usage of patents, or IP more broadly, by the well-developed middle class population. This factor provided the basis for unprecedented levels of innovation in early American industrialisation.[7] Furthermore, these characteristics helped to create a golden age for independent inventors. In

---

    [4]   Block F.: America's Stealth Industrial Policy, available at http://www.longviewinstitute.org/blockstealth.

    [5]   Popper, S. and C. Wagner (2002) 'New Foundations for Growth: The US Innovation System Today and Tomorrow', Science and Technology Policy Institute, 2002, p. 5.

    [6]   Hicks, M.D. (2006) 'A Broad Overview of the US Innovation System', available at http://crds.jst.go.jp/GIES/archive/GIES2006/participants/abstract/12_diana.pdf.

    [7]   Weinhold, D. and U. Reichert (2009) 'Innovation, Inequality and Intellectual Property Rights', *World Development*, V.37, I.5, p. 894.

time, this prompted the growth of specialised inventors and inter-
mediaries, which also contributed to economic catch up.[8] Moreover, there
was a correlation between accessing markets and patenting activity,
which made clear that inventors were responsive to material incentives as
well as to the availability and security of property rights in technology.[9]

The US patent system is outlined in Article 1, Section 8, Clause 8 of
the US Constitution, which states:

> Congress shall have [the] Power ... To promote the Progress of Science and
> useful Arts, by securing for limited Times to Authors and Inventors the
> exclusive Right to their perspective Writings and Discoveries.

In the late nineteenth century, the US started to switch from its historic
status as a borrower of technology to a source of industrial technology.
Simultaneously, Congress acted to strengthen patent law. For instance, at
this time, Congress extended the duration of patent protection. The patent
reforms in the country prompted the development of industrial research.
Furthermore, the reforms anticipated the growth of the market for the
acquisition and sale of industrial technologies. According to Mowery,
while the search for patents incentivised industrial research, the impend-
ing expiration of these patents catalysed establishment of industrial
research laboratories.[10]

Today, the patent system in the US acts as an incentive to innovation. It
is supplementary to other important innovation policy tools. Furthermore,
it requires periodic examination in order to ensure the vitality of the
NIS.[11]

The US patent system is based on the concept of the public good. The
innovation cycle in the US is premised upon the idea that the production
of new knowledge is a public good. It is often argued that the absence of
a patent system may lead to an environment where free riders are able to
take advantage of the knowledge pool without having to contribute to it.
Due to the inability of inventors to capitalise on their inventions within
such an environment, it is stated that innovation will only occur on a
lesser scale. Thus, the patent system is justified as being an essential
component of the innovation cycle in the US. The market exclusivity that

---

[8]   Mowery, D. (2010) 'IPR and US Economic Catch-up' in H. Odagiri, A.
Goto, A. Sunami and R. Nelson (eds) *Intellectual Property Rights, Development
and Catch-up*, New York, Oxford University Press, p. 32.

[9]   Weinhold, supra note 7, p. 894.

[10]   Mowery, supra note 8, p. 45.

[11]   Merill, S. and R. Levin (2004) *A Patent System for the 21st Century*,
Washington, National Academic Press, p. 19.

is granted by patents provides a remedy for potential market failure. Furthermore, it allows inventors to capture the invention's market value.[12]

Nonetheless, the US innovation system has come under much criticism due to the recent increase in patent protection. The reason for this is that increasing patent protection in recent times has not spurred innovation. In fact, there is evidence that it has impeded the development and use of new technologies.[13] Some years ago, the US patent system appeared to be ideal. The system fostered and promoted innovation. Today, however, there are increasing concerns about the effectiveness of the current system. The US patent system has been fiercely criticised for undermining the US competitive advantage in relation to developing new technologies. The US Supreme Court's decision in *Diamond v Chakrabarty*[14] effectively changed the patent laws and, in particular, it changed how the laws were to be applied in the area of biotechnology. The court's decision facilitated the patenting of new organisms. This was justified as a way of promoting the progress of biotechnology in the country. Nevertheless, policy changes have made patents easier to get and stronger in scope. Generally there have been broader claims, of a longer duration, and with extended eligibility.[15] In the meantime, court decisions have generally interpreted patent law in order to make it easier to enforce. For instance, there have been increased levels of monetary damages for breaches in recent times. Given the breadth of the current regime, patents are increasingly used as offensive competitive weapons, rather than as defensive protectors.[16]

Over the past few decades, there has been an extraordinary increase in the number of US patents. Nevertheless, the increase in quantity has led to a corresponding decrease in quality. The fact that it is relatively easy to obtain a patent has given rise to problems such as the presence of patent thickets, strategic patenting, patent trolls and portfolio races. Thus, the patent system, which is intended to foster and protect innovation, has

[12] *See,* Thomas, J. and W. Schacht (2007) 'Patent Reform in the 110th Congress', CRS Report RL33996, p. 4.

[13] Maskus, K. (2006) 'Reforming US Patent Policy: Getting the Incentives Right', Council Special Report, N.19, November 2006, p. 3.

[14] *Diamond v. Chakrabarty,* 447 US 303 (1980). The Supreme Court held that a live, human-made microorganism is patentable subject matter under statute providing for issuance of patent to a person who invents or discovers 'any' new or useful 'manufacture' or 'composition of matter'.

[15] Maskus, supra note 13, p. 15.

[16] Jaffe A. (2005) 'Is the US Patent System Endangering American Innovation? A Congressional Briefing Luncheon', available at http://www.athenaalliance.org/pdf/patent_reform.pdf.

started to generate waste. This has led to uncertainty, which hinders and threatens the innovative process. According to Jaffe, the US system has effectively converted the weapon that a patent represents from something like 'a handgun or a pocket knife into a bazooka, and then started handing out the bazookas to pretty much anyone who asked for one, despite the legal tests of novelty and non-obviousness'.[17] Correspondingly, he asserts that the behaviours of inventors and firms have changed as a result. The overall winners of the innovation wars in the US have ultimately been the big firms. These firms can afford to pay for the best lawyers and thus, they can withstand the risk of litigation. The losers of this war have often been the smaller companies, some of whom have possessed the brightest scientists and the most original, valuable inventions, but have lacked the financial powers to defend their position.[18]

Even though there are growing concerns about the effectiveness of the US patent system, it is increasingly dominant in determining worldwide patenting behaviour. For instance, the previous reluctance of many patent systems to recognise new types of invention, such as software, has changed following the US affirmation of patentability. Thus, the US courts tend to be preferable for companies that are in the process of taking patent litigation cases resulting in worldwide settlement agreements. Gradually, the US patent system and the rulings of the US courts have had the potential to affect more and more innovators in Europe and Japan.[19]

Since 2010, the Supreme Court has used subject matter eligibility to limit long-standing practice of the United States Patent and Trademark Office. The Supreme Court decisions in *Mayo v Prometheus*,[20] *Bilski v*

---

[17]   Jaffe, A. and J. Lerner (2004) *Innovation and Its Discontents, How Our Broken Patent System is Endangering Innovation and Progress, and What to do about It*, Princeton, Princeton University Press, p. 35.

[18]   *Ibid.*, pp. 5–6.

[19]   Bessen, J. and M. Meurer (2008) *Patent Failure*, Princeton, Princeton University Press, pp. 5–6.

[20]   No.10–1150 (US 20 March 2012). 'The Supreme Court invalidated the asserted patents' process claims as not patent eligible subject matter under §101 of the patent statute. The Court decision is justified on three grounds: (1) the process claims were directed to 'laws of nature, natural phenomena, and abstract ideas'; (2) the patent did not contain enough of an 'inventive concept' to ensure that it 'amounts to significantly more than a patent upon the natural law itself'; and (3) the invention involved 'well-understood, routine, conventional activity, previously engaged in by researchers in the field'. For more information *see*,

Kappos[21] and *Ass'n of Molecular Pathology v Myriad Genetics*[22] demonstrate that it is not happy with the extremely broadened scope of patent-eligible subject matter. What is clear, for now, is that the Supreme Court is scaling back on the maximalist tendencies of US patent policy referred to by some as the global IP ratchet.

The Other Drugs: Generics and the Hatch-Waxman Act

The development of the US pharmaceutical industry was illustrated with the example of penicillin in a previous chapter. The mass production of penicillin during World War II, and the antibiotic revolution thereafter, prompted an increase in R&D activities in the US with regard to drug development and discovery. As a result, US pharmaceutical companies soon became world leaders in the global drug market. The institutional and legal framework in the US assisted the industry to sustain and develop. However, during the 1980s, the industry started to lose momentum in innovation with regard to drug development. It became evident that a greater level of R&D expenditure would be required in order to produce advances comparable with those of the past. This prompted an increase in prices and the number of me-too drugs that were produced.

Sherkow, J. (2013) 'And How: *Mayo v Prometheus* and the Method of Invention', 122 *Yale Law Journal Online* 351, available at http://yalelawjournal.org /2013/04/01/sherkow.html.

[21]   561 US (2010). The Supreme Court has recently imposed sharp limits on their patentability of medical processes. The Court stated that in order to be patentable, a method or process must either: (1) be tied to a machine or, (2) transform its subject into something of a different nature. Accordingly, lower courts have already begun to adopt the machine-or-transformation test in conducting §101 analyses.

[22]   The US Supreme Court ruled in June 2013 that isolated human DNA is not patentable subject matter because it is naturally occurring, while complementary DNA (cDNA) is patentable subject matter because it is not naturally occurring. cDNA is a synthetic form of DNA that does not contain introns (nucleotide sequences that don't encode for proteins), while isolated DNA is composed of exons (protein-coding nucleotide sequences) interspersed with introns. Because both isolated DNA and cDNA have important research applications, the Supreme Court's decision in Myriad will have an enormous impact on the future of biotechnology, biomedical research, and diagnostic and therapeutic efforts. For more information *see*, Kılıç, B., A. Benedict and T. Yang (2013) 'Reversing the "IP Ratchet": Global Implications of the US Supreme Court's Ruling in Myriad', CitizenVox, available at http://www.citizenvox.org/ 2013/06/19/reversing-the-ip-rachet-global-implications-of-the-u-s-supreme-courts-ruling-in-myriad/.

The term 'generic drug' usually describes a pharmaceutical product that is intended to be interchangeable with an innovative product. Once the patent expires, the generic drug is manufactured without a licence from the innovator company and it is marketed under a non-proprietary or approved name.[23] Generic drugs use the same underlying substances as the innovator product and thus, these drugs have the same efficiency as branded drugs. However, generic drugs are often cheaper than their branded counterparts and, thus, these drugs pose a challenge to existing market structures.[24] At this time, there were significant barriers and limitations for generic entry into the market. For instance, generic companies were required to carry out extensive clinical trials in order to get an approval from the FDA. Thus, the significant barriers for entry into the market deterred generic companies from undertaking the requisite efforts. In an attempt to accelerate early market entry of generic drugs and to assure market competitiveness in price and variety, the Drug Price Competition and Patent Restoration Act, known as the Hatch-Waxman Act, was enacted in 1984.

The act strengthened patent protection for innovative drugs by extending the patent term. However, it also weakened the market position of brand-name drugs by facilitating the entry of generic competitors once the patent had expired. Hence, the act had two contradictory objectives. First, it aimed to make lower-cost generic copies of approved drugs more widely available. It also tried to assure that there were adequate incentives to encourage investment in relation to the development of new drugs.[25] It established a 'regulatory framework designed to balance incentives for continued innovation among research-based pharmaceutical companies with opportunities for market entry by generic drug manufacturers'.[26] The aim of this was to strike the right balance between public demand for lower price drugs and the need to promote innovation.

---

[23]   'Generic Drugs, Glossary of Globalization, Trade and Health Terms', World Health Organization, available at http://www.who.int/trade/glossary/story034/en/index.html.

[24]   Gassmann, O., G. Reepmeyer and M. von Zedtwitz (2008) *Leading Pharmaceutical Innovation*, 2nd edn, Heidelberg, Springer, p. 21.

[25]   Engelberg, A. (1999) 'Special Patent Provisions for Pharmaceuticals: Have They Outlived Their Usefulness? A Political, Legislative and Legal History of US Law and Observations for the Future', *IDEA: The Journal of Law and Technology*, V.39 N.3, pp. 389–428.

[26]   Prepared Statement of the Federal Trade Commission before the Committee on Judiciary, United States Senate (17 June 2003).

Furthermore, the act provided incentives to generic companies to encourage them to challenge drug patents. Thus, the generic companies were given the opportunity to challenge a patent when they had created a generic version of the patented drug that did not infringe, or when they had established the patent's invalidity. Under the law, the generic company that was first to challenge the patent would be awarded exclusivity, regardless of whether litigation actually ensued thereafter.[27]

Thus, the act promoted generic medicine competition within the US. As of 2007, there were 7000 generic drugs on the US market, whereas before the introduction of the act the number of generic drugs on the market was much more limited. In 1984, for instance, there were approximately 150 drugs that went off patent without the development of any generic follow-on drugs.[28] The reason for this was that it was necessary at the time for generic manufacturers to conduct expensive tests and clinical trials in order to prove the safety and reliability of the drug. This situation created a *de jure* and *de facto* right. It allowed the larger firms to effectively exclude the generic manufacturers and keep them out of the market. After the enactment of the act, generic companies were only required to demonstrate that a product was effectively bio-equivalent to the pioneer drug. In accordance with the Abbreviated New Drug Application (ANDA) system, a company submitting an application for a generic version of a drug that demonstrates bioequivalence may use the extensive safety and efficacy studies conducted by the pioneer drug as evidence of its safety.

Nonetheless, in order to compensate for the negative effects of the Hatch-Waxman Act and extend market exclusivity, the large pharmaceutical companies began to seek, and ultimately obtain, a great variety of patents. Many of these patents were of little scope or merit. The inspection of the system was founded upon the listings of the Orange Book. This includes the listing of drug products that were approved on the basis of safety and effectiveness by the FDA. It is clear from an examination of the Orange Book that most approved products have more

---

[27]   Mehl, A. (2006) 'The Hatch-Waxman Act and Market Exclusivity for Generic Drug Manufacturers: An Entitlement or an Incentive?', *Chicago-Kent Law Review*, V.81, pp. 651–2.

[28]   Understanding Warfarin Bioequilvalency, available at https://www.cedrug storenews.com/userapp/lessons/page_view_ui.cfm?lessonuid=&pageid=81F261 BC00B53EBB51278659FA543232.

than one listed patent. Furthermore, some of these patents claim un-approved uses, crystalline forms of the active ingredient, specific formulation, tablet shape or other subject matter.[29] In most cases, it is clear that a new patent on the same invention appears in the Orange Book shortly before the expiration of the basic patent protection. This creates an additional barrier for generic companies to enter into market as the generic company is required to re-certify to this later-listed patent.

It must be noted that any patent infringement case, which is filed by the patent holder against a generic company within 45 days of receipt of notice, effectively delays market entry of the generic drug for an additional 30 months.[30] The Medicare Act[31] introduced in 2003 modifies certain provisions covering generic drugs that were set forth in the Hatch-Waxman Act. The Medicare Act allows only one 30-month delay, per product, subject to the ANDA application.

In this context, the Orange Book system has been subjected to substantial criticism. It is suggested that the Orange Book ought to be listed by drug product. As a result of this, generic manufacturers must be required to certify the given drug product. According to critics, the FDA is competent enough to determine whether the generic product is equivalent to the original product. This eliminates any potential risk pertaining to misuse of the system. Moreover, the requirement that the generic drug must be bioequivalent to the original product would mitigate any potential problems.[32]

According to the Hatch-Waxman Act, the first generic company that files an ANDA application should get 180 days of exclusive marketing.[33]

---

[29]   Engelberg, supra note 25, p. 415.

[30]   *See, Watson v Henry Bristol Myers Squibb*, 194 F. Supp. 422 (D. Md. 2001).

[31]   Medicare Prescription Drug Improvement and Modernization Act of 2003.

[32]   Caffrey, A. and J. Rotter (2004) 'Consumer Protection, Patents and Procedure: Generic Drug Market Entry and the Need to Reform the Hatch-Waxman Act', *Virginia Journal of Law and Technology*, V.9, N.1, p. 42.

[33]   21 U.S.C 355 (J) (5) (B) (iv):

'If the application contains a certification described in sub-clause (IV) of paragraph (2)(A)(vii) and is for a drug for which a previous application has been submitted under this subsection continuing [sic] such a certification, the application shall be made effective not earlier than one hundred and eighty days after–

(I) the date the Secretary receives notice from the applicant under the previous application of the first commercial marketing of the drug under the previous application, or

During this market exclusivity period, the first-to-file generic company can sell the generic drugs at a higher price before other generic competitors are able to enter the market. The submission period is measured as of the day the ANDA application is filed and the exclusivity period is measured from the first day of *marketing* the listed drug. In most cases, the inevitable long and costly patent disputes delay many generic drugs from entering the market. Hence, it is suggested that in a case of expiry, due to the arbitrary status of the first ANDA application, the second ANDA filer should receive exclusivity for 180 days.[34]

During the 20 years since the Hatch-Waxman Act, diverse opinions have emerged concerning pharmaceutical innovations. Some commentators believe that the exclusivities introduced by the act may provide important incentives. By way of illustration, pharmaceutical firms are given additional incentives to continue to develop new information regarding approved drugs. Firms are also encouraged to engage in more ambitious R&D efforts. However, the act has been subject to considerable criticism by pharmaceutical companies. One of the major criticisms is that lessening patent protection and decreasing the period of exclusivity results in a decrease in profits, while the incentive for companies to invest in further innovation also decreases.[35]

As one of the key lawmakers of the Hatch-Waxman Act, Rep. Henry Waxman, states:

> In drafting the Hatch-Waxman Act, we worked hard to strike the right balance between the need to improve access to affordable generic drugs and the need to reward brand-name drug companies for the costs in the process of developing those new drugs.[36]

Regardless of all the discussions concerning the application of the act, it does represent a careful balance between access and innovation. This balance is essential for economic vitality and public health.

(II) the date of a decision of a court in an action described in clause (iii) holding the patent which is the subject of the certification to be invalid or not infringed, whichever is earlier.'

[34]   Caffrey et al., supra note 32, p. 39.

[35]   Eurek, S. (2003) 'Hatch-Waxman Reform and Accelerated Market Entry of Generic Drugs: Is Faster Necessarily Better?', *Duke Law & Technology Review*, available at http://www.law.duke.edu/journals/dltr/articles/2003dltr0018. html.

[36]   'Hatch-Waxman Compromise Bill in Need of Reform', *Drug Store News*, 17 February 2003, available at http://findarticles.com/p/articles/mi_m3374/is_2_25/ai_97998967/.

Furthermore, it can be argued that the robust generic industry in the US owes its very existence to the Hatch-Waxman Act.[37] It must be noted that Article 30 of the Agreement on Trade Related Aspects of Intellectual Property Rights (TRIPS) establishes general parameters for exceptions to patent rights. Furthermore, the US experience illustrates that the continuum of the business of developing and manufacturing generic medicines relies heavily on safe harbour provisions. Any country aiming to provide initiatives to encourage the local pharmaceutical industry ought to take into account the US experience. It follows that some lessons can be drawn from the US approach to patent exceptions. This is reflected in the Hatch-Waxman Act. It is also necessary to explore the possibilities of using of TRIPS flexibilities and sidestepping any bilateral pressures.

University–Industry Collaboration and the Bayh-Dole Act

There is an unambiguous relationship between the success of the US innovation policy and the enactment of the Bayh-Dole Act of 1980. The Bayh-Dole Act provided incentives for universities, faculty investors, and private companies to engage in the commercialisation process. Thus, the act is regarded as a catalyst for economic growth. The act has proven to be fundamentally important for encouraging the transfer of technology from university to industry.[38] Furthermore, the Bayh-Dole Act takes advantage of patents as a legal instrument, facilitating the transfer of technology, information and know-how.

The main rationale behind the act is the commercialisation of invention. By drawing a strict line between invention and innovation, the act assumes that the true value of an innovation comes after the invention. It follows that IP protection enables the conversion of inventions into assets. These assets can be sold, licensed, developed, and used as collateral for financing. In other words, IPRs turn inventions into commodities that can be traded within the marketplace.[39]

---

[37] *See,* Fersko, R.S., E. Trogan and P.M. Harinstein (2005) 'Hatch Waxman: A work in Progress, Responding to the Conundrum: How to Encourage Innovative New Drugs While Reducing the Cost of Access', *Journal of BioLaw and Business*, V.8, N.3, pp. 20–7.

[38] Boetinger, S. and A. Bennett (2005–2006) 'The Bayh-Dole Act: Implications for Developing Countries', *IDEA*, V.45, pp. 261–2.

[39] Rafiquzzaman, M. and S. Ghosh (2001) 'The Importance of Patents, Trade-Marks and Copyright for Innovation and Economic Performance: Developing a Research Agenda for Canadian Policy', available at http://strategis.

The most remarkable legacy of the act is that it established an environment that encourages companies to take the risk of investing in R&D. Thus, it is clear that university research[40] advances pharmaceutical innovation significantly and directly. Most of the blockbuster medicines that are currently being marketed by American pharmaceutical companies were invented in university laboratories. Nevertheless, drug development cannot be simplified to encompass merely R&D activities. It involves a costly and long innovation and commercialisation process. This process encompasses clinical trials, the regulatory process, the packaging and marketing of the drug and so on. Thus, collaboration between inventive universities and innovative companies is a prerequisite for pharmaceutical innovation.

Since the passage of the Bayh-Dole Act, the levels of medical and biological R&D have grown significantly. Funding for university R&D in the area of medical sciences constitutes the largest portion of financial support. A recent study found that the cost of medical and biological R&D takes up almost 52 per cent of total R&D expenditures in 2005.[41]

Nevertheless, many analysts now assert that the strategy of the Bayh-Dole Act is failing. Many critics argue that co-operation among government departments, companies and academic institutions provides many opportunities for conflicts of interest. This can lead to redirection of research, less openness in relation to the sharing of scientific discoveries, and a greater emphasis being placed on applied research rather than basic research.[42]

The life sciences, and particularly biological and medical sciences, account for the biggest slice of university funding. The federal government continues to be the primary source of funding for university R&D in these areas. In 2002, for instance, 48 per cent of the federal R&D budget was spent on the medical and biological sciences.[43] Therefore, the huge share of life sciences in R&D budget generated concerns due to the

---

ic.gc.ca/epic/site/ippd-dppi.nsf/vwapj/03%20EN%20Gosh-Rafiquzzaman.pdf/$ file/03%20EN%20Gosh-Rafiquzzaman.pdf, p. 9.

[40] In the US industrial funding for university research rose steadily through the 1980s and 1990s, reaching 7.1 per cent in 1997.

[41] National Science Foundation, Academic Research and Development Expenditures: Fiscal Year 2005, May 2007, Tables 2, 53, and 54, available at http://www.nsf.gov/statistics/nsf07318/content.cfm?pub_id=3767&id=2.

[42] Schacht, W. (2000) 'Federal R&D, Drug Discovery, and Pricing: Insights from the NIH-University-Industry Relationship', CRS Report, p. 14.

[43] Neal, H., T. Smith and J. McCormick (2008) *Beyond Sputnik: US Science Policy in the Twenty-First Century*, New York, University of Michigan Press, p. 82.

fact that the benefits that are granted to the pharmaceutical companies come at the expense of the public under the act. The National Institutes of Health (NIH) funds the early stages of research and testing. This research constitutes the groundwork for drug development. Hence, it is asserted that a high proportion of the drugs that have been brought to market in the past 30 years were mostly based on taxpayer-backed research at academic institutions or the NIH. In fact, 45 of 50 top-selling drugs got government subsidies totalling nearly $175 million in 1998.[44]

However, the pace of innovation has been substantially reduced in recent years. Due to the high costs of investment that are associated with in-house R&D, the current efforts of pharmaceutical companies favour the development of me-too drugs and therapies. On the other hand, most of the R&D that leads to blockbuster drugs comes directly from publicly funded universities and government laboratories. Furthermore, this initiates a fierce level of competition among pharmaceutical companies. Nowadays, pharmaceutical companies compete aggressively to licence publicly funded R&D. Thus, they have been subject to considerable criticism for competing not to find new drugs, but for the limited number of drugs that are available to licence.[45] Considering the high drug prices that currently exist in the US, there is a widespread belief that the public, which shares the cost and risk, should also be involved more directly in the benefits.[46] Daniel Zingale, formerly executive director of AIDS Action illustrates this situation very clearly:

> Imagine if General Motors could get the American taxpayer to heavily subsidise its research and development, fund government programs that purchase half of its cars and get many of those same taxpayers to buy a new car each and every year.[47]

Critics also argue that the strategy of the Bayh-Dole Act encourages the patenting of fundamental research which, in turn, prevents further biomedical and pharmaceutical innovation. On this basis, many analysts now assert that the strategy of the act has not been successful. Eisenberg and Rai, for example, have emphasised that certain patents hinder the process. The reason for this is that permitting universities to patent discoveries under federal funding 'draws no distinction between

---

[44] 'Public Handouts Enrich Drug Makers, Scientists', *The Boston Globe*, 5 April 1998, available at http://www.cptech.org/ip/health/econ/bg04051998.html.

[45]   Angell, M. (2005) *The Truth about the Drug Companies: How They Deceive Us and What to do about It*, New York, Random House..

[46]   O'Neill, supra note 514.

[47]   Schacht, supra note 42, p. 19.

inventions that lead directly to commercial products and fundamental advances that enable further scientific studies'.[48]

Active university involvement in commercialisation generates further concerns. It is arguable whether the Bayh-Dole Act has in fact shifted the university away from the pursuit of its traditional goals. Delays in publication and the free flow of information from academia and greater secrecy in the research process have discouraged the advancement of knowledge and prevented scientific progress in universities.[49] According to a survey conducted in university research centres in the US, over half of the research centres permitted firms to request publication delays. Furthermore, 35 per cent of institutions allowed researchers to delete information prior to publication. More interestingly, 63 per cent of research centres allowed publication delays and 54 per cent permitted deletion of information.[50] It has been stressed that commercialisation of academic research has undermined the real value of universities as the nation's primary source of knowledge creation and talent and that university research is skewed toward marketable products rather than basic research.[51]

In spite of all the weaknesses, the resulting system has borne benefits beyond the imagination of the drafters of the act. The act has demonstrated that society can benefit from creativity only if a properly balanced legal and institutional framework is in place. Publicly funded innovations take place in the commercial market place. Thus, academic creativity is transformed into innovative products in the form of new medicines, materials and chemicals.[52]

Concluding Remarks

To sum up, both the legislation and the consequent interaction between federal and private organisations have had significant influence on the success of the US innovation system. Furthermore, several studies have

[48] Rai, A. and R. Eisenberg (2003) 'Bayh-Dole Reform and the Progress of Biomedicine', *American Scientist*, January–February, p. 52.
[49] Schacht, supra note 42, p. 20.
[50] Cohen, W., R. Florida, L. Randazzese and J. Walsh (1998) 'Industry and the Academy: Uneasy Partners in the Cause of Technological Advance' in R. Noll (ed.) *Challenges to Research Universities*, Washington DC, Brookings Institution, pp. 171–200
[51] Schacht, supra note 42, p. 22.
[52] Gollin, M. (2007) *Driving Innovation, Intellectual Property Strategies for a Dynamic World*, New York, Cambridge University Press, p. ix.

shown that both the US antitrust policy and the IP system have helped to drive the US innovation system. US antitrust policy is internationally unique in its scope. It has an unusual structure. Furthermore, the vertical specialisation of US industries affects the interaction of patent regime and antitrust policy.[53]

Arguably the American innovation system requires significant reforms in the areas of patent law and judicial practice. Nonetheless, the American patent law tradition has contributed a great deal to making the US the world leader in technology. The systematic structure of the patent law has helped to promote innovation in the pharmaceutical sector. It has also assisted US companies to become market leaders. The US experience also demonstrates the importance of the careful integration of university-funded research into the commercial market and the importance of interaction between the main actors in the innovation system. Moreover, the Hatch-Waxman Act is highly significant to the US pharmaceutical industry. The system establishes a level of equilibrium in terms of incentives for innovators and generic companies. In fact, the generic industry owes its very existence to this act. The act led to the growth of generic giants such as Teva. Ultimately, the US innovation system suggests a role for an improved strategy of IP protection in promoting innovation. This system encourages system linkages between public and private agencies and ensures vital knowledge flows and diffusion.

THE NATIONAL INNOVATION SYSTEM OF JAPAN

When Freeman proposed the term 'National System of Innovation' in 1987, he had a concrete example in mind. The paradigm example for Freeman was the case of Japan, as he was impressed by its extraordinary success. In an influential article, Freeman praised Japanese performance in relation to R&D intensity. During the 1950s and 1960s, the Japanese system worked on a simple basis involving copying, imitating and importing foreign technology. However, as Japanese products and processes began to out-perform American and European products and processes, this practice gradually became obsolete.[54]

The Japanese system was designed to encourage industrial development through emphasising technology acquisition from abroad, domestic information diffusion and incremental innovation. According to Maskus,

---

[53]   Mowery, supra note 8, pp. 58–9.
[54]   Freeman, supra note 1, pp. 11–12.

when Japanese policymakers designed domestic IPRs laws in the mid-twentieth century, they did so bearing in mind that Japan was a technology follower. As a result they deliberately limited the scope and breadth of patent law. Furthermore, legislators excluded pharmaceuticals from patent protection in order to provide an enabling environment for local innovation. According to Maskus, this constituted the fundamental key to Japan's successful innovation system.[55] However, the IPRs laws had to be reformed as the innovation policies shifted in the direction of R&D. Today, IP protection serves as a tool for encouraging technological, cultural and industrial development in Japan.

During the 1960s, the Japanese government's industrial policy was based upon a selection of would-be winners. These industries included automobiles, machinery, electronics, ships and petrochemicals. The promotion of these infant industries came through close co-operation with the private sector. By way of illustration, it is clear that the Japanese automobile industry today includes some of the best-known auto-brands in the world. Nevertheless, in the 1960s, many people, including the Japanese, thought the Japanese automobile industry was weak. Nonetheless, Japan realised an economic miracle in the automobile sector. Chang illustrates this Japanese miracle by exploring the example of Toyota. When Toyota exported its first cars to the US market, the export proved to be a failure. Customers in the US thought the cars looked lousy. Furthermore, customers were reluctant to spend a substantial amount of money on a family car that came from a place where it was thought that only second-rate products were made. Thus, the cars had to be withdrawn. Following that first catastrophic experience, fierce discussions were held in Japan about the future of Toyota. The received wisdom was that no industrialised country had got anywhere without developing serious industries, for example, automobiles. Thus, Japan needed a strong automobile industry. However, the industry needed more time to grow and become competitive. The Japanese government took the lead on the project and adopted a protectionist approach. This ensured high profits for the automobile industry in the country through high tariffs and draconian controls on foreign investment. The government banned foreign cars. In fact, the government kindly asked General Motors and Ford to leave the market in 1939 and invested public funds in order to save Toyota from imminent bankruptcy. In the meantime, Toyota improved its existing technological capabilities and skills. Crucially, Toyota began to

---

[55] Maskus, K.E. (2000) *Intellectual Property Rights in the Global Economy*, Washington, Institute for International Economics, p. 69.

engage in R&D activities. Eventually, half a century after the first unfortunate experience in the US market, Toyota's Lexus has become something of an icon for globalisation.[56]

Thus, successful policies must provide a strategic link between technological information and private capital. It is also necessary to facilitate the sharing of information between private players.[57] According to Chang, if Japan had not followed a protectionist regime and ruled out revenue tariffs on foreign products, thus preventing a foreign takeover of local markets and companies and protecting infant industries, its economy would not be as strong as it is today. In other words, if Japan had followed the path advocated by the free-trade economists such as Friedman,[58] they would not be exporting Lexus cars. In fact, the Japanese would still be fighting over who owns the mulberry tree.[59]

During the 1970s Japan's catch-up strategy began to shift towards a focus on R&D. The policies developed by the government increased basic scientific research. This increased the rate of technology development and also supported the global scientific community.[60] The government successfully took the necessary measures in order to increase basic research. These measures emphasised that research is an international public good and that it contributes to the world's stock of knowledge.

---

[56]   Chang, H.J. (2008) *Bad Samaritans: The Guilty Secrets of Rich Nations and the Threat to Global Prosperity*, New York, Bloomsbury Press, pp. 19–21.

[57]   Lee, K.T. (2007) 'Comment on 'From Industrial Policy to Innovation Policy: Japan's Pursuit of Competitive Advantage', *Asian Economic Policy Review*, V.2, p. 271.

[58]   In *The Lexus and the Olive Tree*, Friedman categories countries as the ones that are intending to build a better Lexus (during his stay in Japan, his visit to a Lexus factory, mightily impressed him), which are dedicated to modernising, streamlining and privatising their economies in order to thrive in the system of globalisation and the others caught up in the fight over who owns which olive tree. Then he develops a particular set of economic policies for the olive-tree world, which he calls the Golden Straitjacket. The Golden Straitjacket, was pretty much of a 'one size fits all' model, which namely includes most of today's neo-liberal economic policies such as privatisation, low inflation, reduced size of government bureaucracy, liberalised trade, deregulation of foreign investment and capital markets etc., *See,* Chang, supra note 56, pp. 19–21.

[59]   Mulberry trees feed silkworms. Back in the early twentieth century, Japan was the world's larger exporter of raw silk and Toyota's original business was simple textile machinery, Chang, supra note 56, p. 21.

[60]   Tassey, G. (1998) 'Comparisons of US and Japanese R&D Policies', Strategic Planning and Economic Analysis Group, National Institute of Standards and Technology.

Within the innovation cycle, universities in Japan were considered to be of primary importance as the most appropriate performers of basic research.[61] During the 1970s and 1980s Japanese companies successfully utilised external knowledge as a foundation for building up core competencies.

In the 1990s, the Science and Technology (S&T) Basic Law regulating the orientation of science and technology illustrated the government's new approach to R&D policy. The first S&T Basic Plan was implemented in 1996 in order to achieve higher standards of science and technology. The aim of the Basic Law was not only to expand R&D, but to focus more on creativity, as well as sectorial and regional integration of R&D activities. It also sought the promotion of co-operative research mechanisms as well as a more liberal assignment of IPRs.[62]

Japanese Patent Law

Japan took full advantage of the IP system in order to enhance its industrial competitiveness. IP protection has proven to be vital for the stimulation of business innovation in Japan. During World War I, the Japanese government enacted the Wartime Law on Industrial Property, which revoked the patent rights of foreigners whose countries were in a state of war against them. This wartime suspension of foreign patents greatly contributed to the catching up process of the Japanese pharmaceutical companies. Following this, Japanese companies built up their own capabilities in relation to drug manufacturing.[63]

Although the Japanese pharmaceutical companies were able to catch up with the German pharmaceutical companies following World War I, they were isolated from scientific and technological developments during World War II. For instance, they did not have access to penicillin. In post-war Japan, it became evident that wartime damage to infrastructure

---

[61] Odagiri, H. and A. Goto (1993) 'The Japanese System of Innovation: Past, Present and Future' in R. Nelson (ed.) *National Innovation Systems*, New York, Oxford University Press, p. 111.

[62] Tassey, supra note 60, p. 4.

[63] Odagiri, H., A. Goto and A. Sunami (2010) 'IPR and the Catch-up Process in Japan' in H. Odagiri, A. Goto, A. Sunami and R. Nelson (eds) *Intellectual Property Rights, Development and Catch-up*, New York, Oxford University Press, p. 107.

had been significant. Furthermore, Japan's science and technology industries were lagging behind the US and Europe. Thus, a new process of catch-up strategy was required.[64]

The current post-war patent law was enacted in 1959. It clarified the requirements for an invention through the enactment of provisions such as the inventive step rules. Moreover, it fulfilled the requirements of a modern patent law. For instance, the law adopted a standard of absolute novelty, with novelty being anticipated whenever an invention enters the public domain through publication.[65]

Strengthening the patent law has led to the creation of economic incentives for R&D in Japan. The patent law amendment of 1970, for instance, introduced a provision for the publication of yet-to-be examined patent applications within 18 months. This publication system assisted knowledge dissemination in the country and minimised duplicate R&D efforts.[66] As was the case with the German patent system, facilitation the dissemination of technical information was considered to be as important as rewarding innovation. Thus, priority was given to the circulation of knowledge. This accelerated the momentum of further invention in the country.[67]

Japan started to grant patents to pharmaceutical products in 1975. It was introduced much earlier than most European countries, for example, Switzerland (1977), Austria (1987) and so on. According to Odagiri et al., this was a twofold process. Both international and domestic circumstances necessitated this amendment. The international reason was the Lisbon conference in 1958. This conference gathered momentum for the eventual amendment of the Paris Treaty. At this conference, the member countries recommended the adaption of patent protection for chemical and pharmaceutical products. Domestically, the majority of pharmaceutical and chemical firms, as well as members of the academic community, were in favour of the introduction of chemical product patents.[68] The industry had already developed a high level of technical skill by this stage. Moreover, the big Japanese pharmaceutical companies were able to modify foreign technology, for example, antibiotics. Thus,

[64]   Odagiri et al., supra note 61, p. 109.

[65]   Tassey, supra note 60, p. 4.

[66]   Odagiri et al., supra note 61, p. 117.

[67]   Dutfield, G. (2003) *Intellectual Property Rights and the Life Science Industries*, Dartmouth, Ashgate, p. 79.

[68]   In 1970, a survey conducted by Japan Patent Association and the supporters of product pharmaceutical patents outnumbered the opponents. *See,* Odagiri et. al, supra note 61, p. 119.

they focused their efforts on improving and generating less advanced technology.[69] As a result of FDI restrictions in the country, Japanese companies tended to focus on the domestic market, where profits were assured. With minimal R&D effort, the companies were able to receive satisfactory profits.[70]

Nevertheless, it was time for Japanese companies to engage in R&D activities and develop their own medicines. Arguably, the lack of pharmaceutical product patents inhibited incentives for the development of new medicines in Japan. The firms generally used process patents to exclude other firms from circumventing patent protection through the use of different production methods.[71] Hence, the strong patent regime supported the production of globally competitive blockbuster products. The American and European companies were actively pursuing a strong patent regime in the country and there was also a threat that cheap generic drugs, coming from Asian countries, would flood the market. In other words, patent protection for pharmaceuticals did not conflict with local needs. On the contrary, the changing internal conditions of the industrial and technological structures necessitated a strong patent production for pharmaceuticals at that time. Thus, local priorities, coupled with international motivation, led towards the introduction of patents for pharmaceutical products.[72]

Gradually, the Japanese patent law was amended several times in accordance with changing local needs. For instance, in 1988 the system of multiple claims was introduced and the patent term was extended for pharmaceuticals in order to compensate for loss of patent life due to the lengthy approval process. Furthermore, there was a shift from a system of one-patent and one-claim principles, which required numerous individual patent applications for multiple related inventions, to a system of multiple claims. This facilitated a single patent application which covered multiple inventions from one-patent. Further to this, patent protection was extended to a wider range of inventions.[73]

The Japanese patent system has gone through a serious of revisions. The patent act was revised in 1994, 1999, 2003, 2004, 2005, 2006, 2008

---

[69] *Ibid*, pp. 119–20.

[70] Kneller, R. (2003) 'Autarkic Drug Discovery in Japanese Pharmaceutical Companies: Insights into National Differences in Industrial Innovation', *Research Policy*, V.32, p. 1808.

[71] Motohaski, K.: 'Japan's Patent System and Business Innovation: Reassessing Pro-patent Policies', RIETI Discussion Paper Series 03- E-020, p. 7.

[72] Odagiri, supra note 61, pp. 119–20.

[73] Motohaski, supra note 71, p. 7.

and 2011.[74] Each amendment moved Japanese law closer to the US patent system and patent rights in Japan have undergone a significant transition. These rights have been extended and strengthened in order to cover a broad range of technology including software, business models, microbiology and gene fragments. Nevertheless, in contrast to the general belief that patents promote innovation, the study of Sakakibara and Branstetter (2001) has revealed that the recent patent reforms enacted in 1998 had only minor impacts on Japanese R&D and patenting. According to their study, there was no evidence of an increase in innovative effort or innovative output in industries other than the pharmaceutical industry that could be plausibly attributed to the recent patent reform.[75] Alternatively, they perceived that a substantial increase in R&D spending preceded the legal and procedural reforms. Hence, going too far towards a strong patent system is undesirable because it does not incentivise innovation. The enforcement mechanism in the Japanese patent system was traditionally considered to be weak in relation to protecting inventors. Some Japanese inventors give priority to the enforcement aspects of the patent system, rather than strengthening and broadening the patent regime.[76]

Nonetheless, empirical evidence shows that the pharmaceutical industry has received enormous benefits from a gradual strengthening of the patent regime in Japan. The history of the Japanese pharmaceutical industry goes back to the 1970s. This was a time when pharmaceuticals were intentionally excluded from patent protection. The industry tended to import technologies from foreign countries. As the industry built capacity, the technology become more sophisticated, which required protection. Hence, the Japanese legislature intended to provide incentives to the local industry to encourage R&D for new drugs. Consequently, Japanese pharmaceutical companies shifted their approach from catching up towards global innovation and the law facilitated basic research on new chemical compounds. Not long after the introduction of patent protection for pharmaceutical products in 1984, the Japanese Patent Office's survey[77] showed that there was a striking increase in the number

[74]   *See,* WIPO Lex, http://www.wipo.int/wipolex/en/details.jsp?id=6858.
[75]   Sakakibara, M. and L. Branstetter (2001) 'Do Stronger Patents Induce More Innovation? Evidence from the 1998 Patent Law Reforms', *The RAND Journal of Economics*, V.32, N.1, p. 98.
[76]   ???
[77]   Japanese Patent Office, 'The Impact of Product Patent Protection for Materials on the Chemical Industry in Japan', 1984, p. 14; *See also,* Masuda, S. (2008) 'The Market Exclusivity Period for New Drugs in Japan: Overview of

of pharmaceutical companies that were involved in R&D projects for new drug development. The survey revealed the ratio of Japanese companies that had engaged in drug discovery and development had increased to 69 per cent from 40 per cent prior to the enactment of patent protection for pharmaceutical products.[78]

The findings of a survey conducted by the Institute of IP in 2001[79] confirmed the previous findings of Taylor and Silberston regarding the relationship between patents and innovation. Recalling Taylor and Silberston's research, it is clear that the pharmaceutical and chemical industries were the only outstanding exceptions to the general rule that patents are not effective for encouraging investment in R&D. In these industries patents were regarded as highly effective in investing in R&D. Along similar lines, an Institute of Intellectual Property survey affirmed that the pharmaceutical industry in Japan was sensitive to pro-patent policies in Japan and that the industry had experienced major effects from changes to the patent system.

Moving Towards an Advanced Knowledge Economy

The Japanese route of catching up fits well with the conventional list of sequences for innovation. According to these sequences, a country first starts with imitation of foreign technology and the industry develops a basic level of technical skill. In the second stage, incremental local innovation occurs within the context of existing technologies. This typically involves making minor modifications and improvements, each of which is of little significance. However, cumulatively these alterations are of major significance in terms of gains in productivity and product/ service performance.[80] Following the local innovation phase, a country usually begins to produce new innovations, whether new products or

---

Intellectual Property Protection and Related Regulations', *Journal of Generic Medicines*, V.5, N.2, p. 123.

[78] *Id.*

[79] Institute of Intellectual Property (2000), Report on Survey of Patents and the Economy, Report on FY 2001, Survey on Industrial Property System Issues. The National Institute of Science and Technology Policy conducted a survey of Japanese firms using a similar questionnaire as the Yale Survey of technological exclusivity. Thus this characteristic of the pharmaceuticals industry has been confirmed in surveys conducted in both Japan and the US.

[80] The NSW Board of Vocational Education and Training's submission to the Productivity Commission research study into public support for science and innovation, available at http://www.pc.gov.au/__data/assets/pdf_file/0006/37959/sub067.pdf.

processes or improvements of existing ones. This leads to the creation of products that are globally competitive.[81]

In the early phase, the sequence of innovation repeated itself. As a result, Japan benefited from a head start in relation to the imitation phase. Japanese industry rose quickly to the innovation frontier in relation to would-be winner industries. These industries involve reverse-engineering and investment in in-house R&D. It is clear that during the local innovation phase the main emphasis was placed on process innovations, particularly of the organisational type. An example of these processes is the 'just in time' system. This system allowed for the simultaneous exploitation of scale economics as well as ensuring flexibility and led to an efficient level of inventory management. It also facilitated high level of quality and reliability. This, in turn, produced an ability to adjust to the needs of the end-user. Subsequently, the industry in Japan underwent extensive structural change. Finally, it established itself as among the global producers of innovation.[82]

The government and the enactment of institutional instruments have played a dynamic role in Japan's success. This role remains important for Japan's continuing progress towards the establishment of a knowledge-based economy. By the beginning of the twenty-first century, in order to achieve competitiveness in the Japanese market, the government established action plans for the promotion of creation, dissemination, and effective exploitation of rights. The government adopted pro-patent policies to stimulate business innovation. This policy change occurred in the early 2000s. These pro-patent policies included the adoption of procedures for accelerated patent examination, enacting a revision of the tort system, and creating an extension of patent protection in relation to new fields of technology.[83]

The Japanese version of the Bayh-Dole Act[84] created conditions that enabled Japanese universities to become catalysts for economic growth within the innovation system. Before the adoption of the act, universities were not allowed to file for a patent application. Hence, university funded research was not commercialised, and in most cases university inventions

---

[81]   Gervais, D. (2007) *Intellectual Property Trade and Development: Strategies to Optimize Economic Development in a TRIPS-Plus Era*, New York, Oxford University Press, p. 46.

[82]   Fagerberg, J. (2006) 'Knowledge in Space: What Hope for the Poor Parts of the Globe?' in B. Kahin and D. Foray (eds) *Advancing Knowledge and the Knowledge Economy*, Cambridge MA, MIT Press, p. 225.

[83]   For detailed information, *see* Motohaski, supra note 71.

[84]   Law to Strengthen Industrial Technical Ability, 2000.

entered the public domain via publication. Thus, the act gave universities ownership and control of their inventions. Universities were empowered to establish their own technology transfer offices in order to license employee inventions. Nonetheless, innovative behaviour in Japan is still dominated by in-house R&D. By way of illustration, a significant fraction of R&D in pharmaceuticals is still performed in-house by Japanese pharmaceutical companies. Japanese pharmaceutical companies do not rely upon universities, and the corresponding university start-ups, as much as their European and US counterparts.[85]

In an effort to enhance university–industry interaction, the Ministry of Education, Culture, Sport, Science and Technology (Monbukagaku-MEXT) was established. MEXT provides material support for IP personnel at university-oriented venture companies. MEXT also deals with technology transfer from universities to industries, from the early stage of idea development through to industrialisation. As a start-up policy, the 'University-based Structural Reform Plan for Revitalizing the Japanese Economy' was enacted to enable the licensing of university patents.[86]

Thus, the Japanese system is still developing. The Japanese government began a new project in 2001 in order to shape the system of co-operation between industry, academia and the public sector. In order to establish a comprehensive system promoting co-operation among industry, academia and the public sector, four priority measures have been identified:

(1) Consideration of economic and social needs for the promotion of R&D;
(2) Effective return of research results to society;
(3) Support and fostering of ventures growing out of universities; and
(4) Strengthening organisations and fostering personnel to support co-operation among industry, academia and the public sector.[87]

Notwithstanding the efforts undertaken by the Japanese government, policies of this kind have a number of well-known limitations. Recalling the US experience, the relationship between industry and university is a

---

[85] Kneller, supra note 70, p. 1822.

[86] Angelino, H. and N. Collier (2004) 'Research and Innovation Policies in France and Japan: Similarities and Differences', a presentation of the informatics, http://www.nii.ac.jp/openhouse/h16/archive/PDF/704.pdf.

[87] *See,* Japanese Government Policies in Education, Culture, Sports, Science and Technology 2001, http://www.mext.go.jp/b_menu/hakusho/html/hpac200101/hpac200101_2_087.html.

complex one. Thus, the balance should be consistent between public and private interests. Universities should be responsive to the needs of society. However, over-encouragement of universities to undertake research work merely for the purposes of obtaining patents may very well lead universities away from their essential role as educative institutions.[88]

It has been suggested that the Japanese recipe for innovation takes advantage of all the potential ingredients that exist. The Japanese model changes the role of public institutions, which alleviates the administrative burden and also changes the culture in the different components involved in the processes.[89] Still, critics believe that the government's industrial policy needs a new approach. Traditionally, the promotion of innovation through the government-sponsored co-operative research schemes was concentrated on a small number of large, well-established firms. However, according to Goto, considering the important role of small- and medium-sized firms in the innovation cycle is vital. Hence, the government may give priority to the promotion of innovation within these companies in future.[90]

Concluding Remarks

During the years prior to the 1960s, Japan was nothing more than a catching-up economy. As a catching-up economy in the post-war period, Japan took full advantage of being a latecomer. The Japanese drew valuable lessons from the experiences of other developed countries. The Japanese government adopted a protectionist approach. In doing so, it protected its infant industries, banned foreign investment and trade, increased tariffs, and engaged in industrial espionage. As part of this process, it wilfully violated patents and trademarks. Once the economy had matured, and Japan had joined the champions' league of industrialised countries, the government began to advocate free trade in order to prevent the outflow of technologies. Hence, Japan became a strong

[88]   Odagiri, H. and A. Goto (1993) 'The Japanese System of Innovation: Past, Present and Future' in R. Nelson (ed.) *National Innovation Systems*, New York, Oxford University Press, pp. 108–11.
[89]   Angelino and Collier, supra note 86.
[90]   Odagiri et al., supra note 88, p. 111.

protector of IPRs[91] and made its best endeavours to 'take a leading role in the international discussion of the formation of the IPRs system'.[92]

Over the few past decades, the Japanese strategy of catching up has been presented as a success story. Other developing countries may follow this example in their own implementing innovation strategies. There are lessons to be drawn from the Japanese national innovation system. One of the most significant findings that emerged from Japan's case study is that it benefited greatly from a well-constructed IPRs system. This system took account of suitable local needs and realities. Thus, the IPRs system in Japan was built upon the realities of a catching-up country. It was eventually transformed into a strong system that supported the global competiveness of the country. To put it simply, the IPRs system has evolved throughout the years in accordance with the economic and technological development of the country.[93]

Nevertheless, the world has changed in last few decades and so has the international environment. In fact, examining the case of Japan shows the effects of the changing international dynamics. Japan had already passed the imitation and local innovation phase, and transformed its presence into a position of global competitive advantage, long before the TRIPS discussions began in earnest. If TRIPS had been enacted during the mid-twentieth century, Japanese companies such as Toyota or Takeda Pharmaceuticals would have met substantial IPRs-related barriers. Hence, the TRIPS effect might have had negative repercussions for the development of the country.[94]

Thus, the case study of Japan raises an important question of whether the policies and practices that were actively pursued by the Japanese government during the mid-twentieth century could provide useful guidance to developing countries. According to Odagiri et al., the Japanese catch-up policy was founded upon a system that combined a flexible IPRs policy with a strict foreign trade regime and capital policy. However, pursing this policy is unlikely to be possible under the current WTO system. Nevertheless, the Japanese experience still offers some real life lessons for developing countries. These lessons include guidance regarding the path-dependent evolution of the IPRs system. It is also important to nurture IPRs-minded entrepreneurship. Establishing an

---

[91]　*See,* Chang, supra note 56, pp. 64–6.

[92]　Japan Patent Office, Making creativity the font of prosperity, available at http://www.meti.go.jp/english/aboutmeti/data/aOrganizatione/2007/10_japan_patent_office.html.

[93]　Odagiri et. al, supra note 88, pp. 123–5.

[94]　*Ibid*, pp. 123–5.

148   *Boosting pharmaceutical innovation in the post-TRIPS era*

effective competition policy and the correct balance between industry forces and public sector intervention may also be counted as complementary measures in this account.[95]

THE NATIONAL INNOVATION SYSTEM OF SOUTH KOREA

Although the industrialisation of South Korea only began in the early 1960s, its rapid economic development since then has made South Korea an important player in the world economy. Korea has been transformed from an agricultural country into a newly industrialised one during the past quarter of a century. In the 1960s, Korea had the same level of economic development as Ghana. The country was suffering from almost every possible difficulty that a poor country can face. However, by the end of the 1980s, Korea's level of R&D investment and its high level of economic growth approached the levels of some of the most highly industrialised countries of Europe.[96] Hence, Korea's progress in terms of life-change indicators and economic growth may well be illustrated with the hypothetical analogy of a country such as Haiti developing into a country with the economic climate of Switzerland.[97]

The Korean national innovation system is founded upon the presence of strong formalised, government-driven policy planning and decision-making.[98] However, a serious flaw with the Korean system is its weak systematic linkages and its poor levels of interfaces between innovation actors. It also features an inefficient level of duplication of resource allocation and an uncoordinated setting of priorities.[99] The system had been criticised on the basis that it was primarily guided by the catch-up model. For instance, during the 1970s the system lacked the technological capabilities necessary for industrialisation. Hence, the system

---

[95] *Ibid*, pp. 125–7.

[96] Kim, L. (1993) 'National System of Industrial Innovation: Dynamics of Capability Building in Korea' in R. Nelson (ed.) *National Innovation Systems*, New York, Oxford University Press, p. 357.

[97] Chang, supra note 56, p. 12.

[98] 'No nation has tried harder and come so far so quickly, from handicrafts to heavy industry, from poverty to prosperity, from inexperienced leaders to modern planners, managers and engineers'; Vogel, E.F. (1991) *The Four Little Dragons: The Spread of Industrialization in East Asia*, Cambridge, Harvard University Press, p. 65.

[99] Yol-Yu H.: ' Korean National Innovation System', available at http://crds.jst.go.jp/GIES/archive/GIES2006/participants/abstract/41_hee-yol-yu.pdf.

relied on foreign technology and knowledge rather than domestic R&D.[100] Nevertheless, by the 1980s the system had entered into a stage of transition. Over the course of this stage, a high level of investment was targeted towards indigenous R&D and the competitiveness of the country was strengthened by the use of creative imitation of foreign technology and local innovation. At this time, Korean companies developed skills in order to make incremental advances in relation to imported technology. Over the course of the final stage of development, Korean companies engaged in experimental areas, such as research into semiconductors, electronics and biotechnology. Furthermore, Korean companies drastically raised their level of R&D investment in order to strengthen their technological competitiveness.[101]

The government functioned as an effective orchestrator of the catch-up process. In this context, the government's strong commitment to technology-based national development, coupled with the efforts of private industry bodies in relation to competitiveness in the high-tech industries, are strong features of the Korean system. The positive contributions of the R&D activities have been reflected in a remarkable growth of registered patents in Korea. The high rate of R&D activities has also encouraged the establishment of high-tech companies such as those manufacturing semiconductor memory chips, liquid crystal displays and telecommunication equipment. In these areas, Korea has emerged as a world leader.[102]

The private sector has been identified as the major benefactor of R&D in Korea. In consultation with the private sector, the government has protected certain industries. It has done this through tariff protection, subsidies and other forms of support. The government actively protected these industries until they reached a certain level of maturity that enabled the companies to withstand international competition.[103] Consequently, the government has extensively supported the corporate sector in relation to R&D activities through direct R&D subsidies, preferential financing and tax incentives.[104]

---

[100]   Lee Y. (2004) Patent Rights and Universities: Policies and Legal Framework for Korea, A thesis submitted for the Doctor of Philosophy, Queen Mary, University of London, 2004, p. 81.
[101]   Kim, L. (1997) *Imitation to Innovation: The Dynamics of Korea's Technological Learning (Management of Innovation and Change)*, Boston, Harvard Business Press, p. 194.
[102]   Lee, supra note 100, pp. 89–92.
[103]   Chang, supra note 56, p. 14.
[104]   Kim, supra note 101, p. 372.

Examining the Korean Patent Regime

Today, Korea's patent regime is highly advanced when compared to the economies of other newly industrialised countries. The very first patent of law in Korea was based on the US patent system. Thus, the law adopted the first-to-invent regime. However, during the 1960s, Korea switched to a first-to-file rule. As a consequence of the catching-up process in the country, the patent term was shortened from 17 to 12 years. More importantly, pharmaceutical and chemical materials were excluded from patent protection. Korean law provided protection for pharmaceutical processes, but not the products.

Nevertheless, Korea introduced patent protection for pharmaceutical products in 1986 as a result of international political pressure, particularly from the US government. The patent protection term was extended to 15 years from the grant of a patent, or 18 years from the application date, whichever is longer. Moreover, five years of patent-term extensions were introduced in order to compensate for regulatory delays.

In the early years of catch up, it was largely the case that individual inventors applied for patents. Thus, the share of corporate patent ownership was quite limited. However, Korean companies started to use the patent system once they had built up their own technological capabilities and skills. Nevertheless, the corporate share of domestic applications was limited to 10 per cent in the late 1980s. The introduction of pharmaceutical product patents generated economic losses in the short-term for the pharmaceutical industry. At that time, the industry relied heavily on generic drugs. As a result, the industry was incapable of developing globally marketable new drugs. The companies were still involved in the process of adapting and absorbing foreign technologies. Nevertheless, Korean companies soon changed their strategy. Many moved towards more innovative R&D and a number of companies formed alliances with technology-holders abroad. The limitations of imitative R&D were soon realised and consequently, new research laboratories were established. The number of approved research laboratories during the period between 1986 and 1988 was about four times larger than the preceding years. Moreover, in 1987 the proportion of R&D in relation to percentage of sales increased from 0.69 to 1.86 per cent.[105] However, the Korean market was a small one and as a result, the pharmaceutical companies' R&D budget was at a level below 4 per cent of their overall sales. Thus,

---

[105]   Lee, K. and Y.K. Kim (2010) 'IPR and Technological Catch-up in Korea' in H. Odagiri, A. Goto, A. Sunami and R. Nelson (eds) *Intellectual Property Rights, Development and Catch-up*, New York, Oxford University Press, p. 152.

R&D expenditures remained unimpressive during the 1990s when compared with the same levels in other countries.[106] Nevertheless, during the late 1990s Korean companies began to invest heavily in R&D to close the R&D gap. Consequently, Korean firms have managed to invent 16 new medicines, all of which are commercially viable. Currently, Korea ranks tenth in the list of countries capable of drug discovery and development.[107]

The Korean success in the pharmaceutical industry can be illustrated by examining the Hepatitis B vaccine development story. During the 1980s, one of the major health problems in Korea was Hepatitis B. The prevalence of infection was something between 8–15 per cent before the introduction of the Hepatitis B vaccine.[108] Korean businesses typically imported the vaccine. As a result, the vaccine was of limited use. It was only available in small quantities and it was not affordable for everyone in the country. Thus, the government acted promptly in order to encourage local production. Korean companies focused their R&D departments towards the goal of developing a new vaccine. By collaborating with foreign companies, or by obtaining patented technology from abroad, the companies transferred knowledge and technology. Thereafter, companies modified foreign technology to suit their local needs. Hence, they were able to launch their vaccines successfully during the 1990s. Soon after this, Korean companies became global exporters of DNA vaccines. This resulted in a substantial decrease of prices in the international market. According to Lee and Kim, Korean pharmaceutical companies were not significantly inhibited by existing IPRs over vaccine technology. Companies were able to transfer technology within the limits of the IPRs system by establishing joint ventures or collaborations. Thus, companies took full advantage of their position as latecomers. Many companies adopted a stage-skipping catch-up strategy. More importantly, the government played a critical role in the success of the Korean pharmaceutical companies. It not only helped to secure a profitable market for producers but also provided export encouragement and subsidised the building of vacuum factories.[109]

---

[106] La Croix, S. and A. Kawaura (1996) 'Product Patent Reform and its Impact on Korea's Pharmaceutical Industry', *International Economic Journal*, V.10, N.1, p. 121.

[107] *See,* Lee and Kim supra note 105, pp. 153–4.

[108] Juon H., et al. (2009) 'Hepatitis B Vaccinations among Koreans: Results from 2005 Korea National Cancer Screening Survey', BMC Infectious Diseases, V.9, available at http://www.biomedcentral.com/1471-2334/9/185.

[109] Lee and Kim supra note 105, p. 158.

As with the case of Japan and the US, pharmaceutical innovation in Korea has passed through a path-following route. Korean companies primarily built up their skills and expertise in drug manufacturing during an era featuring a lack of patent protection for pharmaceuticals. When product patents were finally introduced in Korea, Korean companies were in a position to enhance their capacities for developing and assimilating new knowledge and technologies. However, they were not able to make modifications to foreign technology and thus, apply new knowledge to old technology. Therefore, in the short term, there was a significant loss of wealth in the industry. The growing threat of Hepatitis B infection and the lack of local production capability prompted the government and the industry to take action. The government provided the necessary incentives and guaranteed a profitable market for the industry. The industry utilised their corporate sources in order to gain access to foreign know-how. Instead of reinventing the wheel, Korean companies took advantage of being latecomers and followed a stage-skipping catch-up route. Thus, they invested directly into research and the latest foreign knowledge. This was achieved through joint venture arrangements in order avoid possible IPRs problems with the technology. The in-house R&D efforts were supported by the latest foreign technology. The successful launch of vaccines during the mid-1990s confirmed that the Koreans had completed the local innovation stage and thus, Korea was ready to move on to the next stage.

The importance of the government's role in the industrialisation of Korea should not be underestimated. The presence of a strong government speeded up the Korean catch-up process. According to Kim, 'the government held the wheel and supplied the fuel, while private firms functioned as engines'.[110] In fact, the government guaranteed the market and it also provided the necessary incentives. Moreover, it took a crucial role in enlarging the export market for the vaccines. The export market encouragement of the government facilitated the industry's move up to the next level. It also fostered the global competitiveness of the Korean industry and today, the two companies who actively took part in vaccine R&D – Green Cross and LG Chem – are the two leading players. Thus, the Korean industry is independently capable of developing new drugs. Companies are no longer associated with imitative drugs. As stated above, the Korean industry has already invented 16 new medicines.[111]

---

[110]   Kim, supra note 101, p. 15.
[111]   Lee and Kim supra note 105, p. 15.

Catching Up to the Future

The industry in Korea has been transformed from being imitative in character to being innovative. In doing so, it has achieved a positive level of industrialised growth. Nonetheless, the Korean national innovation system has lost its competitiveness in recent years. Excessive reliance on private industries in relation to R&D investment is one of the main weaknesses of the system. The lack of distribution of R&D investment across facilities and personnel in Korea constitutes another drawback of the system.[112] The fundamental problem that lies at the root of the Korean NIS is the underdevelopment of the university research capability. Furthermore the mechanism required to turn the basic university research into commercial activities is not always present. Recent evidence suggests that the impact of university basic research in driving long-term innovative behaviour remains limited. It is contended that the Korean system requires structural changes, which ought to be directed towards particular actors and activities. The efficiency of the Korean system depends on the linkages and the division of labour between innovation actors. Therefore, harnessing the new generation of indigenous knowledge and strengthening the university system are of the utmost importance in relation to sustainable innovation policies.[113]

China and other emerging Asian countries – so-called Asian tigers – are strong challengers to the Korean economy. Consequently, the Korean government is currently in the process of restructuring the NIS. The government is developing innovation-driven polices rather than imitative and catch-up oriented ones.[114] Korea still possesses a competitive advantage. Nevertheless, it became evident that an upgrade, not only in terms of quantity, but also in quality, is needed in order for the Korean innovation system to accumulate knowledge in the area of basic science and fundamental technologies.[115] It is suggested that Korea should break its old model and thus, create a new one. This model must be founded upon notions of economic indigenisation. Indigenisation requires the regeneration of the indigenous knowledge base as well as a strengthening of university research capabilities. Deepening the innovation system

---

[112]   Lee, supra note 100, p. 94.
[113]   Suh, J. (2000) 'Korea's Innovation System: Challenges and New Policy Agenda', UNU/Intech Discussion Papers, p. 67.
[114]   Yol-Yu, supra note 99.
[115]   Yim, D.S. (2005) 'Korea's National Innovation System and the Science and the Technology Policy', Science and Technology Policy Institute (STEPI), available at www.unesco.org/science/psd/thm_innov/forums/korea.pdf.

depends upon the re-orientation of the state's business strategy, rather than technological progress. Thus, there is a need for basic policy review that moves towards a more diffusion-oriented regime. Last, but not least, in relation to high and sustained growth, Korea may be able to take advantage of global integration by strengthening both its domestic and international linkages.[116]

Concluding Remarks

The rapid industrialisation of Korea is usually described as a process of upgrading, that is, a progression from imitation to innovation. Over the course of the catch-up process, Korea combined Japanese-style creative imitation with American-style innovation.[117] After the introduction of patents for pharmaceutical products in Korea, there were short-term wealth losses. Thus, the transition had an initial adverse effect on the pharmaceutical industry. However, although the patent system presented serious barriers in relation to catching up, the IPRs system functioned as a push factor for the industry during the catch up. Apart from importing foreign technology and knowledge through joint venture arrangements and costly licence agreements, the industry also invested heavily in the area of in-house R&D. When compared to Japan, the Korean path to growth and competitiveness was tough and filled with obstacles. Nevertheless, the Korean pharmaceutical industry did not get stuck in the patent trap. Korean companies transformed their reverse-engineering skills and activities into in-house, R&D-friendly activities. Supported by government incentives, Korean companies were able to invent and produce drugs that met both local and global needs.

THE NATIONAL INNOVATION SYSTEM OF ISRAEL

Over the past decade, Israel has become the pre-eminent technological powerhouse in the generic drug industry. The Israeli generic drug industry is geographically distinct from many other markets. It is richly endowed with human capital and organisational structures. Furthermore, new high-tech ventures are seen to be an essential element of the economy. Thus, innovative generic industry-oriented technologies are

---

[116]   Suh, supra note 113, pp. 67–8.
[117]   Kim, L. (1997) *Imitation to Innovation: The Dynamics of Korea's Technological Learning (Management of Innovation and Change)*, Boston, Harvard Business Press, pp. 11–13.

supported in order to strengthen the country's technological expertise and enhance competitiveness.

The National Innovation System of Israel offers a 'fascinating illustration of extraordinary success in innovation'.[118] The development of the system has been a high priority of policy due to Israel's geographical, economic and historical conditions. Israel is a very small country with a population of seven million. It stands at a global and historical crossroads. It has very few natural resources and it operates under constant security threats. The roots of the government commitment to the development of NIS in Israel go back to the 1950s, when Israel was poor, peripheral, and highly dependent upon foreign technology.[119]

The boycott by the Arab League started immediately after Israel was established and continued until the mid-1990s. The boycott was essentially divided in three components. The primary boycott was prohibiting direct trade between Israel and all Arab countries. The target of the secondary boycott was companies who were doing business with Israel. Furthermore, the boycott prohibited all Arab countries from maintaining commercial ties with those international companies or dealing with their subsidiaries. Moreover, thousands of companies from all around the world, which either traded with Israel or were owned by Jews, were blacklisted, and Arab states were prohibited from doing business with them in the scope of the last and the tertiary boycott.[120] The boycott started to weaken at the end of the 1970s as a result of peace negotiations with Egypt. Eventually, the Oslo peace process in the mid-1990s put an end to the boycott by Arab countries.

Towards the end of the 1960s, the government of Israel made a strategic decision to transfer resources in order to create a science-based sector in Israel. These initiatives largely involved making financial support available in relation to commercial R&D, as well as making up for market failures in relation to the promotion of exports. It was also

---

[118] Trajtenberg M. (2005) 'Innovation Policy for Development: An Overview', STE Program Working Paper, STE-WP-34-200, p. 2.

[119] Breznitz D. (2007) *Innovation and the State: Political Choice and Strategies for Growth in Israel, Taiwan and Ireland*, New Haven, Yale University Press, p. 6.

[120] *See*, Besok M.: 'A Commentary; Last Days Of The Boycott – 01-Feb-94' Israel Ministry of Foreign Affairs, available at http://www.mfa.gov.il/MFA/Archive/Articles/1994/LAST%20DAYS%20OF%20THE%20OYCOTT%20-%2001-Feb-94; Bard, M. (2007) 'The Arab Boycott', Jewish Virtual Library, available at http://www.jewishvirtuallibrary.org/jsource/History/Arab_boycott.html.

necessary for the state to invest in capital-intensive high-tech sectors.[121] In an effort to provide direct support in relation to innovation, the Office of the Chief Scientist (OCS) was created at the Ministry of Industry and Trade. The Law for the Encouragement of R&D (1985) reorganised OCS as a quasi-independent agency. The agency was formed to provide direct support for R&D, both within firms and within public research institutes.[122]

Israel is a country without water, oil and other natural resources.[123] This required a rational identification of the national assets and enactment of national policies in line with the nation's needs and future prospects. In terms of goals, the provision of a highly skilled labour force, as well as the imposition of strong pro-education cultural values within the school system, were vital in the early years of Israel. As a result, a high level of scientific technological power and intellectual capital became the key features of the country. Therefore, the government prioritised the creation of scientific and technological knowledge. This enhanced the economic vitality and sustainability of the nation. Contrary to Japan and South Korea, the incentives for innovation in Israel were created for small- and medium-sized enterprises rather than big corporations. Thus, the innovation policies were generally focused on encouraging industrial R&D activities through government grants, in relation to the ideas that originated solely in the private sector.[124]

Israel is a very good example of Lundvall's hypothesis. The level of innovation that is taking place in small and medium enterprises (SMEs), with a low level of R&D, generates industrial dynamism and market growth. According to the Lundvall's theory, the success of innovation policies in developing countries lies in the increasing importance of industrial dynamism in SMEs. In order to stimulate innovation across the country and to encourage R&D, the government of Israel directly supported the R&D activities of SMEs. The research conducted by these companies lead to the establishment of new ideas and innovations.

---

[121]   Roper, S. (1999) 'Innovation Policy in Israel, Ireland and the UK – An Evolutionary Perspective', Working Paper Series No. 47, NIERC, pp. 6–7.
[122]   Pugatch, M., M. Teubal and O. Zlotnick (2010) 'Israel's High-Tech Catch-up Process' in H. Odagiri, A. Goto, A. Sunami and R. Nelson (eds) *Intellectual Property Rights, Development and Catch-up*, New York, Oxford University Press, p. 213.
[123]   'Innovation in Israel – advantages in generating ideas', available at, http://innovation.freedomblogging.com/category/innovation-in-israel/.
[124]   Breznitz, supra note 119, p. 7.

The Patent Regime of Israel

The roots of the Israeli patent regime go back to the British mandate in 1924. The patent law, which is still in force today, is the Patent Act of 1967. As it originated from the British act, it provided patent protection in all fields of technology, without discriminating between product and process.[125] It is arguable that the scope of patentability was subject to a narrow interpretation before the amendment of the law in 2000.[126] The law previously defined a patented invention as any invention, which could be used in industry or agriculture. In 2000, the definition of a patented invention was broadened to include any technological field in accordance with the broad interpretation of Article 27 of TRIPS.[127]

Although the 1967 Patent Act provided patent protection to pharmaceutical products and processes, the law included peculiar provisions, which were justified as being for the benefit of local pharmaceutical companies. Particularly in the event of lack or insufficient working of a patented invention, it was possible to establish compulsory licences in the country. The next chapter will give a detailed account of the circumstances under which the local pharmaceutical companies were able to use and benefit from these provisions. Nevertheless, it suffices to say that the local industry built up its capacities and expertise in relation to drug manufacturing by relying on these provisions.

The amendment in 2000 introduced revisions to the statutory provisions regarding compulsory licensing. The relevant provisions have been amended in a manner that is considerably limiting in relation to the cases where compulsory licences may be applied. This puts considerable limitations on the value of the compulsory licence for the holder. The scope of a compulsory licence is narrowed down in a manner fully complying with the requirements of TRIPS.[128]

Israel is the very first country in the world that has signed a truly reciprocal free trade agreement (FTA) with the US. The United States-Israel Free Trade Agreement was signed in 1985, long before the US

---

[125] 'An invention, whether a product or a process, which is new and useful, can be used in industry or agriculture, and which involves an inventive step, is a patentable invention.' Article 3 of 1967 Israeli Patent Act

[126] The Israeli patent law was amended in 2000 in order to provide compliance with the TRIPS Agreement.

[127] Gilat, D. (2003) 'Development in Israeli Patent Law 2000–2002' (Report to Institute of Intellectual Property in Asia, 19 October 2003), available at http://www.institute-ip-asia.org/articles/Israelreport.pdf.

[128] *Id.*

adopted an aggressive IPRs policy. The agreement also took place long before the IPR discussions regarding TRIPS and TRIPS-plus during the mid-1980s.

At that time, the Israeli generic drug industry was not in as strong a position as it is today. As a result, the agreed IPRs provisions were general and flexible.[129] Nevertheless, if Israel and the US engaged in FTA negotiations today, the outcome would be significantly different. The US would probably have asked for a stricter, pro-patent regime. Following the FTA with the US, Israel became a member of the WTO. As a result, Israel was obligated to implement TRIPS in 2000. Thus, the patent law of Israel (Patent Law 5727–1967) was amended in order to bring the law into conformity with the requirements of TRIPS.

Today, the Israeli patent regime fully complies with the provisions of TRIPS. Pre-grant opposition procedure is one of the important features of the Israeli patent regime. Pre-grant opposition facilitates public participation to patent examination. It allows any person, including researchers, NGOs, health organisations, and market competitors to oppose a patent application by submitting information and analysis to patent examiners, under an adversarial administrative process. It is an important instrument in terms of improving patent quality and the accuracy of patent claims. According to the relevant provision, any person can oppose the application within three months after the application.[130] The opposition process can continue up until the Supreme Court takes the final decision. The patent examination process can take a long time, in a scenario where the initial examination can take between three and five years and the opposition process can take up to five years. In addition, the patent registrar acts as the first instance district court, if parties appeal the case, then the average waiting time for the decision is two years. In the final stage, the case goes to the Supreme Court, which adds a further two to three years to the waiting time.

This pre-grant opposition procedure has been subjected to fierce criticism by multinational pharmaceutical companies. They argued that the long examination process causes the loss of a significant part of the period of the patent life and the pre-grant opposition system provides a relatively favourable position for the local generic industry.[131] However, both the Israeli Patent Office and the Israeli local pharmaceutical industry reject the accusations. The Patent Office argued that although there were

---

[129] Article 14, Agreement on the Establishment of a Free Trade Area between the Government of Israel and the Government of the United States of America.

[130] Section 30 of the Israeli Patent Act.

[131] *See,* PhRMA, 'Special 301 Submission for 2007'.

cases where the local companies successfully challenged the patents and cases where companies launched products at their own risk before the final decision of the court, these cases did not constitute a breach of the confidentiality of the Israeli patent application.

The Israeli patent regime has traditionally been subject to considerable criticism from the US government due to Israel's failure to protect undisclosed test data from unfair commercial use. According to the United States Trade Representative (USTR) Special 301 report of 2004, Israel has consistently failed to provide protection on data submitted by US pharmaceutical firms. As a result, the US government urged the Israeli government to enact TRIPS-consistent legislation that will provide a reasonable period of non-reliance on confidential data.[132] Even though Israel implemented the data protection that is embodied in Article 39.3 of TRIPS into its regime in 2000, USTR requested that Israel incorporate data exclusivity in order to provide exclusive protection of the data. The data exclusivity provision was introduced in 2005 following drawn-out negotiations with the US government. The data exclusivity provisions in Israel remained an effective compromise between the local industry lobby and the government.

The specific data exclusivity provisions were very peculiar to Israel. Article 47 of the Pharmacist Ordinance regulates the data exclusivity regime in the country. The protection is only available for new chemical entities and it does not cover formulations, second medical use claims, processes, paediatric usages and so on. The protection period was the most controversial part of the regulation. Initially, the act provided either five years of data exclusivity from the registration day of the drug in Israel, or five and a half years of exclusivity from the day of the earliest registration in any of the recognised countries – whichever is the shortest period.[133] The recognised countries are listed in the Pharmacist Ordinance and covers the US, all the EU countries, Canada, Switzerland, Australia, and so on. The protection was tied to registration in recognised countries. It is not possible to register a drug before it is registered in the US and the EU. The regulatory process usually takes between two and three years in Israel. Hence, in most of the cases, the data exclusivity protection was covering the remaining two to three years. However, the USTR wants uninterrupted protection for five years. In fact, PhRMA claimed that the regulation provides a favourable position to the generic companies by allowing them to rely on registration of the original drugs

---

[132]   *See,* USTR Special 301 Report, 2004.
[133]   *See,* Article 47 D (b) 2 of Israeli Pharmacist Ordinance.

for export purposes. Indeed, this regulation did not apply to applications for export licences from the Ministry of Health and thereby assists the export-oriented local industry to maintain its competitiveness in world generic drug markets. Nevertheless, Israel and the US have somehow resolved the data exclusivity dispute. According to the agreement, Israel would prolong the five-and-a-half-years exclusivity by a further year, and in exchange the US will move Israel from the Priority Watch List.[134] The amendment with respect to data exclusivity was enacted in 2011, and Israel was removed from the Priority Watch List of Special 301s in 2012, though it remained on the Watch Lists of 2012 and 2013 Special 301s. Finally in 2014, USTR announced that Israel is being removed from the Special 301 Report Watch List.[135] The new regime requires marketing approval for pharmaceutical products to be granted within 12 months of an application. Under the new system, the data exclusivity protection can last for five years following a timely application for marketing approval.[136]

As a part of the data exclusivity deal with the local pharmaceutical industry, Israel has modified regulation of its patent term extension certificates. This amendment was heavily lobbied by the local industry, and it is widely referred to as a 'Teva deal'.[137] The amendment introduced a new method of calculating the term of protection afforded in Israel, and the new method renders the term of protection to be as short as possible. According to Section 64J of the Patent Act, the term of protection was limited to five years beyond the term. The drug is required to be granted a patent term extension certificate in any of the recognised countries. The extension period counted from the earliest registration in any one of those countries. The accumulative total term of the extension was required not to be longer than 14 years after the day on which the first marketing approval was issued in any of those countries.[138]

It is also argued that the legislation introduced new and burdensome conditions for patent term extension certificate applications. With the

---

[134]   'US, Israel Resolve Long-Standing Pharma Battle', *PharmaTimes*, 23 February 2010, available at www.pharmatimes.com/WorldNews/articles.aspx?id= 17449, (25.09.2010).

[135]   The USTR kept Israel on the Priority Watch List in 2011, citing, among others, delays in the implementation of the agreement. Israel placed on the Watch List of 2012 and 2013 Special 301s.

[136]   *See,* WTO Trade Policy Review of Israel (WT/TPR/M/272).

[137]   Teva Pharmaceuticals is the largest Israeli pharmaceutical company, which is one of the top 20 pharmaceutical companies worldwide.

[138]   *See,* Section 64I of the Israeli Patent Act.

regulation, the applicant was required to file and obtain a similar kind of application in both the US and at least one EU member country. Thus, the new amendment has been interpreted to reduce the effective patent extension term as it required the patent term extension in Israel be aligned with the shortest of the extension periods typically granted to a patent in any of the recognised countries.[139]

In 2010, Israel agreed to limit the number of countries to permit the filing of an application for extension even if the referenced extensions under the 'two state requirement' had not been granted. The relevant legislation was approved by the Israeli Parliament and entered into force in 2014.[140]

The generic drug industry, particularly Teva, is of utmost importance for Israel. As Teva developed and increased its competiveness in the world generic drug market, the pressure from the US, and particularly from PhRMA, increased. The patent regime in Israel is enacted as a compromise between multinational pharmaceutical companies and the local industry. In the past USTR fiercely criticised the Israeli patent regime for the lack of adequate protection, even though the Israeli regime fully complied with the minimum standards of TRIPS. Nevertheless, PhRMA and the USTR consistently pushed for protection going beyond the minimum standards of TRIPS. Currently the Israeli patent regime includes typical TRIPS-plus provisions regarding data exclusivity and patent term extension certificates. Nonetheless, it is still constructed in a manner consistent to the needs of the national industry. Until the last amendment, the patent term provisions, for instance, were designed in consideration of the public interest and public health issues. Apart from the local pharmaceutical industry, the Ministry of Finance and the Ministry of Health actively lobbied for the well-construction of those provisions. The national health care system has always been the primary concern of these government institutions and thus, they wanted generic drug entry into the market at the earliest opportunity.

The next chapter will cover the case of Teva. It will provide real-life analysis of the usage of the patent regime in the best interests of the local needs and realities of Israel. However, it suffices to conclude here that the Israeli patent regime is carefully formulated according to the level of development of the country and industry.

---

[139] Israel, National Trade Estimate Report on Foreign Trade Barriers (NTE) 2007, PHRMA, available at www.sidley.com/db30/cgi-bin/pubs/US-Israel_Business_Law_Developments_.

[140] *See,* WT/TPR/M/272.

Overview of the Innovation Policies, Issues and Concerns

As with the case of Korea, the innovation policy in Israel is government-driven and has a top-down structure in relation to policymaking and decisionmaking. Although Israel is assumed to be one of the success stories, that is, a case where the government has been very successful in catalysing the establishment of world-class high-tech industries, the policy making and evaluation practices are fairly unsystematic. Overall, the policies lack a clear methodology when compared to Korea.

The success of the system, particularly at early stages of innovation, in a large part depends on the financial incentives granted to SMEs, as well as forward-planning in accordance with local realities. Early recognition of the importance of linking university research to the industry, and the establishment of research authorities and science parks, are the key features that brought success to the Israeli system.[141]

The innovation system in Israel may be defined as ambiguous and inexplicit. The rate of innovation is organised as a by-product of encouraging R&D.[142] This R&D eventually leads to industrial dynamism and provides vitality and sustainability to the economy. Unlike Japan and Korea, the Israeli government did not select the would-be winners or provide an incentive for R&D investment in any favoured sector. Israel is acknowledged as being one of the first states to employ both a horizontal and neutral science technology strategy.[143] Neutrality, in fact, is a distinctive feature of the innovation system, which is highly regarded as a long-time success strategy for Israel. This functions in a manner that considers the market demands and signals. The innovation incentives do not discriminate between the different fields of technology.[144] The government policies are characterised by dynamism, which creates new programs in response to changing needs and updates existing ones in light of market developments.[145]

---

[141]   Teubal, M. (1993) 'The Innovation System of Israel: Description Performance and Outstanding Issues' in R. Nelson (ed.) *National Innovation Systems*, New York, Oxford University Press, pp. 477–97.

[142]   Getz, D. and V. Sagal (2008) 'The Israeli Innovation System: An Overview of National Policy and Cultural Aspects', Samuel Neaman Institute for Advanced Studies in Science and Technology, p. 28.

[143]   Breznitz, D. (2007) *Innovation and the State: Political Choice and Strategies for Growth in Israel, Taiwan and Ireland*, New Haven, Yale University Press, pp. 1465–82; Pugatch et al, supra note 122, p. 213.

[144]   Trajtenberg, supra note 118.

[145]   *Ibid.*

The early recognition of the shortage of natural resources and raw materials in Israel led the founders of the state to develop a strategic policy. This policy was aimed at creating Israel's natural intellectual resources. The educational priorities of the country were set to encourage the technical education of the people.[146] The flow of manpower comes from the Israeli university network, and from immigration. There is a high level of public commitment to supporting commercial R&D. Hence, support for innovative activity is clearly another important component of NIS.[147]

Israel ranks first in the world in relation to R&D expenditure. Each year academic research receives more than a quarter of a million dollars of government funds. This constitutes 4.6 per cent of Israel's GDP.[148] Thus, R&D in Israel generates a vast amount of cutting edge innovations.[149] Nevertheless, this may also give rise to a high level of deadweight, as well as displacement and the undertaking of sub-marginal projects.[150] The high level of public support for R&D in Israel has been criticised by Israeli academics. Teubal, for example, argues that 'there is a feeling today that probably too much R&D may have been done, which means that an unduly small proportion was effectively applied'.[151]

Moreover, multinationals are highly active in the Israeli R&D market. A substantial part of the industrial R&D in Israel is done by local laboratories owned by multinationals. The knowledge generated in these laboratories then flows out to meet the global needs of parent companies. Thus, it may be of little relevance to the future economic vitality of Israel. By way of illustration, Centrino chipsets are designed at Intel's R&D centre in Haifa. Generally, most of the laptops in world are powered by Centrino chipsets. Nevertheless, the country has not received substantial economic benefits from this invention. The reason for this is that the IPRs generated in the Israeli R&D labs are owned by Intel and thus, the revenue flows out of the country.

With regard to the economic aspects of innovation, the geographical location of laboratories is also a feature that potentially stimulates the economy. It does so by creating employment, stimulating enterprise development, and increasing productivity and so on. Nevertheless, for a

---

[146] Getz and Sagal supra note 142, p. 13.
[147] Roper, supra note 121, p. 1.
[148] Davis, H. and D. Davis (2005) *Israel in the World: Changing Lives through Innovation*, London, Weidenfeld & Nicolson, p. 18.
[149] Trajtenberg, supra note 118, p. 22.
[150] Roper, supra note 121, p. 15.
[151] *Ibid*; Teubal, supra note 551, pp. 487–8.

knowledge-driven economy, the role of innovation as a growth catalyst mainly depends on the availability of intellectual capital, the knowledge generated, the know-how created, and the ownership of intellectual property. As Trajtenberg clearly notes:

> The impact of a given innovation on the local economy depends in large measure on who owns the intellectual property (IP) generated, where it flows to, what sort of lateral connections are there, and so on, and not just on the geographical location of the R&D lab.[152]

Although the case of Israel illustrates a success story in relation to innovation, the globally competitive businesses in Israel are few. According to the Forbes Global 2000 list, Israel has only one true global giant: Teva, one of the world leaders in generic medicines. Teva's drugs are estimated to account for one out of every 15 prescriptions in the US.[153] The case of Teva reveals guidance for developing countries and local pharmaceutical industries. Although it will be examined in detail in the forthcoming chapter, it should be noted that the long-term strategy and implementation of this strategy, together with the incentives provided by the Israeli national innovation policy, have helped to make Teva a world leader in generic medicines.

Government's Role and Outstanding Issues

The government is the financial source of innovation in Israel. It provides financial support for all types of R&D, from basic research in universities to all kinds of product and process development in firms. This financial support is mainly focused on applied R&D with commercial and economic viability. Due to the indistinct structure of the Israeli innovation system, Israel does not have a law, or legal standards, to accommodate provisions or regulations in relation to grant rates.

The Law for the Promotion of Industrial Research and Development (R&D Law) was enacted in 1985 as the principal mechanism aimed at enhancing the development of the local science-based industry. It did so by utilising and expanding the existing technological and academic infrastructure and by increasing the manufacture and export of high-tech products developed within Israel. The OCS processes applications by considering a set of criteria. The criteria are as follows: technological and

---

[152]   Trajtenberg, supra note 118.
[153]   Davis, supra note 148, p. 21.

commercial feasibility, merits and risks, and the extent to which the project can be expected to generate spillovers.[154]

The standard grants supporting R&D projects in Israel vary from 50 per cent to 60 per cent, depending on the area of science. This repayment is done in terms of royalty payments as a total of revenues derived from the sale of the developed product. In a comparative study of innovation policies in Israel, Ireland, and the UK, Roper reported that for any individual R&D project up-front grant support is likely to be most substantially beneficial in Israel. According to his study, the proportion of government funded R&D in all civil R&D by business was 26.1 per cent in Israel in 1994, more than two and a half times the proportion in Ireland (10 per cent) and more than four times the proportion in the UK (6.3 per cent).[155]

Incubators Program

The Incubators Program was created during the 1990s. At this time, post-Soviet immigration reached its peak. Most of the post-Soviet immigrants were scientists and highly skilled professionals. They possessed innovative ideas and the necessary background and enthusiasm to realise them. However, they were lacking in virtually all other dimensions required for commercial success.[156] In order to give an opportunity to develop innovative technological ideas and set up new businesses in order to commercialise them, the Incubators Program was put in place.

The program provides incentives to entrepreneurs and start-ups at the earliest stage of technological innovation. It equips them with the basic means in order to implement their ideas and to turn them into exportable commercial products. It also aims to establish a link between the academy and the industry by providing infrastructure and managerial support for projects.

Three criteria were considered for acceptance into the program. First of all, the potential product must be marketable for export and it must be capable of forming the basis of a business. Second, the product must be in a high-tech field. Finally, it has to be manufactured in Israel. Due to the neutrality principle present in the Israeli innovation system, the entrepreneurs in any field of technology were able to benefit from the

---

[154] Spillovers occur when R&D activity undertaken in one organisation creates benefits or cost reductions elsewhere which are not reflected fully in the rewards reaped by the organisation which carried out the research in the first place.

[155] Roper, supra note 121, p. 29.

[156] Trajtenberg, supra note 118, p. 20.

programs.[157] However, the inventions that they proposed were to fulfil the patentability criteria. Thus, all the applications had to be accompanied with a proof of patent application.

Creating a strong biotechnology industry, consisting of start-up companies, is a valid aspiration for Israel. Establishing such infrastructure demands a huge investment in time and resources. The biotech start-ups primarily require financial support for long-term R&D activities and the subsequent clinical trials. The incubators have been created to encourage an environment for scientists, who may lack entrepreneurial skills, to interest investors. This makes the incubators program increasingly popular among biotechnology start-ups. There are many successful biotechnology companies that have grown up as part of the incubators program.

Magnet Program

The Magnet Program brings together industry and academia to work on basic research aimed at eventual commercialisation. The program was created as a subsidy for innovative, generic, pre-competitive technologies in order to boost local innovation and enhance competitiveness.

The program specifically focuses on basic research for new high-tech products and processes. By bringing together inventors and innovators, it aims to promote high-technology research, development and commercialisation. It also aims to foster long-term thinking in R&D. The activities are based on collaboration between companies and academic research groups organised in consortia with several members or as a dual co-operation between academic groups doing research in scientific areas. This is potentially relevant to the technological goals of a consortium and one industrial company operating in the field, depending on the chosen track.[158]

All the new knowledge, which was developed under the consortium umbrella, is open free of charge, to all other consortium members. However, the exclusivity of the know-how stays with the developers. Sharing the intellectual property, and giving an upfront licence to use it, is the main justification of the programme. Eventually, each member acquires more know-how than could be achieved if working alone. The synergetic collaboration of knowledge provides the common denominator of a win-win proposition for both industry and academia. This way of knowledge sharing has proven to be successful in the area of life

---

[157]   There are 24 incubators in Israel, 17 of them are privatised and one is a biotech incubator.

[158]   *See,* Getz and Sagal supra note 142, p. 18.

sciences. The consortiums in life sciences focus on the development of process, and tools, but not products. Successful co-operation has been achieved in the fields of bioinformatics, medical tools and cell therapy.

R&D funds

In life sciences, innovative projects are classified as high-risk projects, that is, projects that have a high likelihood of failure. Due to the high risk involved, the venture capitalists are unlikely to invest in these kinds of projects. Hence, government support becomes indispensable in order for the pharmaceutical and biotech industries to thrive.

R&D funds are offered by the Israeli state in order to serve the aim of encouraging innovation. Any company that possesses inventive ideas can apply for these funds. Each application is dealt with on its own conditions. Nevertheless, there are three general criteria that are used for assessment. These are as follows: first, the type of invention; second, market potential; and third, company eligibility. The patentability of the invention must also be justifiable. Apart from showing the market potential in order to justify the investment, companies are required to provide evidence regarding the absorptive capacity of the R&D activities as well as an overview of the technological and organisational capabilities needed to achieve market competitiveness.

An application in the area of life sciences is usually based upon basic research that is conducted by the universities. The Israeli pharmaceutical industry has a long tradition of co-operating with universities and government laboratories. The most prominent successful example of usage of these funds in relation to pharmaceuticals is Copaxone. Copaxone is Teva's first innovative drug. It has been developed for the treatment of multiple sclerosis. Copaxone was developed by researchers at the Weizmann Research Institute. Teva was only involved during the third decade of the research and has taken advantage of the R&D funds available in Israel for conducting clinical trials.

Concluding Remarks

The Israeli innovation system is founded upon a high-degree of government support and entrepreneurship. There are systems of partnership and social networking between industry and university organisations. This may suggest that creation of a synergy is required in order to assure the optimum use and allocation of resources. The accomplishment of these goals entails not only wise planning and strategy setting, but also structural and organisational changes aimed at encouraging trust, reliance, co-operation, and interdependence in the society. The strong academic research base of the country supports institutional co-operation and restructuring of R&D activities.

The peculiar conditions that are connected to its political and socio-economic structure make Israel a unique example in relation to country case studies. The catch-up process and its continuing economic development have been influenced by these peculiar conditions. The catch-up process in Israel has been characterised by the presence of a strong human capital base and an aggressive commitment to science and technology and entrepreneurship. The existence of a relatively strong patent regime and protection, has played an essential role throughout the catch-up process.

Establishing a domestic self-sufficiency in pharmaceuticals was one of the catch-up goals of the country. Thus, the pharmaceutical catch-up process in Israel was structured around a properly tailored patent regime. Due to the different patterns of pharmaceutical innovation, a different route has generally been taken in order to develop local capacities, skills and expertise. The modification of a strong patent regime as a response to local settings and priorities has accelerated the process of scientific and technological catching up. It has turned the country into an innovation hub.

The conflicting interests of the local industry and multinationals require maintaining balance between local needs and international commitments. This setting may provide a further reference for other developing countries. Many developing countries are in the ongoing process of strengthening their patent regime. In an effort to provide an informative framework, the next chapter accommodates a case study of Teva as representative example of the Israeli pharmaceutical industry. It aims to provide a clear insight in relation to facts and circumstances associated with the company's business strategy. It does this in order to determine the optimal strategic choices that can be made in order to boost pharmaceutical innovation. A number of distinctive patterns will also be identified in order provide guidance to governments in developing countries.

With the exception of Israel, the countries subjected to the case study examination herein are the most commonly surveyed countries. The case of the US is enormously scaled. It is particularly noteworthy for the legal framework within which the innovation system is embedded. It is also notable for the high level of interaction between the key sectors – industry, university and government. Another distinguishing characteristic of the US system is the strength of the IPRs in general, and the patent regime in particular. The case of Japan represents a very good example of a strong determination to catch up with more technologically advanced nations. Japanese success in this area is relatively attributed to the latecomer advantage and to government policies. The patent regime was revised several times in order to accommodate the changing needs of the local industry. Nonetheless, the Japanese national innovation system has been strongly challenged in recent years for becoming rigid in the context of technological and organisational change. South Korea has emerged as one of the fastest growing economies in the region. This has transformed Korea into a newly industrialised country in Asia, and into one of the so-called Asian tigers. The Korean experience is often referred to as Japan 2.0. In fact, the Korean system developed in parallel fashion to the Japanese system. Nevertheless, the Korean pharmaceutical industry was not so fortunate. In Korea, the pharmaceutical product patents were introduced much earlier than Japan, at a time when Korean firms were still in process of capacity building. Nevertheless, the Korean vaccine story provides evidence that capacity building in pharmaceuticals is possible through various channels other than mere imitation.

On the other hand, the Israeli case study is of crucial importance, both for guidance for other national innovation systems and for local pharmaceutical industries in developing countries. Over the past decade, Israel has become the preeminent technological powerhouse in the ICT and life sciences. So far, there has been little literature on the Israeli national innovation system. Teva is the biggest generic multinational pharmaceutical company in the world. Although the Israeli innovation experience is completely different from the other countries, in terms of unique characteristics of the country, there are still several valuable lessons that can be drawn. These lessons involve the importance of strategic protection of IPRs, prioritising local capacity building, facilitating an innovation culture and providing financial support for innovation in the country. Above all, the case study of the Israeli national innovation system revealed that the Israeli local pharmaceutical industry requires close examination in order to determine the process through which technical advance proceeds. This includes analysis of the key policies, regulative laws and the institutional actors. Hence, in order to generate a global approach that is potentially applicable to the whole of the extended industry, the next chapter follows a case-study design, with in depth-analysis of Teva.

6. A real life company case study: Teva Pharmaceuticals Ltd and its distinctive trajectories

Following the enactment of the Agreement on Trade Related Aspects of Intellectual Property (TRIPS), the evidence presented from the experiences of local pharmaceutical industries in developing countries (hereinafter referred as local pharmaceutical industry) strongly suggests that there has been a dramatic change in the business climate. Historically, the traditional business model of the local pharmaceutical industry was based on reverse engineering. The process of globalisation and the emergence of a rules-based multilateral trading system, however, require a new, feasible model, which takes account of the particular circumstances of the global marketplace. As the current patent regime brings new challenges for developing countries, this raises a need for the local pharmaceutical industries to reappraise their traditional business strategy. Moreover, a move towards a new business strategy, one that includes the built in elements of research and development (R&D) and drug development, is widely seen as necessary. However, the lack of (or very limited) expertise, in managing innovation and in driving and sustaining market growth, poses a major challenge for the local pharmaceutical industry in the post-TRIPS era. Specifically, in the light of previous discussions, the question arises whether the local pharmaceutical industry should be acting as collaborative partners for multinationals, or whether these local industries should create their own competitive market? This question has yet to be resolved.

Hence, there is currently a great deal of uncertainty regarding the current and future business prospects of the local pharmaceutical industry. The local pharmaceutical industry in developing countries now faces a strategic choice of either to compete or co-operate.[1] The future of pharmaceutical innovation in these countries will depend upon the choice

---

[1]   Grace, C. (2004) 'The Effect of Changing Intellectual Property on Pharmaceutical Industry Prospects in India and China: Considerations for Access to Medicines', DFID Health Systems Resource Centre, p. 19.

of path they chose or will choose. Both of the strategies outlined here bring potential challenges and opportunities for the industry. However, the growth of the industry in the years to come depends upon the investment made now by the companies. The presence of government policies supporting innovation and funding R&D could also prove to be crucial.

One strategy might be building technological capabilities in order to compete with multinational drug companies. This strategy is strikingly different from a 'business as usual' mindset. Several important aspects of this strategy will be outlined here. As part of this strategy, it would be necessary to adjust the scope of business diversification, to evaluate company goals, and furthermore, to provide a strategy for developing lower risk in new drug applications and follow-on biologics. It would also be necessary to invest in R&D for drug development, to develop strategies for patent challenges and to strengthen legal expertise on patented molecules.

Another strategy would be focusing on co-operation with multi-nationals, which would entail different elements. This strategy would require the establishment of partnerships with multinationals for their sale channels. It would also be necessary to provide contract manufacturing and clinical outsourcing for multinationals, and to supply the relevant active pharmaceutical ingredients[2] (API).[3]

For instance, in another piece of research, investigating the encouragement of pharmaceutical R&D in developing countries, prepared for the International Federation of Pharmaceutical Manufacturers Association (IFPMA), it was stated that the development of an R&D based industry in developing countries is structured around three types of company; a company with a research-based multinational approach, a company with a biotech approach and a generic company with a R&D approach.[4]

The first type of company fits the description of a co-operating company, for which foreign direct investment (FDI) plays an important

---

[2] Active pharmaceutical ingredients are also known in regulatory pharmacopeial parlance as 'drug substance'. The use of API is to produce a drug product, which is the final form of the drug substance administered to patients. The ultimate safety and efficacy of the finally administered drug product are dependent on assurance of the consistency of the physical and chemical properties of the API. *See,* Shargel, L. and I. Kanfer (2005) *Generic Drug Product Development: Solid Oral Dosage Forms,* New York, Dekker, pp. 17–30

[3] *See,* Grace, supra note 1.

[4] IFPMA, 'Encouraging Pharmaceutical R&D in Developing Countries', IFPMA Publication, February 2003.

role as it relies heavily on technology transfer capacities from multinationals. In this scenario, the local companies are generally expected to
team up with multinationals to develop local R&D facilities.

The second group targets biotech start-ups. These companies require
considerable investment in biotechnological R&D through the provision
of government funds for academic research programs and so on. Investing in biotechnology is traditionally regarded as a high-risk business and
the biotech companies are usually considered as 'high risk high-reward
type' companies. Nevertheless, the evidence from the earlier chapters
clearly suggests that investing in biotechnology is likely to prove to be
highly beneficial for developing countries as biotechnology is widely
hailed as the future direction of pharmaceutical innovation.[5] It is highly
probable that the countries and companies that invest in biotechnology
today will be the successful gamblers of the future.

The last type of company embodies generic companies in developing
countries. These companies are gradually initiating and extending R&D
activities and pouring an increasing proportion of their overall turnover
into the discovery of new therapeutic options. This type fits very well
with the concept of a competing business strategy developed for generic
companies.

In the light of the observations made above, it might be assumed that
the particular case of Teva presents very good example of a competing
business strategy combining the second and third type of business models
developed in the IFPMA research.

Teva achieved a milestone in the history of the generic drug industry
when, in 2005, it moved into the top 20 pharmaceutical companies in the
world, with revenues of more than $5 billion.[6] Although Teva's business
strategy focuses on the manufacture of generic drugs, the company has
also managed to develop breakthrough ethical drugs. For example, Teva's
first innovative drug Copaxone, which brings in nearly 30 per cent of the
company's revenue, is the fruit of ten years' intensive research and
tremendous investment. It was developed for the treatment of multiple
sclerosis, and was launched in the late 1990s. Apart from being the first
generic company to develop an innovative drug, Teva represents an
example of good practice for the local pharmaceutical industry in
developing countries. As such, a number of subtle lessons can be drawn
from Teva's competing business strategy.

---

    [5] Gassmann, O., G. Reepmeyer and M. von Zedtwitz (2008) *Leading
Pharmaceutical Innovation*, 2nd edn, Heidelberg, Springer.
    [6] 'Biotechnology Israel' (2006) Special Report, *Nature Biotechnology*,
V.24, N.4, p. 4.

A SPOTLIGHT ON TEVA PHARMACEUTICALS LTD

To find out what lies beneath Teva's success, it is necessary to go back to the early twentieth century. At a time when drugs were loaded onto the backs of camels and donkeys for delivery to customers throughout the land, a small wholesale drug business was founded in Jerusalem to distribute imported drugs. Furthermore, the late 1930s witnessed Jewish immigration from Central Europe. Some of the immigrants were scientists, chemists and technicians. In particular, the immigrants from Germany, which dominated the pharmaceutical industry in those years, brought with them the know-how and expertise that would prove to be crucial for the building up of local capacities and technologies necessary for the success of the Israeli drug industry. Recognising the value of the knowledge brought from Germany, as well as the future potential of the drug industry in Israel, Teva quickly established its first local pharmaceutical plants in Israel.

During the years of World War I, Teva emerged as the only drug supplier in the region. In the years following World War II, the Israeli state was established and this attracted highly qualified immigrants from all around the world. Taking into account the growing local market and the presence of highly qualified human capital in the country, it is relatively easy to see the reasons why Teva has grown into an industry leader. The presence of both highly qualified human capital and a leadership position in the market allowed the company to grow and expand into export markets. Moreover, Teva forged ahead with its business model, which included undertaking mergers and acquisitions in the local market to boost its production capacity.

It is well known that a strong API backbone constitutes one of the key elements of a successful generic business model. Most of the API suppliers are based at low cost manufacturing locations and are usually not involved in the drug production business. Nevertheless, Teva presents a good example of a company that has successfully built up a strong API backbone through acquisitions and backward vertical integrations.[7] The acquisition of two big competitors in Israel, Ikapharm and Plantex, enabled the company to strengthen its position in the market. In this way, Teva began to vertically integrate into the API production business. In the

---

[7] *See,* 'Increasing M&A Activity in the Generics Industry: What Happens Next?', Sci. Tech. Trade Newsletters, 26 June 2008, available at http://scicasts.com/analysis/1826-bio-it-a-biotechnology/1960-increasing-maa-activity-in-the-generics-industry-what-happens-next.

meantime, the company started to export drugs to a number of African countries such as Nigeria and Uganda.

During the 1980s, Teva began to expand its business further. As noted here, this led the company to grow outside the borders of Israel and become a generic drug name across the world. In 1984, the US Congress enacted the Hatch-Waxman Act, which facilitated and accelerated the entry of generic drugs into the US market. The intention of the law was to actively promote generic competition in the US market by allowing generic companies to submit an application for a generic version of a drug that demonstrates bioequivalence. The Hatch-Waxman Act therefore created a huge market for generic medicines. The management of Teva was quick to attempt to take advantage of this, and Teva entered the US pharmaceutical market at this time.

Taking into account the risks of entry into a new market, Teva adopted a business strategy based on a 'think global, act local' philosophy. In order to provide a smooth entry into the US market and to gain awareness of what was happening on the other side of the Atlantic, that is, which skills, services and expertise were in demand in the highly competitive and demanding US pharmaceutical market, it matched up with a US chemical conglomerate – W.R. Grace. A joint company was set up between Teva and W.R. Grace; Teva brought its know-how and expertise, and W.R. Grace contributed almost 90 per cent of the capital. The joint venture company acquired Lemmon, a small generic manufacturer in Pennsylvania, which sold and distributed generic drugs manufactured in Israel. This proved to be a sound business decision and Teva did not have to wait long to collect the fruits of its investment.[8] Regardless of the fact that Lemmon had just started marketing a mere seven generic medicines of branded drugs, the sales went up to $40 million in 1987 from $17 million at the time of its acquisition.[9]

Furthermore, the 1990s witnessed Teva's continued rise in the global generic market. At this time, Teva continued to make aggressive investments in the areas of merger and acquisitions and R&D, as well as increasing its own production capacity. The acquisition of pharmaceutical companies in the US, followed by the acquisitions in Europe, saw the company's business expand into France, Italy, the United Kingdom and Hungary.

---

[8]   Teva was bought out of W.R. Grace's interest in the joint venture following the acquisition of Biocraft in the 1990s.

[9]   *See*, A Report on Teva Pharmaceutical Industries Ltd., Funding Universe, available at http://www.fundinguniverse.com/company-histories/Teva-Pharmaceutical-Industries-Ltd-Company-History.html.

Thus, the 1990s proved to be a crucial decade for Teva. The income from the US market reached triple figures (in millions) and enabled Teva to pour millions into R&D initiatives.

The following case studies of two successfully launched propriety drugs of Teva reveal the company's innovative approach to drug discovery. Furthermore, it is important to note some of the successful business practices that Teva followed during the course of drug development over the past 20 years. This is because the leap from copy to innovate requires a deep understanding of key aspects of the drug development process, and this process is outlined here. Furthermore, it is suggested that the exploration of the development history of both Copaxone and Azilect illustrates a number of principles of good practices. These good practices may provide inspiration and motivation for local pharmaceutical industries in the developing world.

Copaxone: Innovation Made in Rehovot

Teva's first innovative drug was launched in April 1997 for the treatment of multiple sclerosis. Given the fact that multiple sclerosis has not been the focus of significant R&D, as there were too few patients to amortise the development costs, the development of Copaxone has been an important breakthrough for multiple sclerosis sufferers.

Copaxone became the flagship drug for Teva. Even today, Copaxone is one of the key revenue drivers in Teva's product profitability; it has close to a 30 per cent global market share. Furthermore, according to the statistics from the third quarter of 2009, in-market sales continue to increase year-after-year and are now at approximately 53 per cent – sales amount to $540 million in the US market.[10] Copaxone accounted for 17 per cent of Teva's total 2006 sales of $8.41 billion.[11]

Historically, Teva's R&D initiatives for drug development were concentrated in the therapeutic areas of neurological disorder. Nevertheless, the drug development story of Copaxone starts long before Teva's involvement. After 15 years of isolation and research, researchers at the Weizmann Research Institute realised that they had produced a drug

---

[10]   *See,* 'Teva, in Turnabout, Sues to Protect its Multiple Sclerosis Drug Copaxone', available at http://industry.bnet.com/pharma/10005164/teva-in-turnabout-sues-to-protect-its-multiple-sclerosis-drug-copaxone/.

[11]   *See,* 'Teva May Face Generic Rival to Copaxone', available at http://www.marketwatch.com/story/teva-may-face-generic-rival-to-ms-drug-copaxone.

candidate that reduced the relapse rate for people in the early stages of multiple sclerosis 25–30 per cent in clinical trials.[12]

Following this discovery, the existence of strong, established links with university research institutions enabled Teva to team up with the Weizmann Institute and turn the academic research into a blockbuster drug. Although Teva was involved in the drug development process only in the last decade of the research, after ensuring necessary funds from the Israeli state, it committed a substantial amount of the funds and staff in order to take the development of Copolymer 1 further and to perform Phase III of the clinical trials. Hence, it can be said that Teva provided the necessary resources that were required to complete both the chemical manufacturing process as well as the clinical trial process. The story of Copaxone illustrates a successful example of university–industry collaboration. Thus, it can be suggested that Teva's strategic utilisation of academic research provides an important example for the local pharmaceutical industry to follow.

As the first Copaxone patent[13] had expired during the three decades of its long development process, Teva made an application for orphan designation to adopt 'orphan drug'[14] for the treatment of multiple sclerosis. It was granted seven years of market exclusivity,[15] which expired in 2003. Nonetheless, the other patents on the drug, which are exceptionally similar to the initial patent and mainly included improved

---

[12]   *See,* Scheindlin, S. (2004) 'Copolymer 1: An Off-Beat Drug Development Story', Reflections: *Science in the Cultural Context,* V.4, I.1.

[13]   The first Copaxone patent (US Patent No. 3849550), which was filed in 1974, relates to the component of Copolymer-1 as a potential therapeutic agent for MS.

[14]   A drug designed to treat or prevent a disease, which has not been 'adopted' by the pharmaceutical industry because it provides little financial incentive for the private sector to make and market new medications to treat or prevent it. *See,* Medical dictionary available at www.medicinenet.com.

[15]   After obtaining marketing approval by the FDA for a designated orphan drug, a sponsor has seven years of marketing exclusivity for that product. Marketing exclusivity may be the most motivating incentive provided by the Act. The FDA cannot approve the same drug made by another manufacturer for the same indication during the marketing exclusivity period unless it has the consent of the sponsor or the sponsor is unable to provide sufficient quantities. *See,* Villareal, M.A. (2001) 'Orphan Drug Act: Background and Proposed Legislation in the 107th Congress', CRS Report.

compositions of Copolymer-1,[16] were due to expire by 2014 and 2015.[17] When these patents expire, Copaxone is very likely to face serious generic competition. In fact, in October 2009 Teva filed a lawsuit against Mylan Pharmaceuticals, Inc. and Natco Pharma Ltd. for patent infringement in the US District Court for the abbreviated new drug application.[18] Several Copaxone patents citing 'indefiniteness' were invalidated in July 2013 by the US Court of Appeals for the Federal Circuit, Teva's patent on Copaxone expired in May 2014.[19]

As noted above, following the launch of Copaxone, a new era started for Teva and it became a rising star in the dynamic world medical drug market.[20] The company took an inorganic route towards expansion in the global market. However, the company has continued to expand rapidly, primarily through mergers and acquisitions. Hence, the first decade of the twenty-first century has seen a variety of acquisitions and strategic alliances. The existence of these alliances has undoubtedly been a characteristic of Teva's business strategy. These alliances furnished Teva with bio-generic capabilities and the alliances further provided Teva with access to important drug delivery technologies. This, in turn, strengthened its position in API manufacturing. Among all Teva's acquisitions since 2000, the acquisition of Barr Pharmaceuticals,[21] one of the world's largest generic companies, was undoubtedly the most significant. It

---

[16] US Patent No.5981589; US Patent No.6054430; US Patent No. 6342476; US Patent No. 63632161; US Patent No. 6620847; US Patent No. 6939539; US Patent No. 7199098.

[17] *See,* 'Teva Increases Generics Leadership Worldwide with Unexpected Acquisition of Barr Pharmaceuticals', IHS Global Insight, 21 July 2008, available at http://www.ihsglobalinsight.com/SDA/SDADetail13398.htm.

[18] Teva is committed to vigorously defending its Copaxone intellectual property rights against infringement wherever they are challenged and intends to pursue all relevant regulatory avenues via the FDA. *See,* Press Release from Teva Pharmaceuticals, 16 October 2009, available at http://www.tevapharm.com/pr/2009/pr_876.asp.

[19] For more information, please see 'Teva's Copaxone Patent Appeal to Go Unheard, May 2014 Generic Launch Prospects Debated', *Financial Times,* 27 August 27 2013 available at http://www.ft.com/intl/cms/s/2/1657223a-0f24-11e3-ae66-00144feabdc0.html#axzz2gOkj1j00.

[20] In 1997, US brokerage organisation, Gronthal, published a strong buy rating for the Teva Pharmaceuticals share saying; 'We believe that, currently, Teva should be seen as a rising star in the dynamic world medical drug market', available at http://www.allbusiness.com/medicine-health/diseases-disorders-neurological/7478008-1.html.

[21] Barr Pharmaceuticals, Inc., was a global specialty pharmaceutical company that operated in more than 30 countries worldwide. Barr was engaged in the

enhanced Teva's leadership position in the US and consolidated its position in key European markets. Eventually, Teva became the world's largest generic company and ranked among the top 20 pharmaceutical companies in the world.

Azilect – Like Moses in the Desert [22]

It widely acknowledged that there is a lack of R&D in relation to addressing the diseases of the aged, such as Alzheimer and Parkinson's.[23] The number of adequate medicines that are developed to fight such diseases is minuscule.[24] Hence it can be said that the pharmaceutical industry is facing serious limitations as regards to efficiency, dosage or presentation form, as well as side effects. For these reasons, the discovery of the active ingredient rasagiline mesilate brought new hope to people living with Parkinson's disease.

Azilect's history, from initial discovery to pharmacy shelves, goes back 30 years. As is the case in most of the drug development stories, Professor Youdim – the inventor – encountered an effective drug with serious side effects while he was investigating existing drugs against depression. The drug candidate proved to have positive effects against Parkinson's. When he moved to Israel to found the pharmacology department at the Technion, he thought it would be a real adventure because he was 'creating a pharmacology department in a country with no real pharmaceutical companies'.[25] He first approached Teva in 1979 in order to transform his initial discovery to a drug for Parkinson's treatment. Given Teva's particular financial circumstances, and its strategic goals as a generic company up to that time, getting into the drug

---

development, manufacture and marketing of generic and proprietary pharmaceuticals, biopharmaceuticals and active pharmaceutical ingredients.

[22]   'I really believed in Azilect, I was like Moses in the desert – everyone had given up on these types of drugs, I kept at it and we did a lot of work on it.' Professor Moussa Youdim, Technion, See. 'Azilect – The One-a-Day Parkinson's Pill', 4 June 2006, Israel21c: Innovation News Service, available at http://www.israel21c.org/health/azilect-the-one-a-day-parkinson-s-pill.

[23]   *See,* IFPMA report, supra note 4, p. 8.

[24]   *See, Ibid;* Love, J. (2003) 'An Agenda for Research and Development', Meeting on the Role of Generics and Local Industry in Attaining the Millennium Development Goals in Pharmaceuticals and Vaccines, The World Bank, Washington DC, 24–25 June 2003, available at http://www.cptech.org/ip/health/rndtf/.

[25]   IFPMA report, supra note 4.

development business did not seem like a realistic option. Thus, they turned it down.[26]

However, not long after Professor Youdim's proposal had been turned down, Teva's business started to grow rapidly in the US market and revenues from generic sales were going up year-after-year. Hence, the company's business strategy began to change. Teva was now willing to invest in drug development. Thus, Teva approached the Technion with the aim of co-operating in order to create a drug for the treatment of Parkinson's. At this time, Rasagiline was a mere compound, which 'was the earliest stage that Teva has ever begun a collaboration to develop a drug from an existing compound'.[27]

The hard work and dedication by Teva and Techion gave its fruits after 20 years when Azilect was released onto the market. It represents a milestone in the treatment of Parkinson's as it can be used both in the early stage of the disease and in the moderate-to-advanced stages. Furthermore, the clinical studies demonstrated that it has positive effects on slowing the clinical progression of Parkinson's.

Teva has great expectations that Azilect will continue to be a success. In the wake of sales in last couple of years, the current success of the drug suggests that Azilect will become as essential for the treatment of Parkinson's as Copaxone has become for the treatment of multiple sclerosis.[28]

Future Prospects

The branded product sales accounted for 35 per cent of Teva's revenue by 2013, more than double the 16 per cent in 2007.[29] The key pillars of the strategy include investment in the next wave of technology and generics, creating affordable biosimilars (biogenerics) at a lower cost–greater value base, focusing on niche specialty areas, leveraging unique sourcing, as well as development and go-to-market approaches. The company's

---

[26] *Id.*

[27] 'Technion Research Helps Those with Neurodegenerative Diseases', American Technion Society, available at http://www.ats.org/site/PageServer?pagename=about_parkinsons.

[28] *See,* 'Azilect – Innovative Drug: Teva Pharmaceuticals', available at http://www.tevapharm.com/Azilect/.

[29] *See,* 'Teva Seeks Deals to Deepen Branded Business in "Niche" Diseases', 23 February 2009, available at http://www.bloomberg.com/apps/news?pid=20601202&sid=aQhXH2ygDnlk.

balanced business model is fully committed to global generics leader-ship[30] and it seems that there is no prospect of adopting a business model that focuses solely on proprietary drugs in the future.

DISTINCTIVE TRAJECTORIES IN THE TEVA CASE STUDY

Recalling the concept of the competing business strategy referred to above, a company pursuing an innovation strategy for R&D should take into account particular issues. Within the context of this thesis, these issues could be identified as:

(1) Developing technical expertise in patent law and patented mol-ecules;
(2) Investing in R&D;
(3) Establishing strong links with academia and managing complex cross-disciplinary research projects; and
(4) Developing sustainable business strategies for biotechnology.

For a comprehensive understanding of those strategies, one has to present real-life observations in order to illustrate considerations and policy implications for local pharmaceutical companies in the developing world. For instance, in order to outline the paradigm case of a generic company, which aims to move upstream and invest in R&D, one needs look no further than Teva Pharmaceuticals. Indeed, taking a close look at Teva's case reveals the business model that embodies the strategies that will enhance competitiveness in the global pharmaceutical market.

Developing Understanding and Technical Expertise in Patents and the Patent Regime

There is no doubt that one of the key factors behind Teva's success is its technical expertise in patents and the patent regime. A careful analysis of the company's growth route and its development throughout the years reveals that the company has always taken advantage of the patent regime in place at the time.

---

[30] 'Teva's Growth Strategy 2008–2012', Sholomo Yanai, President and CEO, Teva Pharmaceutical Industries Ltd., 21 February 2008, available at www.tevapharm.com/pdf/Presentation21.02.08.pdf.

The transformation of Teva from a small wholesale drug company to Israel's biggest generic company took place during the second half of the twentieth century, in between the last two quarters. Under the current Israeli Patent Act enacted in 1967, patents are granted for any invention, whether product or processes, in any technological field which are new, non-obvious and susceptible of industrial application. The Israeli patent regime does not discriminate against the fields of technology. Nor does the patent regime specifically differentiate between product or process inventions. Put differently, patents have been available for pharmaceutical products and processes in Israel since 1967. This is a significant point to consider because the lack of patent protection or flexible application of patentability criteria is often regarded as the most important factor underlying the substantial growth of the pharmaceutical industry, and particularly the generic industry, in developing countries. Local pharmaceutical companies in certain countries such as India, China, Brazil and Turkey became strong competitors in the international pharmaceutical market as a result of domestic patent policies. Thus, the patent regime introduced by TRIPS, and the non-discrimination clause in particular, received considerable critical attention from those countries. Eventually, the pharmaceutical industry in those countries started to face the consequences of the dramatic post-TRIPS era.

So the question arises; how did a company such as Teva manage to expand and grow as a business in a legal environment where patents were available for pharmaceuticals? The answer largely depends on a discussion of how the patent regime should be employed so that it can best serve the interest of the local industry.

Compulsory licences
Even though Teva's development into a big pharmaceutical giant is associated with the Arab boycott of companies doing business with Israel, it should be noted that Teva owes only a small part of its existence to the Arab boycott. In fact, a large part of Teva's success depends upon the compulsory licensing provisions of the Israeli Patent Act.

The Arab boycott between 1948 and 1990 prevented Israelis from accessing many western products, especially pharmaceutical. Yet, in order to alleviate the shortage of medicines, Israel fought back through patent law.[31] In fact, the Israeli Patent Act was enacted in 1967 during the Arab boycott. The 1967 act included highly controversial and flexible

---

[31] 'An Israeli Giant in Generic Drugs Faces New Rivals: Arab Boycott Gave Teva Edge: Now it's No.1 in Industry, but US Market Toughens', *The Wall Street*

provisions, especially on compulsory licensing. For instance, it was possible to establish compulsory licences in Israel on the basis of lack or insufficient working of a patented invention. In the case of non-working patented medical inventions,[32] compulsory licences could be granted at any time after the patent had been granted.

Indeed, the compulsory licensing provisions in the Paris Convention stem from the obligation to work a patent in the country; hence the legal institution of compulsory licences was adopted as to ensure the exploitation of a patent. As such, compulsory licences were established when there was a lack of patents or insufficient patents in a large number of countries following the Paris Convention.[33]

In this context, compulsory licences were considered to be a strategic weapon for local generic companies in Israel. Due to the flexible provisions in the Israeli Patent Act at that time, the proceedings were regarded as little more than a formality by the patent office. In the event where there was no large scale local manufacturing of the patent, and local generic companies were granted licences in all cases.[34]

Nevertheless, contrary to general belief, the number of compulsory licences granted in Israel at that time remained low. However, the generic companies were able to use the act's provisions on compulsory licences as a threat to obtain voluntary licences in order to manufacture generic versions of patented drugs.

As Ladas puts it, the practical value of the existence of compulsory licence provisions in the patent law is that the threat of it usually induces the grant of contractual licences on reasonable terms, and thus the objective of actually working the invention is accomplished.[35] In fact, as in the case of Israel, the threat thereof increased the willingness of patent

Journal, 28 October 2004, available at http://online.wsj.com/article/SB 109890935431257528.html#articleTabs%3Darticle.

[32] '1. A substance capable of being used as a medicine or in the production thereof; 2. a process for producing the substance set forth in (1) supra; and 3. any device usable for medical purposes': Julian-Arnold, G. (1993) 'International Compulsory Licensing: The Rationales and the Reality', *The Journal of Law and Technology*, V.33, I.2; Cohn, C. (1990) 'Compulsory Licensing in Israel under Pharmaceutical Patents – A Political Issue?', *Patent World*, V.27, I.22.

[33] *See*, Correa, C.M. (1999) *Intellectual Property Rights and the Use of Compulsory Licences: Options for Developing Countries*, Geneva, South Centre.

[34] Luzzatto, K. (2008) 'Pharmaceutical Patents in Israel', available at www.luzzatto.com/articles/11.12.08(7).pdf.

[35] Ladas, S. (1975) *Patents, Trademarks and Related Rights – National and International Protection*, Cambridge, Harvard University Press, p. 427.

owners to grant a contractual licence on reasonable terms to local generic companies.

According to Cohn, the importance of compulsory licences from the point of view of the Israel pharmaceutical industry considerably exceeds the results achieved in a restricted number of decided cases, important, as they may have been. He notes that it is extremely difficult to arrive at the relevant facts, but nevertheless it could be safe to say that the very existence of compulsory licence provisions as statutory provisions, and the demonstration by a relatively small number of decided cases that under the right circumstances those provisions were applied, induced foreign patent owners to find ways for granting licences without the need for a compulsory licence.[36]

Teva, as a still-young company, solely focused on building technological capabilities and expertise for drug development and took full advantage of the vitality of the system to get exclusive licences from multinational pharmaceutical companies. Eventually, Teva started to manufacture and market ethical drugs for companies such as Pfizer, Merck and Novartis. More importantly, it benefited from voluntary licences in the sense of exploitation of pharmaceutical products, technology transfer and building domestic technological capabilities in drug development. Unlike other generic companies in developing countries, in a legal environment where pharmaceuticals were susceptible to patent protection, voluntary licences were Teva's only option to learn by imitating and building up capabilities for generic drug manufacturing. Moreover, the relevant profit margins of the multinationals were arguably at a reasonable level due to the fact that Teva paid significant royalties. It might be considered as a win-win situation for both parties.

Nevertheless, the Israeli approach to compulsory licences had been subject to considerable criticism from multinational pharmaceutical companies for creating a bias in favour of the local industry. In line with this criticism, in 1995, the District Court of Tel Aviv reinterpreted the application process for compulsory licences, and took a more restrictive approach. The court held that evidence showing the existence of an actual shortage of a drug should be included as part of the application process.[37] Not long after this decision, in 2000, TRIPS was implemented in Israel and the TRIPS-compliant compulsory licence provisions were adopted.

In reality, neither the holding of the District Court of Tel Aviv nor the coming into force of the TRIPS-compliant compulsory licence regime

---

[36]   COHN, supra note 32, p. 25.
[37]   Prozac case. *See*, Luzzatto, supra note 34.

affected Teva's business substantially. By then, Teva had already become competitive in the production of generic drugs at the global level. Furthermore, by this time Teva had already built up excellent facilities and it had also established strong alliances in the areas of drug development and manufacturing. Nonetheless, the existence of the compulsory licence system allowed Teva to build up its expertise in drug manufacturing and development. This, in turn, helped Teva to transform into an international pharmaceutical giant, which competes globally both in generic and proprietary drug markets. The case of Teva, described above, is broadly comparable with the case of a number of companies, which operated within the German dye industry during the early 1900s. Despite the late start, the German companies quickly developed the institutions and techniques essential for global competitiveness in the dye sector. The principle reason for the success of the German dye industry, at this time, provides for an interesting comparison with the case of Teva. Within Germany, dye companies took advantage of the lack of patentability for chemical products. In a similar vein, many of the German companies built up their own capabilities by free riding on foreign technologies.[38] As the industry matured and built up its technological capabilities, patents were introduced to the industry.

The vital role that the existence of compulsory licences played in Teva's development supports the argument that compulsory licences should be adopted as 'a tool that may be useful in a variety of circumstances in order to mitigate the restrictive effect of exclusive rights and strike a balance between the title-holders' interests and those of the public in the diffusion of knowledge and the access to, and affordability of the outcomes of, innovation and creativity'.[39] Furthermore, it illustrates that the legal institution of compulsory licences may also serve as an effective tool for technology transfer, growth of the local industry and the promotion of innovation.

Active involvement in judicial process

Patent disputes between ethical and generic companies are frequent in Israel. As a result, the generic companies often retaliate by challenging patents, with some success.

In line with this, Drahos stresses the importance of patent opposition as a regulatory tool for pharmaceutical patents. Nonetheless, it is

---

[38] For more information *see,* Beer, J.J. (1959) *The Emergence of the German Dye Industry*, Urbana, University of Illinois Press.

[39] Correa, supra note 33, p. 24.

regarded as a viable option only in very few countries. The viability of litigation depends upon essential factors such as the existence of lucrative pharmaceutical product markets, that is, markets worth contesting. Further to this the existence of a strong generic sector and the presence of a cultural disposition towards litigation are required. Finally, it is often necessary that there exists both a profession capable of servicing the litigation and of course, litigants with deep pockets. For Drahos, only the US scores well on all of these factors and even then, the costs of patent litigation in the US are increasingly seen as a problem.[40] Indeed, the Orange Book system under the Hatch-Waxman Act provides incentives to generic companies to challenge drug patents in the midst of their terms. The generic companies are given the opportunity to challenge a patent when they create a generic version of the patented drug that does not infringe, or when they establish the patent's invalidity. The generic company that is first to challenge the patent, stating either that the patent is invalid, or the generic drug in the ANDA does not infringe the patent, is awarded exclusivity, during which no other generic company may enter the market, regardless of whether litigation ensues thereafter or not.[41] It has been noted that the award of a 180-day period of market exclusivity was designed to maintain a balance by rewarding generic firms for their willingness to challenge unenforceable and invalid innovator patents, or design non-infringing drug products.[42]

Subsequently, generic companies have challenged numerous patents over the past 20 years and these companies have managed to prevail 73 per cent of the time in patent suits.[43] It is worth noting that without this incentive, some brand companies would have engaged in the practice of evergreening patents that would result in lack of access to affordable generic medicines for consumers for many years to come.[44]

---

[40] Drahos, P. (2007) 'Trust Me: Patent Offices in Developing Countries', available at http://ssrn.com/abstract=1028676.

[41] Mehl, A. (2006) 'The Hatch-Waxman Act and Market Exclusivity for Generic Drug Manufacturers: An Entitlement or an Incentive?', *Chicago-Kent Law Review*, V.81, pp. 651–2.

[42] 64 Fed. Reg. at 42882. The FDA's notice explains that '[t]he Hatch-Waxman Amendments benefit consumers by bringing lower priced generic versions of previously approved drugs to market, while simultaneously promoting new drug innovation through the restoration of patent life lost during regulatory proceedings'.

[43] Drahos, supra note 40.

[44] Jaeger, K. (2006) 'America's Generic Pharmaceutical Industry: Opportunities and Challenges in 2006 and beyond', *Journal of Generic Medicines*, V.4, p. 18.

Stiglitz approaches the issue from an economic angle, and according to him, the asymmetry between granting a patent and challenging a patent gives rise to a bias towards excessive patenting, especially in granting and enforcing patents in the US. He ascertains that when a patent is granted, a firm is encroaching upon the commons and making private what would otherwise be public. In other words, the firm is receiving private return, irrespective of whether the invention in question deserves patent recognition or not. On the other hand, when a patent is successfully challenged, a public good is created as that piece of knowledge enters the public domain, which is universally accessible. For this reason, he considers patent challenging to be a public good. He further elaborates that this will lead to an underinvestment in relation to fighting low quality patents, and an overinvestment in relation to attaining these kinds of patents.[45]

Stiglitz's theory appears to accord well with the relevant evidence from recent US patent litigation statistics.[46] Specifically, the last decade witnessed fierce patent battles being fought between multinationals and generic companies in the US; in a large part these disputes were driven by the low quality of patents. In fact, the innovativeness of the industry is highly questionable due to the fact that pharmaceutical patent quality has substantially decreased in recent years.

According to the National Institute of Health Care Management, 54 per cent of FDA-approved drug applications filed between the period of 1989 to 2000 were structurally very similar to already known drugs, with only minor differences; these are often classified as me-too drugs. Further to this, only 238 out of 1035 drugs contained new active ingredients and were given priority ratings on the basis of their clinical performance. Hence, it can be said that, from a strictly medical point of view, 77 per cent of the new drugs are that the FDA approves can be described as redundant.[47]

[45]   Stiglitz, J. (1999) 'Knowledge as a Global Public Good', available at http://www.worldbank.org/knowledge/chiefecon/index2.htm.p.1715.

[46]   Over the last 20 years, the number of disposed cases has more than doubled, from 1013 in 1986, to 2362 in 2004. The rates of adjudication dipped a bit during this time, going from 19 per cent to 14 per cent during the same period (and settlements went from 81 per cent to 86 per cent). *See,* Janicke, P.M. and L. Ren (2006) 'Who Wins Patent Infringement Cases?', *American Intellectual Property Law Association Quarterly Journal,* Vol. 34, pp. 1–37.

[47]   Boldrin, M. and D. Levine (2008) *Against Intellectual Monopoly,* New York, Cambridge University Press., p. 222.

In the research-based pharmaceutical business model, each additional year of market exclusivity can lead to billions in extra revenue for a big pharmaceutical company with a blockbuster drug. Moreover, it is often the case that each successive patent application, related to the original invention, aims to extend the patent term and thus, market exclusivity. It is therefore becoming common practice within the pharmaceutical industry to file a patent application that covers everything from manufacturing processes to new coatings for the drug.[48]

In this context, patent challenging lies at the core of Teva's business strategy both for the US and Israeli market. It is widely known that Teva has been pursuing an aggressive patent litigation strategy in the US in order to take full advantage of the 180 days exclusivity incentive. Nevertheless, this situation is not unique to the US. Patent litigation also acts as a significant regulatory tool for pharmaceutical patents in Israel. The generic companies challenge almost every patent application in order to prevent the issuance of low quality pharmaceutical patents.

Arguably, the business strategy of the local industry largely depends upon patent challenging. Over the years, the local industry has developed advanced knowledge about existing patents. This provides the local industry with the skills to challenge patents successfully. Furthermore, the local industry possesses technical expertise regarding important patent law issues, such as the loopholes in the patent regime, the scope of patentability requirements, and the patent claim and continuation limits.[49] This technical expertise in patent law, coupled with market knowledge, provides the local industry with a sustainable competitive advantage.

The assessment process for Teva starts when the optimal entry to the market is likely to occur. Initially, the patent department assume that all the product's patents are valid. Therefore, they first try to bypass the patent. According to Livneh – head of patent counsel – in order to bypass the patent instead of getting the entire patent disqualified, a substitute can be used, for instance, magnesium rather than calcium. Nevertheless, he accepts that it is not always possible to bypass the patent, as there are different kinds of patents.[50] In theory, the generic drugs are considered to

---

[48] Gawlicki, S.: 'IP Litigation is Virtually Assured for Generic Drug Makers', Intellectual Property – A special Report from Corporate Legal Times, available at www.sutherland.com/files/Publication/.../GenericDrugMakersIP.pdf.

[49] To file a continuation with new claims on the invention is a common means to extend the life of an existing patent. *See,* Chapter 2 for the 'evergreening' efforts of the pharmaceutical companies.

[50] 'Teva's Patent Marathon Runner', *Globes,* 24 April 2006, available at http://www.ivc-online.com/ivcWeeklyItem.asp?articleID=6969.

be the therapeutic equivalent to the proprietary drugs, which have the same amount of active ingredient or ingredients, same dosage form as the original formulation and the same effects with regards to efficiency and safety.[51] For Livneh, it is important to understand where the patent lies, that is, is the patent on the active ingredient or the formula? This is the point where the patent department comes into play, on the front line between science and law. Indeed, in the event that the patent is on the active ingredient, he notes that it is very difficult to bypass it; thus challenging the patent is often seen as the only option. On the other hand, in the case of patents covering the formula, involving both an active ingredient and secondary ingredients, they usually choose to attack the patent with other secondary ingredients.[52]

Nonetheless, the patent department at Teva has a twofold role,[53] first, it must aim to protect their patents and, second, it should look for loopholes in other patents as the company has both proprietary and generic products. In fact, Teva must now vigorously defend its patents against challenges by other generic companies seeking to sell generic versions of Teva's innovative drugs. It is important to note that Teva's first innovative drug is soon coming off patent and Teva's fellow generic companies, Mylan Inc., the US-based generic company, and Natco Pharma Ltd., one of the leading generic drug companies in India, filed an application to challenge the Copaxone patents and make and sell their own version. The

---

[51]   Marzo, A. and L.P. Balant (1995) 'Bioequivalence: An Updated Reappraisal Addressed to Applications of Interchangeable Multi-Source Pharmaceutical Products', *Arzneim-Forsch/Drug Res* V.45, pp. 109–15.

[52]   *Id.*

[53]   Indeed, in the annual report of 2000's fiscal year, submitted to the United States Securities and Exchange Commission, reports that the success of Teva's innovative products depends on the effectiveness of the patents owned:

'Our success with our innovative products depends, in part, on our ability to protect our current and future innovative products and to defend our intellectual property rights. If we fail to adequately protect our intellectual property, competitors may manufacture and market products similar to ours. We have been issued numerous patents covering our innovative products, and have filed, and expect to continue to file, patent applications seeking to protect newly developed technologies and products in various countries, including the United States. Any existing or future patents issued to or licenced by us may not provide us with any competitive advantages for our products or may even be challenged, invalidated or circumvented by competitors. In addition, such patent rights may not prevent our competitors from developing, using or commercializing products that are similar or functionally equivalent to our products.'

FDA has accepted their filing for an abbreviated new-drug application for a generic version of Teva's flagship drug.[54]

It should be noted that Teva is not the only one battling against the multinational pharmaceutical companies in Israel. Unipharm,[55] another local generic company from Israel, has also taken many high-profile cases against multinational pharmaceutical companies. Furthermore, in most of the cases the relevant patents were declared void.[56] Thus, it may be concluded that the Israeli patent regime provides an effective pre-grant avenue for patent oppositions. Yet, it is clear that the industry in Israel has been proactive in this area.

Developing technical expertise in patent law and strong lobbying power
It is important to note that a further reason for the success of Teva is arguably its strong lobbying power in Israel. The Israeli patent law is relatively constructed according to the interest of the local pharmaceutical industry, which is mainly represented by Teva. Considering the fact that the roots of today's international patent regime spring from initiatives created by the US pharmaceutical industry, it is highly contentious to criticise the Israeli regime for explicitly favouring its local industry. Given the fact that Teva is the only company from Israel that is currently on the Forbes 100 list, and in light of the fact that Teva has plants and facilities in Israel, providing jobs for thousands of people, its contribution to the Israeli economy cannot be ignored. Under these conditions, Teva's local lobbying power, coupled with its advanced knowledge of patent law (including its loopholes), led to the creation of a patent regime in Israel that is explicitly favourable to the local industry. Recalling the relevant TRIPS-plus provisions of the Israeli Patent Act on data exclusivity and patent term extensions, there is still a room for the local industry to take advantage of the law.

---

[54] *See*, 'Teva Shares Off: Mylan Files for Generic Copaxone', Marketwatch, 14 September 2009, available at http://www.marketwatch.com/story/teva-shares-off-mylan-files-for-generic-copaxone-2009-09-14.

[55] Unipharm Ltd, a generic drug manufacturer based in Tel Aviv, Israel. For more information, *see* http://www.unipharm.co.il/page.aspx?PageID=1.

[56] The Rosiglitazone case illustrates the effective patent litigation strategy adopted by Unipharm. Rosiglitazone is active ingredient of an anti-diabetic drug in the thiazolidinedione class of drugs, which is marketed by GlaxoSmithKline. The court held that the issue in question – relating to use of the relatively gentle borohydride reducing agent on the thiazolidinedione – was an inventive step and ruled that the correct standard was obvious to try, not obvious to succeed. Thus, the application lacks inventive step.

In this respect, it is submitted that the Israeli regime can provide an example for other developing countries. For instance, the Israeli patent regime has provided patent protection for pharmaceuticals from the earliest stages, and it now embodies TRIPS-plus standards including data exclusivity and patent term extensions. One may argue that it represents a good illustration of a strong patent regime. Nevertheless, a closer look at the provisions of the Patent Act reveals another side to the law. As noted above, the patent term extension provision which exists in Israeli law, includes certain caps and limitations; it is, in principle, designed to provide the shortest term of protection possible and this is also the case in relation to the data exclusivity provision; what results is a piece of legislation that is potentially inefficient.

The provisions in question were drafted in close consultation, and with the active involvement of, the local industry. The legislature engaged in intensive interaction with all stakeholders, and this dynamic led to a situation where a number of options were being explored including economic and social trade-offs for the country and local industry. The critical importance of Teva's contribution in the drafting process should not be overlooked or underestimated. No one can ignore the strong lobbying power of Teva in Israel, as the country's flagship company, and this power is coupled with an advanced knowledge of patent law and international patent standards. Thus, Teva gave a voice to the concerns of the local industry, and the latter provisions were established with relatively high input from the company. Thus, the outcome operates to the maximum benefit of the country, by providing an appropriate balance between the rights holders and local industry.

It can be noted that Teva's crucial role in Israeli intellectual property (IP) policymaking, in relation to pharmaceuticals in particular, presents similarities to the role of the pharmaceutical industry in the US. The pharmaceutical industry is one of the key collaborators in relation to the enactment of IP strategy in the US, and each year pharmaceutical companies make submissions about the IP practices in countries all around the world, which provide the basis for the Special 301 reports. Teva's strong lobbying power in Israel leads to an interesting reversal of roles, that is, Teva acts as PhRMA in Israel.

Israel remained on the Priority Watch List of the United States Trade Representative (USTR) Special 301 Report until 2012, because the US often persuasively requested Israel to provide a higher level of protection, that is, a level that reflects its status as a partner in the US–Israel FTA and its objective of becoming a member of the OECD.[57] Specifically, the criticism focused on the claim that Israel did not facilitate sufficient protection as regards patent term extensions and data exclusivity. Each year, PhRMA, submits country comparisons that ultimately determine the levels of IPRs protection accorded to pharmaceuticals in each country. By comparison, each year, Teva is actively involved in the process of submissions to USTR through manufacturing associations or the government, explaining why Israel should be removed from USTR's list.

In fact, Teva's consultative involvement[58] in policymaking encourages the patent regime to be more industry-centred and economically sustainable, in relation to the wider policy framework for innovation and growth. It may present an ideal model for the local pharmaceutical industries in countries that are close to completing the TRIPS implementation process.

One may conclude that the case of Israel and Teva emerges as a model of good practice for developing countries. Such an assumption seems to accord well with the evidence from comprehensive studies on the experiences of developing countries[59] with regards to the patent regime and local capacity building. This argument is based upon the idea that consultative involvement of the local pharmaceutical industry to the IPRs policymaking is of crucial importance for economic and social development. The national IPRs initiatives include new policy rules and instruments establishing a framework that is novel to all actors in developing countries including governments, industries, academia and the general public. To sum up, an improved participatory policy regime facilitates a wider policy framework that aligns innovation policy actions and prioritises local capacity building.

---

[57] USTR (2007) Special 301 Report.
[58] In consultative involvement, the government and institutions are the decision makers but stakeholders have a degree of influence over the process and outcomes.
[59] By examining the experiences of India, Cuba, Iran, Taiwan, Egypt and Nigeria, Mytelka concluded that the opening policy space for local firms and creating incentives for local innovation might be important triggers in driving subsequent innovation processes. *See,* Mytelka, L.K. (2006) 'Pathways and Policies to (Bio) Pharmaceutical Innovation Systems in Developing Counties', *Industry and Innovation*, V.13, I.4, pp. 415–35.

Establishing an R&D Strategy

i. University–industry collaboration
It is widely acknowledged that universities play a major role in the innovation process, that is, universities substantially contribute to scientific progress and the development of human capital. Hence, collaboration between university and industry has become one of the key issues in national innovation policies. In line with this, academic research is regarded as an endogenised and integrated part of the economic cycle of innovation and growth.[60] For developing countries, in relation to the building up of capabilities and the development of manufacturing capacity in specific areas, the presence of government manufacturing, or public-private partnerships, perhaps between some combination of universities, governments, foundations and generics manufacturers, are widely regarded as necessary.[61]

Indeed, university collaboration is a prerequisite for the pharmaceutical industry to boost innovation in the area of drug development. The evidence demonstrates that much of the basic research for new drugs is being conducted in universities.[62] According to an industry survey conducted in the life sciences industry in 1994, 90 per cent of the 210 companies involved in the survey developed relations with one or more academic institutions. Furthermore, 59 per cent supported academic research and almost 11.7 per cent of the industry's budget, an estimated amount of $1.5 billion, was allocated as R&D funding. In that year, more than 60 per cent of the companies investing in academic research reaped the rewards, for example, through patents, products, and sales thereof.[63]

---

[60]   Debackere, K. (2000) 'Managing Academic R&D as a Business at KU Leuven: Context, Structure and Process', *R&D Management*, V.30 N.4, p. 326; Dooley, L. and D. Kirk (2007) 'University-Industry Collaboration: Grafting the Entrepreneurial Paradigm onto Academic Structures', *European Journal of Innovation Management*, V.10 N.3, p. 317.

[61]   Maybarduk, P. and S. Rimmington (2009) 'Compulsory Licences: A Tool to Improve Global Access to the HPV Vaccine?', *American Journal of Law & Medicine*, V.35, p. 334.

[62]   Maxwell and Eckhardt found that out of the 32 most 'innovative' drugs almost half were directly derived from non-industry sources (that is, universities, government labs and research hospitals). *See,* Maxwell, R. and S. Eckhardt (1990) *Drug Discovery: A Casebook and Analysis*, Totowa, NJ: Humana Press.

[63]   Blumenthal, D., N. Causino, E. Campbell and K. Seashore (1996) 'Relationships between Academic Institutions and Industry in the Life Sciences –

The university–industry research partnerships usually include the exchange of knowledge and resources in a very specific area of science, for example, biotechnology and enabling capabilities for research advancement resulting in a more iterative process where discoveries are taken from laboratory to land and developed by industry.[64] In this context, the emergence and success of the local pharmaceutical industry in Israel might be attributed, in part, to Israel's policies in stimulating collaboration between university and industry. In fact, as noted above, Teva has a long history of university collaboration; the development of Teva's two innovative drugs both followed the common path in which the basic research was conducted in university research centres. Teva then transformed this research into drugs. In fact, neither Copaxone nor Azilect would have been developed if Teva had been reluctant to invest in academic research in Israel. Hence it can be concluded that Teva's success in the creation of these proprietary drugs to some extent depended upon the quality of Israel's university[65] research.

ii. Addressing target diseases

Israeli research institutions have technical capabilities and expertise in a broad range of medical fields. The current research in the country focuses specifically on cardiology, oncology and the central nervous system.[66] Interestingly, Israel is becoming an R&D centre for the treatment of multiple sclerosis; two out of the top three medications to treat multiple sclerosis were developed at the Weizmann Institute of Science, in Rehovot. Apart from Teva's Copaxone, Rebif, the commercial name for interferon-beta-1a, was developed at the Weizmann Institute and it is used by 70 per cent of multiple sclerosis patients worldwide. It is branded under Serono[67] and had worldwide sales of up to $1.3 billion in

---

An Industry Survey', *The New England Journal of Medicine*, V.334. N.6, pp. 368–74.

[64] Dooley, supra note 60, pp. 319–20.

[65] Israel has world-class research institutions: Hebrew University of Jerusalem, the Technion-Israel Institute of Technology and the Weizmann Institute of Sciences.

[66] About 50 per cent of university research projects in therapeutic drugs and two-thirds of biotech drugs in the pipeline are in these therapeutic areas.

[67] Rebif was produced by Interpharm in Rehovot. But Serono almost completely closed down Interpharm and moved production to Europe.

2005.[68] Furthermore, another Israeli biotech company Glycominds is currently working on a predictor test for multiple sclerosis.[69]

The expertise in pharmaceutical research is not limited to the treatment of multiple sclerosis. It has also led to other blockbuster drugs such as Novartis's Exelon, which is principally used for the treatment of Alzheimer's disease, and which originated from research conducted at the Hebrew University. Another example is Johnson & Johnson's Doxil, a chemotherapy drug that was developed at the Hadassah Medical Center.[70]

In the developed world, and particularly in Europe,[71] it is possible to observe an ageing population. People are living longer lives and, hence, the diseases of the aged are becoming more prevalent. Hence, the medical and social needs of older people in the developed world now provide huge markets for drugs to treat the diseases of the aged. Thus, there are wide ranges of opportunities for pharmaceutical companies to enter these markets. It is widely acknowledged that for many of these diseases, such as Alzheimer's or Parkinson's, there are very few options for treatment.[72] Nonetheless, the lack of adequate medicines for such diseases presents a major opportunity for the development of innovative medicines in Israel. The existence of academic research on these diseases in Israel over the past two decades was a factor in the development of successful drugs. It created a competitive advantage for Israeli pharmaceutical companies, such as Teva. However, Israel is not the only country that is building up a portfolio of novel medicines for Alzheimer's and Parkinson's; drugs for the treatment of these diseases and neural disorders are high on the list of targets for Indian pharmaceutical companies.[73]

---

[68]   *See,* 'Life Sciences in Israel', Israel Ministry of Industry Trade and Labor Foreign Trade Administration, available at http://www.israeleconomicmission.com/index.php?option=com_docman&task=doc_download&gid=18&Itemid=1.

[69]   The simple blood test addresses the problem of doctors being unable to tell if a patient who has suffered a single neurological event will develop a mild or active form of multiple sclerosis.

[70]   *See,* Shadlen, K. (2009) 'The Political Contradictions of Incremental Innovation in Late Development: Lessons from Pharmaceutical Patent Examination in Brazil', APSA 2009 Toronto Meeting Paper, August 2009.

[71]   According to Science/Business report, the experts forecast that by 2050, there will be just two workers per pensioner, compared with four workers today, available at www.sciencebusiness.net/documents/demandside.pdf.

[72]   IFPMA Report, supra note 4, p. 8.

[73]   Sharma, N.L and S. Goswami (2009) 'The Nuances of Knowledge Creation and Development in the Indian Pharmaceutical Industry', *Journal of Knowledge Management*, V.13 N.5, p. 320.

Therefore, it is crucial to ensure that the main focus of the research undertaken as part of the collaborative process is an area in which the university possesses a high degree of competence. For instance, it is important that the university is recognised as competent in this area by other universities.[74] Indeed, the particular focus of the research is highly crucial in the pharmaceutical R&D strategy; the focus of the research that the company wishes to undertake must match the research base of the university. A well-defined strategy that concentrates on pharmaceutical R&D along the lines outlined above is quite likely to provide a return over the long term and bring economic growth to the industry.

The current product portfolio and innovation pipeline of Teva largely depends on the existence of relevant university research in Israel, that is, research in the areas of oncology, immunology and the central nervous system. Furthermore, Teva's internal research pipeline generally focuses on niche specialty disease categories such as multiple sclerosis and amyotrophic lateral sclerosis. Nonetheless, Teva is seeking to expand its innovation horizon by buying the rights to treatments for cancers and neurological and autoimmune disorders[75] and Teva also wants to gain access to innovative, pre-clinical programmes from all around the world through research collaboration. In this vein, a unit of Teva pharmaceuticals, Teva Innovative Ventures, is providing funding for projects from beginning to end that would fit the specialty pharmaceutical profile, where Teva is undertaking 100 per cent of the development costs.

The process that has been proposed includes a fairly rapid and collaborative evaluation process, which aims to develop collaboration from day one. In the event that the compound is found to be interesting, a finding based on non-confidential information shared between the parties, a confidential disclosure agreement would usually be signed by both parties. Henceforth, an internal evaluation committee would assess the compound within 14 days of receipt of the full confidential package. If the compound passes the internal evaluation, a material transfer agreement is usually concluded. In most cases, according to the agreement, all rights to the compound remain with the innovator until business terms are negotiated and agreed.[76]

---

74   Dooley, supra note 60, p. 330.
75   *See,* IFPMA report, supra note 4.
76   *See,* www.tevapartners.com.

iii.   Under the spotlight: Teva's R&D strategy

Casting the spotlight on Teva's R&D strategy provides an innovative and sustainable business model for generic companies investing in innovative R&D. Thus, it is of crucial importance to extend the analysis to Teva's R&D strategy. Yet, perhaps the most salient aspect of Teva's R&D strategy for drug development is its collaboration with external innovators, particularly with universities. In other words, Teva outsources the elements of basic research to external innovators.

Indeed, outsourcing is a common inorganic growth[77] strategy in the innovative drug industry, and one that has long provided fundamental research knowledge for new product streams. Pharmaceutical companies routinely outsource the basic research to external innovators such as universities, institutes and government laboratories. For instance, Hoffman La Roche is a case in point. It was among the first to formalise such collaborative relationships, in other words, to develop drugs using knowledge discovered by external innovators. In the 1950s, through the La Roche Institute, it provided researchers with support, independence and facilities that few universities or independent laboratories could equal.[78] Further to this, at least one-third of the blockbuster drugs marketed in the US were initially developed either in universities or small biotech companies.[79] To optimise resources and cut R&D costs, the companies may also consider collaborating with universities and research institutes as this offers increased opportunities for building a cost effective and innovative drug development chain.

The second point that is worth noting here is that it is necessary to target specialty disease categories for innovative R&D. The target-based drug development initiatives of Teva are very much along the lines of diseases in which the country has built up research capabilities and competences. Given that Teva relies heavily on academic research in

---

[77]   Companies focus on external (inorganic) growth when they decide to expand outside of their current operations and buy access to new products or markets. Apart from mergers and acquisitions, the companies may grow externally by entering into strategic alliances, which are agreements between firms in which each commits resources to achieve a common set of objectives. The familiar examples of strategic alliances in the pharmaceutical industry are university–industry collaboration or outsourcing of R&D. *See,* Dhar, S. (2006) *Case Studies on Growth Strategies – Volume II*, Hyderabad, ICFAI Books..

[78]   Quinn, J.B. (2000) 'Outsourcing the Innovation: The New Engine of Growth', *Massachusetts Institute of Technology Sloan Management Review*, V.41, N.4, pp. 14–15.

[79]   Angell, M. (2005) *The Truth about the Drug Companies: How They Deceive Us and What to Do about It*, New York, Random House, p. 67.

Israel for proprietary drug development, the drug targets are identified accordingly. It is, therefore, critical for the companies to understand the foundational elements and capabilities of the university research conducted in the country and then to tailor their particular strategy within the context of their future prospects.

The study of previous successful university–industry collaborations provides empirical evidence that the specific cultural needs, existing in both the industrial and academic environments, should be accommodated in collaboration initiatives. On one side, the industry needs to make concessions on receiving the unexpected from academia and the industry should develop mechanisms to identify and further develop discoveries accordingly. On the other side, academia might consider responding to industry's priorities, and to commercialise any IP resulting from the academic research. In order to have a successful collaboration, it is necessary to develop mutual understanding and ensure respect for priorities. Within both relevant institutions, that is, the company and the university, mutual understanding and respect would usually be a prerequisite for any well-defined and transparent research collaboration. Once these conditions are in place, it should be possible to further transform the investments in basic sciences into discoveries for more and better public health goods.[80]

Developing a Sustainable Business Strategy for Biotechnology

Following the convention established in previous chapters, the received wisdom is that investing in biotechnology is likely to be highly beneficial for the pharmaceutical industry. In fact, biotechnology is widely regarded as the new wave for pharmaceutical innovation and one that will shape the future of the industry. Over the next decade more than half of all new active substances will be the result of antibody research and biotechnology products such as monoclonal antibodies.[81]

According to World Bank's Global Forum on Science, Technology, and Innovation, there is a constant need for developing countries to build up skills and research capacity in biotechnology. In particular, from the standpoint of innovation, the World Bank persuasively argues that discussion should not concentrate on whether developing countries need to build science and technology capacities that promote biotechnology innovation, rather, the focus should be on what type of capacity to build

---

[80] Gray, N. (2006) 'Drug Discovery through Industry – Academic Partnerships', *Nature Chemical Biology*, V.2, N.12, p. 652.

[81] IFPMA report, supra note 4, p. 25.

given the economic realities of developing countries, and how best to implement these capacity building action plans therein.[82]

It is crucial for developing countries to invest in biotechnology – regarded as the most powerful investment sector of the twenty-first century. It is also necessary for developing countries to establish a wide range of networks between university and industry. This would require strong commitments from all stakeholders involved, that is, the triple helix of university, industry and government. At present it appears that this commitment is not present in many developing countries. Hence, in developing countries, investing in biotechnology has rarely been considered as a viable strategy.

Nonetheless, development economists have long recognised that investing in R&D is a step that developing countries must take, in order to be successful in the area of biotechnology.[83] Indeed, it is arguable that the area of biotechnology presents great opportunities for the pharmaceutical industry in developing countries, not only in the development of new drugs and vaccines but also in relation to the development of generic medicines.

Biosimilars (biogenerics), that is, the development of cost-effective generic forms of biopharmaceuticals,[84] is an emerging one. The area of biopharmaceuticals offers significantly improved outcomes in difficult-to-treat diseases such as cancer and autoimmune disorders. As a result, these are the most expensive drugs available in pharmacies today and sales of these drugs account for 10–15 per cent of the developed world's pharmaceutical market. Furthermore, it is anticipated that biologics would represent 19 to 20 per cent of the total market value by 2017.[85]

---

[82]   Global Forum (2007) Building Science, Technology, and Innovation, Capacity for Sustainable Growth and Poverty Reduction. Washington DC.

[83]   IFPMA report, supra note 4, p. 25.

[84]   It is pharmaceutical, inherently biological in nature and manufactured using biotechnology. Compared with drugs, biopharmaceuticals are composed of many more atoms – with molecular masses usually two or three orders of magnitude greater – and involve many additional levels of structural complexity (e.g. forming polymeric chains with varying and diverse structures and chemical modifications). *See,* Rader, R. (2008) '(Re)Defining Biopharmaceutical', *Nature Biotechnology,* V.26, N.7, pp. 743–51.

[85]   'The Global Use of Medicines: Outlook through 2017' *IMS Institute,* November 2013, available at http://www.drugstorenews.com/sites/drugstorenews.com/files/IMS%20Health%20Global%20Use%20of%20Medicines%20FINAL%5B1%5D.pdf. .

The report of the Medicare Payment Advisory Commission reveals that biotech drugs achieve sales of $13 billion a year in the US alone.[86]

Thus, it can be said that the market for biopharmaceuticals is a substantial one. The biotechnology companies, along with the multinationals, do not want to miss any opportunities to gain an advantage within this market. Hence, these companies tend to resist opening the doors to lower cost generics or follow-on protein products.[87] The possible introduction of biosimilars, as the generic alternative to biopharmaceuticals, has been subject to fierce debate, both in Europe and the US. This debate is controversial because of the complex nature of the inventions involved as well as concerns regarding equivalence.

In fact, it is arguable that biopharmaceuticals are highly complex and these drugs 'have a number of characteristics that set them aside from low-molecular-weight drugs; their activity depends on their conformation, which is based on secondary, tertiary and sometimes even quaternary structures. If conformation is altered, activity can also be altered. As the conditions in which biologics are produced largely define the final product, any alteration to the manufacturing process could result in a completely different product'.[88]

This issue is part of a much wider discourse; the bioequivalence tests conducted by generic companies for the traditional therapeutic medicines are not functional for biopharmaceuticals. In order to prove the safety and efficiency of biosimilars, some additional test data, and in some cases, clinical trial data, is required. Proponents of biosimilars are also required to demonstrate that the chemical identity of the active substance is therapeutically equivalent. In addition to proof of essential similarity, a lack of technical infrastructure, the existence of weak academic network ties and the high cost of production pose serious challenges for the generic companies in developing countries.

---

[86] 'Generic Biotech Drugs: Cure or Quagmire?', *Businessweek*, 15 June 2009, available at http://www.businessweek.com/technology/content/jun2009/tc20090615_361364.htm.

[87] Follow-on protein products generally refers to protein and peptide products that are intended to be sufficiently similar to a product already approved or licensed to permit the applicant to rely for approval on certain existing scientific knowledge about the safety and effectiveness of the approved protein product. Follow-on protein products may be produced through biotechnology or derived from natural sources. *See,* Rader, R. (2007) 'What is s Generic Biopharmaceutical? Biogeneric? Follow-on Protein? Biosimilar? Follow-on Biologic?', *BioProcess International*, V.5, pp. 28–38.

[88] Griffiths, S. (2004) 'From the Analyst's Couch: Betting on Biogenerics', *Nature Reviews, Drug Discovery*, V.3, p. 197.

Relying on the complex nature of biopharmaceuticals, biotechnology companies, partnered with multinationals, often claim that it is nearly impossible to prove that any two-protein cultures are identical. Furthermore, these companies often highlight the potential, and very serious, safety and efficiency problems that may arise due to the slight differences among drugs.

In line with this, Griffiths reports evidence that even when a company is able to use the same manufacturing process, there may still be serious difficulties in producing the same drug. By a way of illustration, Johnson & Johnson recently commissioned a new manufacturing facility to produce commercial quantities of epoetin alfa (Procrit/Eprex). Even though the manufacturing processes were the same, certain batches of the product were withdrawn due to safety concerns. According to Griffiths, if an experienced manufacturer is unable to consistently reproduce its own manufacturing process, there will be significant obstacles on the path to generic biopharmaceutical drugs. Furthermore, regulatory bodies are likely to treat the manufacture of biosimilar products with a measure of caution.[89]

Indeed, the introduction of a regulatory approval process system of biosimilars has proceeded at a slow pace. Taking into account the challenges thereof, legislatures both in Europe and the US have, thus far, preferred to be cautious, while clearing up the uncertainties surrounding regulation of the biosimilars. Further to this, the legislation that applies to the biosimilars regulatory system was introduced in Europe only in 2003.[90] In the US, the Biologics Price Competition and Innovation Act (BPCIA) of 2009 provides an approval pathway for follow-on biologics and 12 years of exclusivity – four years of data and market exclusivity and an additional eight years of market exclusivity – for biologics. However, the discussions are ongoing as regards to the data exclusivity period. The White House had proposed reducing the length of exclusivity to seven years in its budget for the fiscal year 2014 in order to control healthcare costs. The budget proposal claimed that such changes to US

---

[89]   Griffiths, supra note 88, p. 197.

[90]   Directive 2004/27/EC of the European Parliament and of the Council of 31 March 2004 amending Directive 2001/83/EC on the Community code relating to medicinal products for human use. The European Medicines Agency (EMEA) is the main regulatory body that grants 'marketing authorization' on the basis of a scientific evaluation of the product. *Official Journal of the European Union* L 136, 30/4/2004 P.0034–0057.

law would result in $3 billion in savings over ten years to federal health programs.[91]

Thus it can be said that the regulatory system of follow-on biologics is multi-faceted. It both poses challenges and offers opportunities for generic companies. The challenges mainly revolve around the requirements that a great deal of independent data,[92] proving safety and efficiency, be shown by generic companies, as well as the potentially long term data exclusivity periods; it is already ten years in Europe and 12 years in the US.

Nonetheless, some of the generic companies are expanding their horizons into the area of follow-on biologics. In order to develop a set of competences, they are aiming to transform their existing capabilities into biotechnology. Furthermore, it is not only the propriety drug companies that are linking up with biotechnology companies to acquire expertise; the generic companies are also taking advantage of biotechnology research and start-ups.

In this context, Teva is putting science and technological systems in place in order to manufacture safe and effective biologics.[93] Indeed, Teva can easily be regarded as one of the important components of the life sciences industry in Israel. Every sector of Israel's life sciences industry is, to some extent, affected by Teva and the company has exclusive access to every kind of biotechnological research. Further to this, Teva has

---

[91]   Office of Management and Budget, Fiscal Year 2014 Budget of the US Government, available at http://www.whitehouse.gov/sites/default/files/omb/budget/fy2014/assets/budget.pdf.

[92]   EMEA, requires extensive testing demonstrating the same quality, safety and effectiveness as the reference product before approval. EMEA takes a case-by-case approach requiring 'differences between the similar biological medicinal product and the reference medicinal product to be justified by appropriate studies.' Such studies will typically include clinical trials. Biosimilars are required to undergo post-marketing monitoring just like new innovative biologics. In the US, FDA requires expensive immunogenicity studies and clinical trials for biosimiliars.

[93]   'I feel very strongly that we have the science and systems in place to manufacture safe and effective biologics,' said Marvin Samson, a vice president of Teva Pharmaceutical Industries Ltd. 'Teva already produces biologics in Eastern Europe for countries where patent protection is not enforced' and, he adds, 'The situation is like in the 1980s with Hatch-Waxman, where the brand-name industry said we didn't have the science and capabilities to analyze their products and reproduce them. We did have the ability then, and we do now.' *See,* 'Biotech Drugs' Generic Future Debated; Medications are Hard to Afford', *The Washington Post,* 10 February 2005, available at http://www.washingtonpost.com/wp-dyn/articles/A12377-2005Feb9.html.

shares in the ownership of investment funds for biotechnology and biotech incubators and it possesses a long list of start-ups. Hence, it is possible to observe a number of small, but strong, start-up companies, particularly in the field of biotechnology. This can be said to be a characteristic of the Israeli life sciences industry.[94] The Teva example serves as a model of ideal investment in the life sciences area. In this context, the start-up companies generate an internal innovation pipeline for Teva, and the companies have a substantial R&D budget, for example, around $383 million in 2005.[95]

Moreover, apart from its work with Israeli universities and biotechnology start-up companies, Teva also links up with biotechnological and biopharmaceutical companies in other countries, and particularly companies in the US. By a way of illustration, Teva has established a partnership with a Canadian biopharmaceutical company, Oncogenex,[96] which is committed to the development and commercialisation of new cancer therapies. Oncogenex also aims to develop and commercialise OGX-011 – a phase III cancer therapy designed to inhibit cancer treatment resistance.[97]

Biotechnology, biopharmaceuticals and biosimiliars are the latest R&D concepts that are likely to underlie the future of the pharmaceutical industry. Furthermore, these areas will be at the forefront of public health discussions, both in the developed and developing world. Therefore, in terms of access to affordable medicines in future, it is critical that generic companies develop innovation strategies that prioritise the building up of capabilities in specific biotech areas as well as initiating the transfer of technology from laboratory to land.

CONCLUDING REMARKS

It can be suggested that Teva's steady growth, from a company that manufactures generic drugs, to a company developing innovative drugs, was achieved through a mix of organic and inorganic growth strategies.

---

[94]   The research in field of therapeutics including drug discovery, cell therapy and genetics constitutes almost 60 per cent of the biotechnology activity in the country.

[95]   *See*, Biotechnology Israel, supra note 6, p. 5.

[96]   http://www.oncogenex.ca/.

[97]   'Teva Signs Drug Development Deal with OncoGeneX', 29 December 2009, Silico Research, available at http://silico.wordpress.com/2009/12/29/teva-and-oncogenex-sign-global-licence-and-collaboration-agreement/ (02.01.2010).

The organic growth strategies[98] focused on existing conditions; these were then combined with the local realities in order to provide better prospects for success. The distinctive trajectories of Teva have included using local institutions to positive effect, as well as focusing on local realities. These can be assessed as a part of an organic growth strategy, which has led the company's growth in the pharmaceutical market. On the other hand, Teva has also adopted an inorganic growth route. The company's inorganic growth[99] was largely achieved through mergers, acquisitions and strategic partnerships. In line with this, recent mergers and acquisitions have increased Teva's market share, particularly in the US market.[100] Furthermore, the success of these mergers has reduced competition and it has added new brands and products to Teva's portfolio. In this context, both the nurturing of university–industry collaboration and the provision of R&D outsourcing can be seen as examples of good practice strategies for achieving effective inorganic growth. Moreover, Teva's aggressive patent challenging strategy is seen as vital to the company's inorganic expansion activity in the US market.

Hence, the strategies adopted by Teva reveal a business model that embodies targets to achieve inorganic growth through mergers and acquisitions; these mergers help to enhance competitiveness in the global pharmaceutical market. It should also be noted that merger and acquisition strategies, or the expansion strategies more broadly, may be serve as

[98] Organic growth is the most reliable and sustainable way for a company to grow. It tends to rely on factors such as hiring more employees, growing the customer base, opening new company-owned locations or developing new products through internal R&D. The implementation of an organic growth strategy is going to vary with the individual characteristics of each firm, its culture, and its position in the market place. An ability to innovate is considered as one of the drivers of organic growth in the company. *See,* Dhar, supra note 77.

[99] Mergers are one common form of inorganic growth. Mergers occur when two or more firms combine operations to form one corporation, perhaps with a new name. One goal of a merger is to achieve management synergy by creating a stronger management team. Acquisitions, a second form of external growth, occur when the purchased corporation loses its identity. The acquiring company absorbs it. The acquired company and its assets may be absorbed into an existing business unit or remain intact as an independent subsidiary within the parent company. Acquisitions usually occur when a larger firm purchases a smaller company. *See,* Dhar, supra note 77.

[100] The acquisition of Barr Pharmaceuticals in the US pushed market share of Teva to 24 per cent from 18 per cent. It further increased Teva's market share to 16 per cent in the global market. See, 'Two Marriages and a Funeral' Outlook Profit, V.1, N.12, August 2008, p. 50.

valid aspirations for companies that are considering methods of penetrating new markets overseas. In fact, a growing number of pharmaceutical companies from developing countries appear to be considering such strategies as a part of a successful expansion policy. For instance, the Indian pharmaceutical companies can provide a good illustration of such efforts. They have successfully adapted to the realities of globalisation and these companies have been able to penetrate western markets, in part through the use of mergers and acquisitions. Thus, the overseas expansion of Indian pharmaceutical companies has focused on the European market, as well as the US market. In line with this, a leading Indian pharmaceutical company, Dr Reddy's Laboratories (DLR), acquired a German generic company, Betapharm,[101] in order to strengthen its position in the European market. DLR has also adopted a patent challenging strategy as part of its inorganic growth strategy in the US and UK markets.

Hence, there are a number of competitive business strategies that could prove useful to the local pharmaceutical industries in developing countries. Furthermore, the findings herein indicate that, in most cases, the pharmaceutical companies are very likely to adopt the same known growth route for innovation driven businesses. Indeed, the analysis of Teva's business model, which evolved from developing generics to developing innovative drugs as well, shows one strategy. Further to this, analysis of the recent efforts of the Indian pharmaceutical companies, which have attempted to exploit opportunities in the global market, and achieve growth through innovation, reveals that the emerging pathways to innovation in the pharmaceutical industry often follow the same routes.

Teva's case study reveals mechanisms that might be put in place in order to drive long-term global growth and to develop wide-ranging capabilities for R&D success. These thematic mechanisms that have been used by Teva include:

- Developing technical expertise in patent law (including compulsory licensing and patent challenging and active involvement in judicial process);
- Strong lobbying power (intervention into law-making and the Special 301 submission process);

---

[101]   Betapharm is the fourth biggest generic drug manufacturer in Germany. The $572 million Betapharm acquisition was a key strategic move in the Dr. Reddy's expansion plans in terms of boosting its presence in Europe. *See,* BBC News, 16 February 2006, available at http://news.bbc.co.uk/1/hi/business/4718692.stm.

- Sustainable R&D Strategy (addressing target diseases, biotechnology);
- R&D partnerships (university–industry collaboration); and
- Mergers and acquisitions

The overall aim of this chapter has been to present real-life observations, shown with the example of a generic company, which has climbed up the innovation ladder and has grown into a pharmaceutical giant, so that the evolution of Teva can provide an example for other companies in the developing world.

However, the wider debate on these issues continues. Thus, the question must be posed as to whether a similar level of success could be achieved by other pharmaceutical companies. Unfortunately, there is no clear answer as the countries in question are different, that is, the company structures can vary significantly between different developing countries and even the market conditions can be different from one country to another. Nevertheless, the growth route and strategies adopted by the Indian pharmaceutical companies appear to have strong similarities to those adopted by Teva. Hence, such cases may present a compelling rationale in favour of the practicality of Teva's business strategy as a model of good practice.

The trajectories examined herein are the most distinctive ones within the framework of research in this area, and these trajectories gave Teva its current high profile in pharmaceutical market. Even though the potential applicability of these trajectories to the actions of other companies remains questionable, there are some important lessons to be drawn. More importantly, the success of Teva has the potential to inspire the growth aspirations for other companies in the developing world.

7. Real life lessons for the developing world

The emergence of the Agreement on Trade Related Aspects of Intellectual Property Rights (TRIPS) has long been a subject of controversy. Much attention has been devoted to the the alleged destructive consequences of its implementation in developing countries. The global implementation process has raised important issues in relation to patent barriers, and access to medicines. More importantly, it has added a layer of additional complexity for local generic drug companies in relation to local technical expertise and scientific infrastructure.

It is widely accepted that TRIPS, and the global patent rules that it has introduced, potentially affects the ability of developing countries to catch up. This is particularly clear in the area of pharmaceuticals, where patents are strongly and positively correlated with research and development (R&D) activity.[1] Given the fact that local pharmaceutical production in developing countries has traditionally concentrated on the area of generic drugs, boosting local pharmaceutical innovation is not an easy task for developing countries. However, it is not an impossible task.

Unfortunately, there is no ideal recipe for developing a strategic plan, nor is there a best model that each country may adopt. Nevertheless, there are certain ingredients that are common to innovation and R&D policies. The previous chapters attempted to identify these ingredients, that is, the provision of a fine-tuned intellectual property rights (IPRs) system, which incorporates TRIPS flexibilities and the enabling of a reliable innovation system tailored to the local realities and needs of the country. This policy will include, but is not limited to, policies complementing the IPRs regime.

---

[1] Odagiri, H., A. Goto and A. Sunami (2010) 'Conclusions' in H. Odagiri, A. Goto, A. Sunami and R. Nelson (eds) *Intellectual Property Rights, Development and Catch-up*, New York, Oxford University Press, p. 427.

A FINELY-TUNED INTELLECTUAL PROPERTY REGIME

TRIPS has been promoted as a necessary component of the innovation/ development process. Developing countries were assured that by enacting the agreement, they would receive a jump-start in relation to economic growth.[2] Today, almost 20 years after the emergence of TRIPS, it is still unclear whether patents, or IPRs more broadly, are necessary or desirable for promoting innovation in developing countries. Furthermore, there is limited evidence that TRIPS has positively affected the development process within catching up or low-income countries.

Nevertheless, the experience of the developing countries over the last 18 years shows that the mere protection of IPRs is not sufficient to achieve developmental objectives. As noted previously, the optimal level and impact of IPRs in the innovation process can vary. The size of the market and the nature of local R&D capabilities in a country largely determine the potential effect of IPRs in relation to innovation and development. Governments are more likely to strengthen their IPRs regimes when IPRs are more likely to maximise national wealth. It is usually the case that governments postpone the enactment of a strong national IPRs regime until domestic firms are able to develop creative works that can be traded internationally.[3] IPRs regimes co-evolve in conjunction with the development of innovative capacities within a country.

The IPRs regime, in many cases, may be characterised as necessary to effectively facilitate successful innovation strategies. Nevertheless, the relationship between IPRs and innovation is at least as complex as the innovation profile of each industry. The research findings indicate that industries differ greatly in terms of R&D propensity. Furthermore, these differences greatly influence the industrial attitude towards IPRs protection. Clearly, there are a number of conditions under which each industry determines its attitude towards patents. The structural characteristics of the industry and the nature of its field of activity significantly shape the innovation process. In turn, this shapes the role of patents as an appropriability mechanism. Consequently, each industry treats patents

[2] Gervais, D. (2009) 'Policy Calibration and Innovation Displacement' in N. Netanel (ed.) *The Development Agenda*, New York, Oxford University Press, p. 52.

[3] La Croix, S. and A. Kawaura (1996) 'Product Patent Reform and its Impact on Korea's Pharmaceutical Industry', *International Economic Journal*, V.10, N.1, p. 110.

differently. Among all the industries examined, patents are most crucially conducive to innovation in the pharmaceutical industry.

The pharmaceutical industry attributes a great deal of significance to patents. Patents are unusually strong in pharmaceuticals. For instance, a slight change in the molecular compound could radically influence the efficiency of the drug. Thus, pharmaceutical patents have clear boundaries. Nonetheless, ease of imitation is an issue of great concern. In essence, ease of imitation determines the power of patents within the industry. For instance, the success of the aviation industry does not depend on patents. The reason for this is that inventions are difficult to reverse-engineer. On the other hand, patents have long been recognised as a crucial element of innovation in the pharmaceutical industry. This is because drugs are easy to reverse-engineer and disclosure is imminent. In line with this equation, it can be concluded that innovation patterns vary significantly across industries.

All segments of the aerospace industry are highly capital-intensive. Given the huge investment of time and money associated with building up capabilities, companies start inventing and innovating right from the very beginning in order to capture a competitive position in both the national and international market. However, imitation may well be an option. Still, an imitator will not be in a favourable position, because it is too costly to acquire resources and capabilities for reverse engineering. Hence, when latecomers have acquired all the resources and capabilities necessary to copy an aircraft, they have typically already begun to innovate. The structure of the industry and the innovation patterns therein, justifies why the patent regime is relatively unimportant in these types of industries. This also clarifies why there is little or no discussion about the patents or the TRIPS regime more broadly, in relation to the possible impact on the aerospace industry.

Going back to the main topic of interest, the pharmaceutical industry, it is clear that the innovation patterns differ significantly from the aerospace industry. A great deal of importance is attached to the patent regime in a country with a pharmaceutical industry. Recalling the traditional innovation sequence, where innovation starts with imitation and then proceeds through to innovation, a great deal of importance is attached to the imitation phase in terms of capacity building and knowledge assimilation. The historical analysis of pharmaceutical innovation in previous chapters has shown that imitation, or reverse engineering, has been consistently part of the behaviour of pharmaceutical companies. The foundations of today's pharmaceutical market were established on the imitation practices of companies in relation to each other's inventions. Given the ease of imitation and the availability of complementary assets, it has become relatively difficult for the pharmaceutical companies to protect their competitive advantage in the market. In an effort to protect structural market advantages, IP assets have become essential for the continuum of pharmaceutical innovation, particularly in developed countries, which contribute to the harvesting of benefits in terms of structural market advantages in pharmaceuticals.

Clearly one industry that has been significantly affected by the global patent rules is the pharmaceutical industry. As latecomers, pharmaceutical companies from developing countries now face enormous initial disadvantages when compared to the position of their Western rivals. This raises the serious question of whether it is possible to develop a strong local pharmaceutical industry in post-TRIPS era; there is no clear answer to this question.

A fine-tuned IPRs system appears to be a prerequisite for successfully building up domestic capabilities in the highly competitive pharmaceutical industry. The historical evidence reveals that in the past countries have derived great benefits from freely designing their own IPRs system. By providing limited scope and reflecting development needs, they were able to capture comparative advantages and maximise their levels of skill and knowledge. The success story of the German dye industry represents compelling evidence to support the validation of this argument. The specifically tailored patent regime in Germany helped to facilitate the successful absorption of foreign technology through reverse engineering. In Japan, it is clear that the Japanese patent regime has strengthened only when Japanese companies have been able to market innovative and globally competitive drugs. In a similar pattern, Korea has carefully pursued a development strategy aimed at promoting its ability to 'imitate, absorb, assimilate, replicate or duplicative imitation of foreign inventions'.[4] The IPRs system has also been constructed in a manner consistent with the economic and social policy goals of Korea. However, Korean pharmaceuticals were not in as fortunate a position as their Japanese rivals. The reason for this was the existence of strong patent provisions, which were introduced long before the companies were able to truly compete globally. Thus, companies utilised other sources for technology transfer and full capacity building. The Korean vaccine story in previous chapter is evidence for the fact that joint ventures and international collaborations can lead to success.

---

[4] Kumar, N. (2003) 'Intellectual Property Rights, Technology and Economic Development: Experience of Asian Countries', RIS Discussion Paper No.25/2003, p. 4.

Notwithstanding this fact, in the post-TRIPS era, countries appear to have very little flexibility in designing their national IPRs systems. Furthermore, innovation without patents, particularly in the pharmaceutical industry, seems to be exceptionally difficult. Today, pharmaceutical innovation is associated with TRIPS. Hence, the local patent regime has a large impact on the innovation process. Nevertheless, pharmaceutical innovation is a long-term process. It requires not only a well-designed patent regime, but also a huge investment of time and money. The existence of a patent regime is important, but it is not the only component of the pharmaceutical innovation process. As it turns out, the patent regime may well contribute to innovation process, but only in cases where certain conditions are put in place. These conditions depend upon the technological capabilities that a given country actually possesses and the extent of the government's dedication.

It is therefore important to distinguish between developing countries at different stages of development. It is necessary to bear in mind that developing countries do not form a homogeneous group. For the purposes of this book, the term refers broadly to countries that already have a certain level of technological and scientific capability and an internationally renowned local generic drug industry. The research findings here are aimed at contributing to the body regarding new policies that aim to boost levels of pharmaceutical innovation in these countries. Given the terms of the global patent regime, the development of a strong pharmaceutical industry in a country with limited, or no, technological capabilities is increasingly implausible. The latecomers' R&D prospects largely depend upon the existence of access to the external knowledge base. In other words, technology transfer is crucial.[5]

Nevertheless, there are certain initiatives that could prove useful in relation to establishing alternative programmes for pharmaceutical capacity building in countries that possess limited or no technological capacities. An example is the public pharmaceutical compounding program for African countries. As in the Korean example, joint ventures or international collaborations may also be an option for countries with no or limited technological capacities.

Still an important question remains to be answered – how can a TRIPS-complaint patent regime be utilised for boosting pharmaceutical innovation in the developing world?

---

[5]   Mahoney, R., L. Keun, L and Y. Mikyung (2005) 'Intellectual Property, Drug Regulation, and Building Product Innovation Capability in Biotechnology: The Case of Hepatitis B Vaccine in Korea', *Innovation Strategy Today*, V.1, N.2, available at www.biodevelopments.org/innovation/index.htm.

TRIPS is widely accepted as a framework that sets general and minimum standards of protection for IPRs. A large portion of the discussion in the previous chapters has centred on the suggestion that the agreement allows some margin of appreciation in relation to the devising of a patent system. There is considerable room for manoeuvre in relation to different interpretations of the words. While designing the patent regime, the country's local needs and technological capabilities must be taken into account. In this fashion of thinking, countries with a standard level of technological and scientific capacity are in better position to pursue their own policy objectives for the local pharmaceutical industry.

Developing countries have traditionally been regarded as importers of technology developed abroad. During the pre-TRIPS era, taking the full advantage of the absence of patent protection for pharmaceuticals, these countries developed their own skills and capabilities in drug manufacturing by imitating foreign technology. Most of these countries had already completed the imitation phase at the time of the emergence of TRIPS. Although the implementation of the TRIPS regime had substantial impacts on prices, the destructive effect of TRIPS was not as notable as it was in developing countries that possess limited or no technological capacities. Nevertheless, due to the changing structures of the global market, the focus of investment shifted from companies that manufacture imitative generic drugs to companies that created innovative products. The possibility of taking a leap from imitate to innovate became of great interest to these countries. Confirming this, India adopted a new vision 'to use the industrial base built up mainly for the domestic market over the preceding 30 years, to move out into world markets'.[6]

India

The share of local pharmaceutical company's investments in R&D of new chemical entities has risen significantly in recent years. In an effort to realise this vision, countries started to implement TRIPS in their best interest. India, for instance, is the fourth largest producer of prescription drugs in the world. With 22 per cent of the market share in generics, India appears to be a prominent example of a developing country that has

---

[6] 'Inaugural Address by Shri Bhuvnesh Chaturvedi, Minister of State, Prime Minister's Office and Science & Technology; *See,* Drahos, P. (2009) 'The Jewel in the Crown: India's Patent Office and Patent-Based Innovation' in C. Arup and W. van Caenegem (eds) *Intellectual Property Policy Reform, Fostering Innovation and Development*, Cheltenham, UK and Northampton, MA, USA, Edward Elgar.

successfully implemented TRIPS.[7] The balanced approach taken by the Indian Government in terms of policy implementation aimed at decreasing the social costs associated with patents. The Indian government has also tried to provide the necessary incentives for the local pharmaceutical industry. In stark contrast to western patent regimes, the new Indian patent law does not consider second or third use for a known substance to be patent eligible subject matter unless a derivative of a known substance demonstrates a significant difference in its properties with regard to efficacy. In so doing, the Indian patent regime aims to block monopoly extensions through follow-on patents.[8] The act considers derivate forms of known substances, for example salts, esters, ethers and polymorphs to be the same substance, unless it is proved that the new derivative has a more substantial effect than the known substance.[9] Given the fact that evergreening has become a widely used practice among multinational pharmaceutical companies in recent years,[10] this provision may provide moderate benefits to the local industry. Notwithstanding the local characteristics of innovation in the country, it is also very likely to hurt the local industry, and thus, the rate of indigenous innovation in the country. On the other hand, the critics argue that this kind of assumption can often be misleading given that it stands upon weak data and fails to account for the dynamic character of the local industry.[11]

Taking action to preserve and enhance the competitiveness of the local industry, India has also adopted a higher standard of inventive step.[12] To be patentable in India, an invention has to be not only non-obvious to a person skilled in the art but it must also involve a technical advance when

---

[7]   *See,* IndusView 'Special Report: Opportunities for India in Generic Drug Space', V.2, I.8, available at www.theindusview.com/.../pdf/Vol2Issue8Special_report_NA.pdf.

[8]   Section 3(d), Patent (Amendment) Bill, 2005.

[9]   'For the purposes of this clause, salts, esters, ethers, polymorphs, metabolites, pure form, particle size, isomers, mixtures of isomers, complexes, combinations and other derivatives of known substance shall be considered to be the same substance, unless they differ significantly in properties with regard to efficacy.'

[10]   In the last decade, a significant proportion of pharmaceutical patents claimed various forms of existing products.

[11]   Krishnaswamy, S. (2009) 'Mashelkar Report on IP Rights Version II: Wrong Again', *Economic & Political Weekly*, V.XLIV. N.52, p. 32.

[12]   'Inventive step is a feature of an invention that involves technical advance as compared to existing knowledge or having economic significance or both, making the invention non-obvious to a person skilled in art.' Section 2 (ja), Patent (Amendment) Act, 2005.

compared to the existing knowledge, or have economic significance. Some scholars interpret this as a non-obviousness-plus standard, which grants explicit discretion to patent office officials and courts when determining a claimed invention's economic significance.[13]

These, and other examples of prominent provisions on oppositions such as compulsory licensing, experimental exception and technology transfer,[14] indicate the possible consideration of national interests within TRIPS. Nevertheless, the enforcement of the patent regime in India still remains surrounded by uncertainties and continues to generate immense concern across the industry. It has been argued that the Indian patent regime has been constructed in a more restrictive manner than is required by TRIPS. The critics of the patent regime assert that the procedure for challenging patents needs to be strengthened in order to maintain high standards of patent eligible subject matter and patentability in India.[15]

Likewise, the compulsory licensing system has been subject to substantive criticism which argues that it is not simple or easy-to-use.[16] Nevertheless, India issued the first-ever compulsory licence in 2012 to the Indian generic manufacturer Natco Pharma Ltd. for Bayer's anticancer drug Nexavar (*Sorafenib tosylate*). Bayer appealed the compulsory licence decision to the Indian Intellectual Property Appellate Board (IPAB). The IPAB upheld the decision but increased the royalty payable to Bayer by Natco from 6 per cent to 7 per cent.[17] The decision of the

---

[13] Mueller, J.M. (2007) 'The Tiger Awakens: The Tumultuous Transformation of India's Patent System and the Rise of Indian Pharmaceutical Innovation', *University of Pittsburgh Law Review*, V.68, N.3, p. 564.

[14] *See*, Vijayaraghavan, B. and P. Raghuvanshi (2009) 'Impact of the Amended Indian Patent Act on the Indian Pharmaceutical Industry', *Journal of Generic Medicines*, V.5, pp. 111–19.

[15] 'Indian-TRIPs Compliance Legislation under Fire', *Bridges Weekly Trade News Digest*, V.9 N.1, 2005, available at http://ictsd.org/i/news/bridgesweekly/7273/.

[16] Chaudhuri, S. (2005) *The WTO and India's Pharmaceuticals Industry: Patent Protection TRIPS and Developing Countries*, New Delhi, Oxford University Press, p. 316.

[17] *See*, 'India's First Compulsory Licence Upheld, but Legal Fights Likely to Continue', Intellectual Property Watch, 4 March 2013, available at http://www.ip-watch.org/2013/03/04/indias-first-compulsory-licence-upheld-but-legal-fights-likely-to-continue/.

IPAB led to concern and condemnation among multinational pharmaceutical companies and triggered unprecedented lobbying efforts against the Indian patent regime.[18]

It seems that India has long way to go on patent reform that would satisfy the majority of expectations. Still, the Indian Patent Act appears to be a successful attempt at striking a balance between protecting IPRs and promoting local innovation sustainability. More importantly, the Indian Patent Act is 'neither the fully-westernised panacea hoped for by its pro-TRIPS advocates nor the unmitigated disaster for the Indian public predicted by its fiercest critics'.[19]

Brazil

Moreover, India is not the only notorious example of a country taking advantage of the flexibilities within TRIPS. The Brazilian approach to the patent regime is regarded as neo-developmental due to the fact that it explores and broadly utilises the available options for gearing IPRs management towards the attainment of national development objectives.[20] For Shadlen, while neo-developmental patent regimes supplement the traditional focus on knowledge-use, they also put a clear focus on knowledge generation in order to encourage incremental innovation. This is of particular importance for middle-income countries, which are in between the imitation and innovation phase. Typically, these countries have already acquired the necessary imitative capabilities, but they still do not possess sufficient innovative abilities. Neo-developmental patent regimes, therefore, appear to provide the best option.[21] Brazilian policy, for instance, is strictly based on the consideration that incremental innovation is an essential step towards the goal of moving up the ladder of global innovation. The Brazilian patent regime does not limit patents

---

[18]   *See*, 'Members of US Congress Seek Pressure on India Over IP Rights', Intellectual Property Watch, 20 June 2013, available at http://www.ip-watch.org/2013/06/20/170-members-of-us-congress-pressure-india-on-ip-rights/.

[19]   Mueller, supra note 13, p. 639.

[20]   Shadlen, K. (2004) 'The Politics of Property and the New Politics of Intellectual Property in the Developing World: Insights from Latin America', Paper Presented at the Annual Meeting of the International Studies Association, Canada, available at http://www.allacademic.com/meta/p72999_index.html.

[21]   Shadlen, K. (2009) 'The Political Contradictions of Incremental Innovation in Late Development: Lessons from Pharmaceutical Patent Examination in Brazil', APSA 2009 Toronto Meeting Paper, August 2009, available at http://ssrn.com/abstract=1449086 (05.02.2011), p. 2.

to radical inventions. By regulating patentability for incremental inventions, the regime facilitates local industry participation in the patent system. This has been confirmed in the statement of the President of the Brazilian National Authority of Industrial Property. It was stated:

> The [Brazilian] firms that have developed innovative capacities demonstrate the need to retain the patentability of incremental innovations, because it is not possible for a new actor in the scenario of innovation to immediately become a radical innovator. The entryway to the system of innovation is incremental innovation.[22]

In contrast to Indian practice, Brazilian patent law encourages incremental innovations, particularly in pharmaceuticals. It does this in order to incentivise local R&D in terms of secondary uses or new drug delivery methods. Nevertheless, in order to provide balance between incremental and radical innovation and more importantly, to prevent the attempts of evergreening by originator companies, Brazil has developed a health-oriented patent examination system. Although there are still ongoing discussions as regards to the Brazilian prior consent system, it is suffice to say that the Brazilian system appears to be progressing well, and the system is operating in a manner conducive to improving the capacities and competitiveness of local firms.[23]

Speaking of Brazil, particular attention must be paid to the provisions concerning compulsory licenses. Over the last 15 years following TRIPS, Brazil has been one of the few countries that have exploited compulsory licence arrangements. In 2007, Brazil issued a compulsory licence in order to allow the import of a generic version of a patented antiretroviral Efavirenz, which was granted for public interest and for non-commercial use. Moreover, Brazil has also used the threat of compulsory licences in the past to reduce the price of patented medicines. This provides evidence to show that even the capacity to manufacture generic drugs potentially increases the bargaining power of the developing countries. In this vein, it provides flexibility when addressing public health crises.

---

[22] President Jorge Avila's testimony to the Brazilian Congress (3 July 2008 hearings, p. 4); *see, Ibid,* p. 13.

[23] For more detailed discussion in this subject, please see the seminal work of Shadlen, supra note 21.

Israel

Likewise, Israel is another prominent example of a country that has taken full advantage of compulsory licence provisions. Even the mere threat of compulsory licences promoted the voluntary licensing of patented inventions. This laid the foundations of Teva, which is now a giant in the world pharmaceutical market. Compulsory licences have proven to be of great potential, not only as bargaining mechanisms for lower drug prices, but also as effective tools for technology transfer. This encourages the growth of local industry and the promotion of innovation therein. Although the post-TRIPS compulsory licence provisions are not as flexible as the past regimes, they still offer some room for manoeuvre in this area for developing countries.

A well-functioning IPRs system also depends on the local industries' levels of technical expertise in relation to the patent regime. Previous country and company case studies have revealed that local industries acted as a regulatory tool for pharmaceutical patents. The very existence of a strong local industry and the presence of a cultural disposition towards patent opposition helped to improve the legal and institutional environment to foster local innovation. It is important that the local industry possesses technical expertise regarding important patent law issues, such as the loopholes in the patent regime, the scope of patentability requirements and the range of patent claims. Teva, for instance, possesses a high level of expertise in patent law, and the company is equipped with a capacity and dedication towards innovation and learning. This enhances the synergy between the local industry and the IPRs system. Furthermore, industry participation may contribute to the improvement of the wider policy framework, that is, in order to anticipate and respond to local social and economic conditions and priorities.

To sum up, it is clear that tailor-made solutions, particularly in the field of IPRs, are necessary to encourage economic and social development. Nevertheless, providing these solutions is not easy to do. In the past, countries were able to design structures and institutions in order to promote and foster technological and scientific development. The technological gap between countries was much smaller than it is today. More importantly, the global economic structure was increasingly diversified. There was no unified global attempt to dictate a globalisation policy.

Nevertheless, TRIPS is a package deal. Aside from the challenges it has posed for developing countries, the agreement also offers opportunities for innovation and development. Once again, it is necessary to note that TRIPS only draws the general framework of the global IPRs regime. It sets the minimum levels of protection. Furthermore, there is still room for developing countries to recalibrate their own patent policy in a manner compliant with the agreement.

A NATIONAL INNOVATION SYSTEM

Notwithstanding the increased awareness of IPRs within developing countries, there is a lack of research at the interface between national innovation systems and the IP regime on one side, and policy development on the other. Greater integration of economic, legal and technological considerations into each country's national innovation system is the way forward. The national innovation system is necessary in order to build a sustainable pharmaceutical industry in a country. It is a well-established fact that a fine-tuned IPRs regime is a prerequisite for creating an innovative and sustainable local pharmaceutical industry. However, IPRs alone do not suffice to determine the local extent of technological innovation, access and productivity.

Over the last decade, there has been a dramatic change in the IP landscape. In fact, developing countries now have a better understanding of IPRs. It has become evident that IPRs must be complemented by other economic, social, institutional and political elements. This is necessary to contribute to promoting an effective and sustainable national innovation system.

Given the major challenges created by the globalisation process, a question arises regarding how to design a national strategy of innovation within the framework of TRIPS. In this context, the rationale and the priorities behind the policy design are vitally important. It is widely recognised that promoting innovation is an imperative for developing countries. For innovation to be successful, it is necessary to enable technology transfer. Hence, the national innovation strategy should be driven by the social dynamics of a country. This essentially requires an overall institutional design aimed at enhancing local capacities to assimilate, develop and apply new knowledge.

In this context, the concept of national innovation system (NIS) involves the set of organisations, institutions, policies and linkages that affect creation, development, commercialisation and diffusion of new technology within a national economy.[24] It requires a particular approach to adjust policies and instruments to the new paradigm for technological

---

[24] *See,* Nelson, R. and N. Rosenberg (1993) 'Technical Innovation and National Systems' in R. Nelson (ed.), *National Innovation Systems*, New York, Oxford University Press, pp. 4–5.

innovation. This involves a systematic and intensive exploitation of the available knowledge bases and a focus upon the strategies of recombination within the context of the specific realities and needs of a country.[25]

It is necessary to establish a dynamic network encompassing policies, institutions and people. This can facilitate knowledge flows across national borders and within local industries, helping to shape the innovation system in a country. In an attempt to catch up, and fill existing technological gaps, NIS serves as an efficient socio-economic platform for developing countries. Developing countries usually invest in physical assets, R&D and human capital in order to accelerate catching up. However, given the global economic conditions of today, these initiatives alone will not be sufficient to capture the benefits of local economies. The countries that are willing and able to take advantage of the knowledge economy, must engage in a technological learning process. This process must be centred on the accumulation and creation of knowledge.

The nature of an innovation system is dynamic. The institutional components of the system, that is, the laws, social rules, cultural rules, routines and habits, govern the social interactions between the innovation actors. The flow of information, resources and regulations occurs between innovation stakeholders, generating dynamism within the system itself. In other words, the actors and their linkages, that is, their interaction with each other, are vital to the system. In general, the actors are usually considered to be an integral part of the system. Hence, paying attention to merely one component or a single issue, such as the enactment of a strong IPRs regime, or an investment in physical assets is unlikely to produce significant results in terms of economic growth and prosperity.

In designing the necessary policy mechanisms and support schemes it is necessary to determine the structures and institutions that are typically involved in the innovation process. It is widely recognised that IPRs are a necessary, but not sufficient, requirement of a system. IPRs help to generate benefits, either as a direct or complementary asset, in relation to innovation and development. However, drawing from the previous discussions, the effect of IPRs appears to be destructive, unless certain social and economic thresholds have been reached. Thus, it is clear that the impact of IPRs on innovation can vary. Economists have long theorised that socio-economic factors are related to a country's ability to adapt,

---

[25] OECD, *Accessing and Expanding the Science and Technology Knowledge Base*, Paris 1994, http://www.oecd.org/pdf/M000014000/M00014640.pdf.

assimilate, and develop new knowledge and technologies, all of which play major roles in this process.[26] Chapter 4 gave a detailed analysis of contemporary economic research. This research has established the links between innovation, development and IPRs. In an effort to integrate an IPRs regime into a broader view of a national innovation system, complementary socio-economic measures were also drawn from the standpoint of innovation. These complementary measures are as follows. It is necessary to set priorities and enhance domestic innovation capabilities, serve local needs and demands, set up organisational innovation, encourage linkage of the university system to local industry, restructure public sector institutions and organisations, establish policies for the funding of R&D, and encourage foreign direct investment.

Drawing from the country and company case studies, the analysis herein seeks to build upon these previous complementary measures. The main aim of this section is to highlight the examples of horizontal measures. These measures serve not only as powerful inducers for IPRs policy, but also as contributors to efforts to maximise global competitiveness.

Fostering Local Innovation Capabilities

While developing and sustaining national innovation strategies, the focus for developing countries should be on the country's local realities, that is, the economic and social circumstances, technological capabilities, and industry profile that are present. Countries, particularly developing countries, have encountered serious difficulties in their attempts to conceptualise their own national systems. Simply replicating a system that has been successfully applied in other countries is a common failure of policymakers in developing countries. There is no 'one size fits all' method for designing a national innovation system. A country's specific advantages and disadvantages must be examined by policy makers. Countries may aim to encourage would-be-winner industries, as demonstrated by the cases of Japan and Korea. Alternatively, the priorities may be determined based on a number of other factors, such as the market demand, system linkages and the current technology base. As in the case of Israel, the government may adopt a neutral approach towards technologies and innovative activities.

---

[26]   UNIDO, (2006) 'The Role of Intellectual Property Rights in Technology Transfer and Economic Growth: Theory and Evidence', Vienna, Working Paper.

Nonetheless, government support and planning is a prerequisite for the building up of a strong pharmaceutical industry in a country. The presence of incentives facilitating the use of existing knowledge, and the dissemination of this knowledge through a variety of mechanisms is important. This will help to create new knowledge in relation to pharmaceutical innovation. The process of technology adaptation is a collective effort between the government and the pharmaceutical industry. In other words, the adaptation of foreign technology must be on a country's own terms. This requires the long lasting co-operation and commitment of government and industry.

Advancements in existing technology provide new avenues for future R&D. As a result, a great deal of attention must be paid to designing industrial policies that reflect the nature of the industry. This requires in-depth analysis of the domestic innovation system and a detailed identification of the core competences required for technological knowledge production. In an effort to enhance local innovation capabilities, government and industry must work together throughout all the phases of policy development, implementation and evaluation.

The scope of government intervention in the field of pharmaceuticals potentially covers a wide spectrum of areas including technology, industrial policy, IPRs, and financial support. Beyond the economic consequences, the national policies are usually focused on the major strategic imperatives regarding maximising competitiveness and increasing productivity. By way of illustration, the Brazilian patent regime is constructed so as to accommodate incremental learning and innovation. The pharmaceutical industry is one of the main industries subject to government intervention in Brazil.[27] In order to encourage industry and enhance R&D local capabilities, the patent regime seeks to provide an environment that encourages local industry's participation in the patent system. This incentivises local R&D in terms of secondary uses and new drug delivery methods.

Nevertheless, the adoption of a successful policy approach necessarily requires the active involvement of the local industry. The vast lobbying power of the industry, coupled with the industry's legal and technical expertise, must be taken into account in relation to institutional capacity building. The most prominent example of this kind of industry intervention in institutional policy making can be seen with the example of Teva

---

[27]   Four industries have been identified as strategic to Brazil's economic development: semiconductors, software, capital goods, pharmaceutical products and medications. *See,* Industrial, Technological and Foreign Trade Policy (PITCE) of 2003.

in Israel. Recalling the previous chapter on the company case study of Teva and its distinctive trajectories, it may be concluded that consultative involvement of the company in policymaking process has the potential to improve the patent regime, ensuring that it is industry-centred and economically sustainable.

Throughout the history of pharmaceutical innovation, the active participation and intervention of the pharmaceutical industry in the policymaking process has been key to the development of a strong pharmaceutical industry in a country. For instance, the German dye industry intervened to influence patent regulation in Germany. In Britain, the chemical industry pressurised the government to set priorities for the local production and take measures against unfair trade practices of German dye companies. Since the antibiotic revolution, the American pharmaceutical companies have been actively involved in policymaking processes, both at a national and an international level. Before the Japanese patent law was enacted, the Japanese government conducted an industry survey in order to determine whether a strong patent regime was in the interest of the pharmaceutical industry. The Japanese patent law was amended only when the industry supported the introduction of product patents for pharmaceuticals.

New policy rules and instruments on innovation and sustainability, particularly on IPRs, usually establish a framework that is potentially conducive to development. Thus, any engagement effort that seeks to establish intensive interaction with all stakeholders, either industry or university, is very likely to lead to an increased focus on priority setting for local innovation. An extensive institutional interaction between the local industry and the government appears to be essential for enhancing local capabilities and encouraging the support of local innovation.

Responding to Local Needs and Demands

The innovation policy in a country must be linked with the economic realities and local R&D capabilities of the country. Additionally, local needs and demands must be considered when formulating strategies aimed at driving innovation in the country. These innovation initiatives, distributed widely across the whole spectrum of R&D activities among public and private agencies, ought to be consistent with local market characteristics.

There are many lessons that could be drawn from the German dyestuff industry. The German companies were the first companies to respond to customer demand. German companies carefully studied the market conditions and established close relationships with their customers in order to learn about new market opportunities.[28]

Innovation in developing countries usually describes the reverse-engineering process. This involves the transfer, usage and adaption of technology developed abroad. Therefore, developing countries are frequently associated with imitative, adaptive technology. Nevertheless, the adaptive nature of technology in these countries gives rise to a greater degree of invent-around technology. Rather than inventing through new inventive technologies, and producing cutting-edge products, inventors in developing countries tend to pursue a customer-pull approach to product development. This kind of approach reacts to the voice of the customer. It tries to solve customer dilemmas without relying on novel science the innovation process is designed around customer needs and demands.[29]

The whole process of pharmaceutical manufacturing in developing countries is based on the generic drug business model. The absence of patent protection in developing countries for a substantial period of time has facilitated the transfer and usage of technology developed abroad. These countries were able to build up excellent facilities and establish strong alliances in the drug manufacturing industry. These countries developed their skills in relation to reverse engineering. The generic companies in India, Brazil, and China had already become regionally, and even globally, competitive in the area of generic drug production. Most of these countries have now completed the imitation phase.

The capabilities and skills developed in the area of reverse engineering, coupled with the adaptive nature of technology, have led to the implementation of local solutions to local customer needs. The generic drug companies have started to modify and improve technologies in order to suit domestic demands. Rather than simply manufacturing copycat drugs, companies have started to consider cost-effective alternative treatments. Indian generic companies, for instance, have achieved self-sufficiency in drug production, and engaged in R&D activities in order to respond to local market needs. Cipla, an Indian generic company, released its own triple combination AIDS drug in 2001. It contained the

---

[28]   Mowery, D. (2010) 'IPR and US Economic Catch-up' in H. Odagiri, A. Goto, A. Sunami and R. Nelson (eds) *Intellectual Property Rights, Development and Catch-up*, New York, Oxford University Press, p. 47.

[29]   Sull, D., A.R. Ruelas-Gossi and M. Escobari (2004) 'What Developing-World Companies Teach Us about Innovation', Harvard Business School, Working Knowledge, available at http://hbswk.hbs.edu/item/3866.html.

separate antiretroviral drugs Stavudine,[30] Lamivudine[31] and Nevirapine.[32] Cipla's radically lower-priced and lower-dosed product Triomune was launched as a cocktail tablet to be taken twice a day. While the alternative AIDS cocktails, that is, combinations of drugs, were costing around $10 000–$15 000 a year per patient in the US or Europe, Triomune was selling only at $600 per year.[33] Cipla strategically and successfully exploited the national circumstances in order to respond to the demand of local users in the healthcare system. At that time, pharmaceutical products were exempted from patent protection in India. Thus, Cipla was able to work on and re-engineer three separately patented drugs. The very existence of Triomune is jointly due to the flexible patent regime in the country and the reverse-engineering skill base that existed within the company. Nevertheless, the success of Triomune should not be degraded as a mere case of reverse engineering. Its innovative potential cannot be ignored. This proves that Cipla, and Indian generic companies more generally, are capable of producing drugs for local users within the healthcare system. Their efforts at inducing research focused on domestic healthcare problems, coupled with the enactment of sound R&D policies and incentives, are having a significant impact on the future of pharmaceutical innovation in India. This kind of strategy can also be illustrated by the Korean case of the Hepatitis B vaccine. In the 1980s, Hepatitis B became a major health problem in Korea. This generated a great deal of interest in developing a Hepatitis B vaccine. Thus, the Korean government assured companies that there was an initial market for the vaccine. Hence, Korean companies engaged in higher domestic R&D activates in response to local demand. Less than a decade later, companies were able to launch their own vaccines.

Focusing on domestic healthcare needs is a R&D strategy that has proven to be highly effective for developing countries. In fact, today, 85 per cent world's population live in emerging markets. This makes emerging markets and specific medical needs of patients living in these

---

[30] The fourth antiretroviral drug on the market, originally patented to Bristol-Myers Squibb. The US patent expired in 2008.
[31] The fifth antiretroviral drug on the market, originally patented to GSK. The US patent is due to expire in 2010.
[32] Nevirapine was the first non-nucleoside reverse transcriptase inhibitor approved by the US Food and Drug Administration, originally patented to Boerhinger Ingelheim.
[33] *See,* Ramani, S. and V. Mukherjee (2010) 'CSR and Market Changing Product Innovations: Indian Case Studies', UNU-MERIT Working Paper, 2010–026, pp. 13–14.

regions quite attractive for multinational pharmaceutical companies. Lately, pharmaceutical companies have been investing in local R&D to discover and develop medicines specifically to treat local diseases in these regions. AstraZeneca, for instance, launched the Asia Oncology Strategic Alliance aimed at evaluating novel treatments for stomach and liver cancers. As a part of local regional development programme, GlaxoSmithKline is seeking R&D partnership opportunities to develop a product specifically for the medical needs of emerging markets.[34]

There is also a lack of effective treatments and drugs for any disease that disproportionately affects the poor. Supporting this view, a study in 2002 found that over the period between 1975 and 1999, out of 1393 new chemical entities marketed, only 16 were for tropical diseases and tuberculosis.[35] Thus, developing and sustaining R&D strategies for the treatments of the diseases that particularly affect the developing world is likely to provide a return over the long term, regardless of market conditions.

It is also vital for countries to address target diseases. This strategy has proven to be successful in creating a competitive advantage for Israeli pharmaceutical companies, and Teva in particular. The case study of Teva and its distinctive trajectories reveals that there is a lack of adequate medicines for certain diseases, in particular Alzheimer or Parkinson's. This presents a major opportunity for upcoming companies to develop innovative medicines. Apart from Israel and Teva, Indian generic companies are also building up a portfolio of novel medicines for target diseases.[36]

Nevertheless, it should be borne in mind that the concept of innovation is based upon a complex structure of interactions between various organisations and institutions. A strategic planning system that anticipates and responds to the changing needs of the market must combine different elements. Furthermore, pharmaceutical companies constitute only one element of the pharmaceutical innovation process. A well-functioning system depends on interaction between actors. Hence, university-industry linkages are critically important. Furthermore, the particular focus of

---

[34]   *See,* 'Evolving R&D for Emerging Markets', *News and Analysis, Nature Reviews: Drug Discovery,* V.9, June 2010, pp. 417–20.

[35]   Trouiller, P. et al. (2002) 'Drug Development for Neglected Diseases: A Deficient Market and a Public-Health Policy Failure', *Lancet,* V.359, 9324, pp. 2188–94.

[36]   *See,* Sharma, N.L and S. Goswami (2009) 'The Nuances of Knowledge Creation and Development in the Indian Pharmaceutical Industry', *Journal of Knowledge Management,* V.13 N.5, p. 320.

research that companies wish to undertake must match the research base of the university system in the country.

University–Industry Collaboration

A growing body of empirical research appears to support the view that innovation increasingly stems from institutional spheres outside of corporate firms. Innovation today largely comes from research at universities. Thus, lateral relationships across boundaries become crucial.[37]

In the early part of the last century, the success of the German dye industry was partly due to the strong collaboration that had established with major German research institutes. The German universities helped the German companies to develop a better understanding of the formation of dye molecules. Moreover, the university system in Germany had a scientific focus. This provided essential training for chemists who populated the German firms' R&D laboratories.

Taking inspiration from the German university structure, Johns Hopkins University, the first US research university, was founded in 1876. In a very short period of time it began to show success in collaborating with industry.[38] In the period following World War II, the US government extensively funded scientific research at universities. The antibiotic revolution, which changed the course of medicine, began with the discovery of penicillin. However, an expanding body of scientific knowledge on antibiotics was developed later through the collaboration of university, industry and government. Thus, the American pharmaceutical industry emerged as the world leader in the pharmaceutical market partly because of the excellence in in-house R&D, but mainly because of the strong linkages established with the university sector.

On the other hand, although British scientists had invented penicillin, the reluctance of British pharmaceutical companies to collaborate with British universities was the main reason why the penicillin was taken to the US. Long after the discovery of penicillin, Ernst Chain, who shared the Nobel Prize in 1945 with Fleming and Florey, detailed the painful story of penicillin. He focused particularly on the fact that British industry missed a golden opportunity. He stated that British industry

---

[37] Etzkowitz, H.: 'The Triple Helix of University–Industry–Government Implications for Policy and Evaluation', Working Paper 2002–11, Science Policy Institute, p. 1.

[38] Mowery, supra note 28, p. 35.

could only survive in future through closer collaboration between academic and industrial research laboratories.[39] After missing the opportunity to commercialise penicillin, it took a while for British industry to realise the importance of university–industry collaboration. As a slow starter, the British industry became competitive in the international pharmaceutical market only in the late 1980s.[40]

Hence, universities play an increasingly important role in innovation and socio-economic development. In general, some conclusions and key practices can be drawn from the case studies given in this book. First of all, it is evident that university–public research advances industrial innovation significantly, and directly advances pharmaceuticals. This results in an increasing level of R&D intensity and productivity.

Basic university research is a necessary precondition for the development of a country's ability to absorb and assess scientific knowledge and to apply it to advanced technology. Scientific knowledge is a basic part of technologic development in the life sciences. This involves a 'trial and error and experimentation without a clear prior understanding of how and why the drugs should work'.[41] By way of illustration, in 1997, Cockburn and Henderson investigated the development history of 21 drugs with the greatest therapeutic impact over the period between 1965 and 1992. The study revealed that only five, that is, 24 per cent of the drugs were essentially developed without any input from the public sector. The findings led the authors to the conjecture that, over time, public sector research has become more important than private sector research.[42] In fact, available evidence collected from the case studies supports the view that most drugs are discovered, and the best research results are obtained, in a collaborative environment.

Knowledge flows and technological diffusion within the pharmaceutical industry strongly suggests that the financial support of basic scientific research should remain under government responsibility.

---

[39]   Palombi, L. (2009) *Gene Cartels, Biotech Patents in the Age of Free Trade*, Cheltenham, UK and Northampton, MA, USA, Edward Edgar, p. 115.

[40]   Only by the late 1980s had the British pharmaceutical sector managed to increase their share of the world market to level behind the US. *See,* Dutfield, G. (2003) *Intellectual Property Rights and the Life Science Industries*, Dartmouth, Ashgate, p. 105.

[41]   Balconi, M., B. Stefano and L. Orsenigo (2008) 'In Defence of the Linear Model: An Essay', KITeS, Working Paper 216, p. 24

[42]   Cockburn, I., R. Henderson, L. Orsenigo and G. Pisano (1999) 'Pharmaceuticals and Biotechnology' in D. Mowery (ed.) *US Industry in 2000: Studies in Competitive Performance*, Washington, National Academy, pp. 369–71

Encouraging university research through public policies aimed at fostering university-industry linkages is an ambitious, but realistic, innovation policy initiative for developing countries.

On the other hand, taking university research out of the laboratory and turning the basic research into a drug is a more complex exercise. This typically entails a mechanism that diffuses basic university research into commercial activities. From the earlier discussions, it is clear that invention typically refers to a technical idea that can lead to new products or that can be used to solve an industrial problem. Notwithstanding this, innovation refers to a distinct economic process. This process of innovation describes the journey of a mere invention to a commercialised product. This sharp distinction between invention and innovation can also be applied to university research. Research conducted by universities largely represents the concept of invention. Nevertheless, not all inventions can be turned into an innovative product. The notion of innovation is clearly much broader than participation in basic research. In this context, innovation can be described as an act of transferring this technology from the laboratory to land. The story of penicillin presents anecdotal evidence in support of this argument. Penicillin, which was discovered by Fleming, is widely regarded one of the greatest inventions of the last century. However, it later became an innovation that changed the course of medicine. This occurred partly because of the actions of the US government and the US pharmaceutical companies, but it occurred mainly because of the actions of Florey. Florey's enthusiasm transformed the speculative experiment of penicillin into a research programme. The majority of the drugs marketed today are invented in university laboratories. Nevertheless, these drugs reached their therapeutic potential because the technology was successfully transferred from the laboratory to land. At present, it is not possible to observe comparable individual innovators such as Florey. Instead, it is the pharmaceutical industry that facilitates the commercialisation of university research.

In this equation, where the university is the inventor and industry is the innovator, it is the government that ultimately takes the responsibility regarding policy making. This is necessary in order to establish interactive linkages, knowledge flows and technological diffusion among public and private sectors. This so-called triple helix model of innovation aims to enhance the synergy between university and industry, to diffuse basic university research into a commercial activity and thus, to stimulate knowledge-based economic development.[43]

---

[43] Etzkowitz, supra note 37.

The introduction of the Bayh-Dole Act of 1980, provided incentives for universities, faculty investors, and private industry in order to engage in the commercialisation process. This act is widely regarded as an example of good practice. It ensures co-operation between government, industry, and academia. Although the act had a significant and beneficial impact on the encouragement of innovative behaviour, it had serious deficiencies in the sense that it promoted closeness in the sharing of scientific discovery. Furthermore it placed a greater emphasis on applied research rather than basic research. Nevertheless, the Bayh Dole Act is a strong societal statement in favour of university–industry collaboration.

It is a well-established fact that the future of the pharmaceutical industry lies in the area of biotechnology. The biotechnological revolution in drug development empowered university research via the innovation process. This led to the emergence of a dense network of collaborative relationships between university start-up companies and the multinational pharmaceutical companies. It is evident that a process of innovation in drug development does not follow a linear path. Hence, a single firm is not able to develop all the requisite ingredients in order to bring a biotech product to the marketplace. A higher-degree of government involvement is required in order to develop and sustain innovation strategies based on biotechnology. Consequently, a triple helix nexus becomes a strong basis for policy initiatives building biotechnology clusters.

In an effort to promote university–industry linkage, a growing number of policy initiatives are being undertaken by developing countries. In reality, research has always been an integral part of university activities. Not only European or American universities, but universities all around the world are currently conducting scientific research that focuses on the most important frontiers of biotechnology. No matter whether it is Boston, Accra, Istanbul or Delhi, universities everywhere are capable of creating, discovering and inventing. Invention can be achieved in any university research laboratory. Nevertheless, taking this research out of laboratory and putting the scientific findings to practical use in the form of the provision of a commercially viable drug is a real challenge, particularly for developing countries. University policies and practices in such countries do not necessarily encourage such acts of collaboration. The organisational structure of universities in developing countries is typically cumbersome. This must be changed in order for developing countries to respond effectively to the needs of the industry. In most cases industry is not fully aware of academic research and, therefore, the new inventions emerging from university laboratories. Moreover, most of the industries are still sceptical about the benefits of academic research.

Companies tend to see the potential of expanding academic scientific research in their home countries as an unrealistic and utopian goal. The reluctance of industry leads to a lack of technological diffusion between university and industry. This creates circumstances where inventions stay in research laboratories and innovation opportunities are completely missed.

Thus, the governments of developing countries must enact creative policies aimed at enhancing the synergy between university and industry. Indeed, a well-functioning system largely depends on the existence of a balanced legal and institutional framework, which is accompanied by certain safeguards. This entails priority setting and careful assessment of the university system. It also requires an in-depth analysis of academic culture and structures, including the encouragement of entrepreneurial attitudes. Despite all the difficulties in developing countries, the opportunity still exists to create a collaborative environment that can foster and enrich links and resources.

Reforming Public Sector Organisations and Institutions

A knowledge-based innovation system involves complex interaction between various stakeholders. The high level of interaction between these stakeholders is usually enhanced by the use of intermediating institutions. These institutional and policy contexts determine how actors and organisations behave throughout the innovation process. The public actors involved in research and innovation activities take on a role, which is particularly important for knowledge generation, local capacity building and the absorption and efficient use of technology. Thus, the systematic differences, the habits, the practices and the mindsets of the public actors can often play a central role in the overall innovation process.

The public sector organisations in developing countries are usually characterised by political weaknesses, systematic differences and long-running bureaucratic disputes. The vast number of public organisations, coupled with the lack of communication between these organisations, usually erodes effective implementation of innovation strategies. Hence, successful innovation systems must give priority to the reform of the public sector.

Conceptually, these reforms involve the establishment of independent organisations with an innovation remit. However, it is very difficult to provide an optimal set of measures for restructuring the public sector. Once again, it must be stated that there is no 'one size fits all' approach. A practice that has proven to be successful in one country may not necessarily be optimal for another country.

Hence, first and foremost, country variables must be identified in order to encourage sustainable reforms in the public sector. Country variables include priorities, local realities, cultural attitudes, habits and mindsets. The next step is to replace a planning approach with a learning approach. Knowledge-based innovation systems typically involve a complex learning process from top to bottom. In an effort to recalibrate the habits, practices and cultural attitudes, the learning process must be enhanced in each stage of the innovation cycle. By way of illustration, a fine tuned IPRs system, which takes account of TRIPS flexibilities, is a prerequisite for pharmaceutical innovation in a country. It is a widely known fact that most developing countries lack the legal and technical competencies to take full benefit of these flexibilities. TRIPS put developed countries under an obligation to provide technical assistance to least-developed country members of the WTO. Nevertheless, the current experience proves that such kinds of assistance have only been provided in a partial way. Most assistance has been aimed at promoting strong IPRs regimes and the surpassing of TRIPS flexibilities. While the implementation of the TRIPS flexibilities has started to receive increasing attention from NGOs and international organisations, developing countries are still unable to establish the correct balance between public interest and innovation. To this end, the conventional wisdom suggests that avoiding general myths about IPRs, recalibrating the mindsets of the public sector towards IPRs, and adopting an approach based on learning are the three most effective strategies for improving the understanding of the global IPRs regime within developing countries. This reforming approach is likely to speed up the pace of the innovation process in the country. It should also be adopted while reformulating university–industry relationships, setting priorities or goals, and enhancing local innovation capabilities.

The existing public sector structures present in developing countries involve the interaction of numerous organisations. These organisations deal with various aspects of industrial policy and innovation. However, they lack the institutional capacity to undertake effective innovation functions. The lack of technical and managerial competencies, coupled with the absence of system linkages between these institutions and private agencies, has become a major impediment to innovation reforms. A well-functioning system depends on institutional and organisational flexibility. Hence, independent organisations must anticipate and respond to the needs of all stakeholders. This becomes vital for developing and sustaining innovation strategies. In Israel, for instance, the Office of Chief Scientist executes government policies for supporting industrial R&D. In Korea, in an effort to restructure the public sector, the Office of

Science and Technology Innovation was established to build momentum in innovation.

Once again, the notion of innovation is much broader than merely R&D. Innovation involves a complex and dynamic interplay between stakeholders, institutions and policies. The complexity of the system requires the increased competency of the public sector. Hence, the adoption of a more strategic approach is a prerequisite for the reformed public sector.

The Government Funding of Innovation

The existence of global patent standards and the introduction of patent protection for pharmaceuticals are very likely to cause short-term wealth losses for the local pharmaceutical industry. The impact of strong IPRs standards on wealth and industrial growth in a large part depends upon the industry structures, technological capabilities and the intensity of R&D rates. In the short term, the industry faces losses. Losses usually occur in terms of price increases, loss of revenues, decreases in profits and so on. The use of extensive government intervention becomes crucial at this stage for the financial recovery of the industry.

It must be noted that the local pharmaceutical industries in developing countries are still incapable of developing globally competitive drugs. Making the leap from the generic area to the innovative area requires a clear strategy. It also requires the financial and economic resources necessary to put the strategy into practice. The encouragement of drug development requires a long-term strategy. It also usually requires better utilisation of financial mechanisms. Hence, market intervention becomes evident in order to improve an industry's access to financial resources. This can be achieved through direct or indirect funding of the industry or through the provision of credit enhancements and tax incentives. The Korean government, for instance, played a critical role in the development of the Hepatitis B vaccine in Korea. Initially, the government created an attractive domestic market for the industry. Moreover, the government provided funds to Korean companies to build their own factories. Similarly, the Israeli government provided tax exemptions to Teva in exchange for investment in the less developed areas in Israel.

Alternatively, governments can adopt mechanisms for funding research. The range of funding instruments capable of supporting the R&D and innovation process can be incorporated within the national innovation policies. These can exist in the form of R&D programmes, such as incubation programmes or R&D funds. The development of such programmes may significantly impact upon the efficiency and effectiveness of innovation rates. These programmes also contribute to the technological infrastructure of the country. In Israel, for example, a well-functioning innovation system increasingly depends upon the existence of an R&D support system. This can be applied to all phases of innovation, from R&D planning to the commercialisation of the product.

The Chinese government launched the 'New Drug Creation and Development Program' in 2008 within the framework of China's 11th five-year plan for the pharmaceutical and biotechnology industry,[44] to promote local R&D and to own the IPRs of newly developed drugs. The initiative provides funding for collaborative research between academia and the local pharmaceutical industry. Several strategic alliances have been established between the Shanghai Institute of Materia Medica and the Chinese pharmaceutical companies, that is, Jiangsu Hengrui Medicine Company and Shiyao Pharmaceutical Group for innovative drug discovery.[45]

Due to the changing nature of pharmaceutical innovation, small and medium sized enterprises (SMEs) have become increasingly critical for the innovation process, particularly in relation to pharmaceuticals. In the past, the whole process of innovation was conducted by big multinational companies. Nevertheless, the biotechnological revolution in drug development has changed the patterns of innovation. Now, SMEs contribute greatly and actively to the innovation process. Today, most inventions, particularly in the biotechnology area, come from SMEs. Thus, R&D support mechanisms must be primarily tailored towards SMEs or start-ups, that is, business incubators. This is critical for fostering linkages and enhancing knowledge diffusion between public and private sectors.

Public investment aimed towards developing and sustaining innovation strategies must be centred on the establishment of an environment favourable to business creativity and private sector R&D. This support comes in the form of integrated packages that apply to all levels. This potentially involves a wide range of investments, not only in R&D.

Foreign Direct Investment

In the previous chapters, it was stated that foreign direct investment (FDI) and innovation are positively correlated. FDI may contribute to the

---

[44]   The need for the growth of local innovative R&D, specifically with regard to owning the IPRs of newly developed drugs has been emphasised in this plan.

[45]   *See,* 'China Spurs Pharma Innovation', *News and Analysis, Nature Reviews: Drug Discovery,* V.9, 2010, pp. 581–82.

innovation process in developing countries in several ways. FDI can create more sophisticated technology generation, lead to increases innovation outputs, facilitate knowledge transfer, increase local innovation capacity, and provide greater efficiency in the innovation process.

The pharmaceutical industry is an R&D intensive industry. It involves several stages of basic, applied and clinical research. The innovation process is usually described as a complex, costly and time-consuming activity. Given the tremendous costs and the long time scale associated with bringing a new product to market, a peculiar importance is attributed to IPRs. Patents are unusually strong in relation to pharmaceuticals in comparison with other industries. Hence, IPRs protection has a strong deterring effect on the FDI decisions of pharmaceutical companies.

The range of FDI activities of multinational companies differs from country to country. The FDI flows within the pharmaceutical industry are usually focused on cross-border merger and acquisition activities. In fact several studies have revealed that merger and acquisition activity has dominated the FDI flows in recent years.[46] The main motivations of the FDI activities of multinational companies concern sales, distribution and manufacturing. The multinationals invest in developing countries in order to utilise the market and trading potential of the country, and to open up new distribution channels. The geo-political situation of the country is taken into account, that is, its trade and investment policies, its currency advantages and the availability of cheap infrastructure.

Baskaran and Muchie identified ten major components within the concept of a well-positioned national innovation system that influence the nature and shape of investment decisions in R&D. These components are as follows: the presence of a stable investment climate; the presence of a stable economic structure; the availability of scientific and engineering skills; the presence of a good education system; the presence of R&D performing institutions; the presence of institutions doing a high level of basic research and publications; the presence of strong links between knowledge institutions and production enterprises; the presence of a strong IPRs regime; the presence of dynamic science parks; the presence

[46] UNCTAD, (1998) World Investment Report, Geneva; OECD, (2006) International Investment Perspectives, Paris; Lippoldt, D. (2006) 'Intellectual Property Rights, Pharmaceuticals and Foreign Direct Investment', Groupe d'Economie Mondiale de Sciences Policy Brief, available at www.gem.sciences-po.fr/.../lippoldt_IPRs_Pharma_FDI1106.pdf.

of a diverse range of firms and institutions; and the presence of a diversified industrial structure.[47]

In theory, the presence of all these components, or most of them, in a country's national innovation system suffices to make the country attractive for FDI in R&D. It is argued that such a country is likely to enjoy a high level of FDI at both the medium- and higher-level of technological and innovation complexity.[48]

Recent evidence suggests that the foreign R&D investments of multinational pharmaceutical companies are limited to 35–40 per cent of their R&D activities.[49] A large proportion of R&D activities in the pharmaceutical industry are still taking place in developed countries. Nevertheless, China and India are also receiving a significant proportion of investment in this area.

Interestingly, China, India and Brazil are the countries that currently have the highest proportion of overall annual FDI inflow in R&D. Nevertheless, when it comes to pharmaceuticals, the level of FDI in Brazil is significantly lower than in China and India. This is despite the fact that Brazil possesses a high level of local capabilities in the pharmaceutical industry.[50]

This is an interesting finding in terms of pharmaceutical innovation, IPRs and developing countries. During the TRIPS negotiations, the developing countries were promised an increased level of FDI in high-tech areas such as pharmaceuticals. Brazil implemented TRIPS in 1999, long before China and India did. Moreover, most of the FDI determinants are present in Brazil, in addition to the high-level of local capabilities present in the country. Nevertheless, the level of FDI in pharmaceutical R&D is much lower than in China and India.

Thus, the previous findings indicate that the FDI decisions of multinational pharmaceutical companies increasingly depend upon factors other than the presence of an IPRs regime or the level of local capabilities. Clearly, China and India have been major recipients of global FDI. Certain factors associated with location, cost, specialised resources and skills may have contributed to make these countries the winners of the game.

---

[47]   Baskaran, A. and M. Muchie (2008) 'Foreign Direct Investment and Internationalization of R&D: The Case of BRICS Economics', Diiper Research Series Working Paper, N.7, pp. 6–7.

[48]   *Ibid,* p. 7.

[49]   UNCTAD, (2005) World Investment Report, Geneva.

[50]   Baskaran et al., supra note 47, p. 17.

Notwithstanding the high level of FDI for pharmaceutical R&D in these countries, China and India were successful in developing wide-ranging capabilities in the complex field of drug development. For instance, Roche established a research centre in China in 2004 to improve global research prospects on medicinal chemistry. Another multinational pharmaceutical company Sanofi–Aventis has also established a strategic research agreement with the Shanghai Institutes for Biological Sciences. The Chinese government increased the amount of funds transferred to public research in order to attract multinational pharmaceutical companies to participate in collaborations with Chinese academic institutions.[51] On the other hand, India is one of the few countries which has achieved self-sufficiency in relation to drugs manufacture, with production capacity covering over 70 per cent of the bulk drugs and 80 per cent of the formulations. Moreover, some Indian pharmaceutical companies have established partnerships or have been co-operating with large pharmaceutical companies in terms of providing API, contract manufacturing for already existing drugs or research candidates, clinical out-sourcing and research partnerships.[52] By way of illustration, an alliance has been established between Dr Reddy's Laboratories and GSK to develop generic drugs. According to the deal, Dr Reddy's undertakes the pharmaceutical development of the drug until the last phase, the human equivalence studies, and GSK does the clinical studies. In other words, each party of the deal does what they do best.[53]

Taken as a whole, the empirical evidence highlights the fact that there is an ambiguous relationship between FDI and pharmaceutical innovation in developing countries. Even for countries such as Brazil, which have more to offer rather than a relatively strong IPRs regime, the FDI flow in relation to R&D has been a trickle rather than a stream. Nevertheless, there is a multiplicity of possibilities ahead for boosting local innovation capacity in the country. More importantly, under certain circumstances, a lack of FDI increases the bargaining power of the country in terms of IPRs protection and the use of TRIPS flexibilities. Brazil issued compulsory licences in 2007 against Merck. Since this time Brazil has been using compulsory licences as part of a hard-line negotiation strategy with originator companies. The local capabilities in the area of generic drugs

---

[51] *See,* supra note 44.

[52] Grace, C. (2004) 'The Effect of Changing Intellectual Property on Pharmaceutical Industry Prospects in India and China: Considerations for Access to Medicines', DFID Health Systems Resource Centre, pp. 23–4.

[53] Ramani, S. and V. Mukherjee (2010) 'CSR and Market Changing Product Innovations: Indian Case Studies', UNU-MERIT Working Paper, 2010–026.

manufacturing and the domestic market power has provided Brazil with a greater flexibility in addressing public health problems. As it turns out, the lack of substantial pharmaceutical FDI in the country prevents any sanctions that pharmaceutical companies may invoke, that is, reduced FDI, reduced technology transfer and local R&D from being applied.[54]

Even though a significant share of FDI, particularly in pharmaceutical R&D, has been channelled to China and India, developing countries may still be able take advantage of future FDI. Contractual mechanisms can be established between local industry and multinational pharmaceutical companies to enable technology transfer. These mechanisms include, but are not limited to, licensing, joint and co-operative R&D agreements, and joint ventures and research consortiums. These initiatives could put developing countries in an advantageous position in terms of acquiring frontier technologies. Thus, this will enable a stage-skipping catch up process for the local industry, rather than a path-following one. Instead of reinventing the wheel or going down the conventional path, they may jump directly to latest technology in order to keep up with developments.

The case of the Korean innovative vaccines illustrates this kind of collaboration very clearly. Like the Korean pharmaceutical companies, local companies in developing countries may collaborate with innovative pharmaceutical companies on projects dealing with local health problems. This may improve their ability to combine local knowledge with global knowledge and frontier technology.

The quality of international collaborations and partnerships between companies is crucial in order to determine the extent that FDI actually contributes to local innovation. Greater international collaboration may well reduce the technology and capacity gap between local and foreign industries. To this end, governments may consider creating attractive domestic markets for foreign companies. This requires a number of structural policy changes in many areas, from improving the research capacities of a country, to ensuring that NIS is attractive to foreign investors.

CONCLUDING REMARKS

The country and company case studies of this book have provided a number of insights regarding patent regimes, or IPRs more broadly, in relation to local pharmaceutical industries and innovation strategies. This

---

[54] For more information *see* Benoliel, D. and B.M. Salama (2009) 'Towards an Intellectual Property Bargaining Theory: The Post-WTO Era' available at http://www.escholarship.org/uc/item/4c03k7v7.

chapter has identified the common threads that exist across these country studies. These are categorised as real-life lessons. The real-life lessons are presented as observations from different countries, illustrated considerations and policy implications. The overall aim is not to reproduce a best model or a recipe, but rather to identify the main determinants of a policy aimed at restructuring and boosting the local pharmaceutical innovation capacities of developing countries.

To this end, a finely tuned IPRs system must match the development needs of the country. It must establish a balance between patent protection and local innovation. This is the first and foremost lesson that can be drawn from the experiences of other countries. The findings herein strongly suggest that there is a non-linear relationship between IPRs and economic development. As a country moves away from a position of borrower to a position of innovator, the IPRs regime becomes significant. Although the global patent rules today does not provide generous flexibilities to modify the IPRs regime as in the past, it is arguable that with the appropriate and right policies in place, developing countries will be able to succeed in drug development.

Nevertheless, the IPRs system alone is nothing more than a set of rules unless it is embedded in a setting. This setting must integrate social, legal, economic, political, and technological considerations into a national system of innovation. NIS effectively determines the local extent of technological innovation. The concept of national innovation describes a dynamic network of organisations, institutions, and policies. These linkages affect the creation, development, commercialisation and diffusion of new technology within a national economy and facilitate technology diffusion and knowledge flows across national borders as well as within local industries. More importantly, NIS serves as an efficient socioeconomic platform for catching up, because the system fills the existing technological gaps and thus, enhances the local innovation capacities.

The integration of the IPRs regime into a broader view of a national innovation system entails the enactment of complementary socioeconomic measures. These measures are identified in Chapter 5. In this chapter, these measures were combined with country and company case studies in an effort to assess their impact on the pharmaceutical innovation process. Nevertheless, what is provided herein are some, but not all, of the pieces of the innovation puzzle. The degree to which each piece is applicable in a particular developing country strictly depends upon the particular social, economic, technological, and institutional variables of that country. Of course, it also depends upon the willingness of policymakers to take the appropriate steps towards developing a sound innovation system.

The research findings herein illustrate the fact that the innovation system potentially creates an intriguing puzzle for developing countries. Within this puzzle, some pieces are harder to put together. The sizes of the different institutions, policies, relationships and potential synergies that exist between all the stakeholders necessarily vary across countries. Thus, some pieces may not initially fit easily into the overall picture. Certainly, there is still much to learn about the missing pieces of the innovation puzzle in developing countries.

Fortunately, public awareness of the importance of NIS continues to increase within developing countries. This will potentially lead to further recognition of the IPRs systems as a vital, but merely one, component of this innovation system.

MOMENT OF TRUTH

The literature on the global IPRs regime is wide and various, and steadily growing. Over the years there have been a significant number of books and articles devoted to TRIPS, its origin, background, content as well as its implementation process. Much has been written and discussed about the impact of TRIPS on developing countries, particularly on the local pharmaceutical industry. Policy options and best practice models have been presented for the developing countries. Consequently, developing countries are well advised to implement TRIPS in an effort to promote innovation and technological development in the country.

In recent years, innovation, development and sustainability have become central in wider attempts to conceptualise and analyse the patent system. Although the patents system has primarily developed to promote economic ends, economists have long relinquished the field. For a while, patent lawyers were glad to see them go, nevertheless, the post-TRIPS experiences of the developing countries showed that strengthened patent rights, or IPRs more broadly, does not bring economic development and innovation in its own. Their impact in a large part depends on the competitive nature of the economy. They do, however, support the flow of knowledge and innovation in the country and contribute to the national innovation system.

As it turns out, economists are coming back into the picture and economic arguments have been dominating the IPRs discussions. Recent developments in the field of IPRs have led to a renewed interest in law, economics and innovation. The conventional wisdom suggests that IPRs regime is but one component of the national innovation system. More-over, the evidence is emerging that unless it is well supported by appropriate complementary socio-economic essentials, an IPRs regime is unlikely to support innovation and development in a country.

On the other hand, legal scholars still tend to ignore economic and social aspects of the issue and usually focus on legal issues surrounding the IPRs. Alas there is a lack of reception of IPRs rights and their relation to innovation theory. Nevertheless, it is becoming increasingly difficult to ignore these economic and social structures that shape the innovation process. The current state of the discussion on the topic proves that legal scholars still have much to learn from economists.

In an effort to incorporate economics and social policy into IPRs law, this book combined socio-cultural, legal, economic, political and technological factor analysis. The primary aim was to improve holistic understanding of the concept of innovation and assess IPRs as part of a national innovation system. Building upon previous findings and discussions, it then highlighted examples of innovation strategies and policies in terms of patents, innovation and local pharmaceutical industry. The case studies of the countries and companies throughout the book presented real-life observations on how the respective structural and institutional characteristics of the countries affected the process and outcome of pharmaceutical innovation practices.

In an effort to boost local pharmaceutical innovation, the previous discussions of some of the practical considerations and policy implications aim to provide some guidance for developing countries. It should be noted that the real life lessons learned from the country and company case studies provide no indication of a 'one size fits all' model to be followed or a magical recipe for boosting innovation in local industry. Nevertheless, they present valid aspirations for countries and they may eventually be incorporated into the country models of innovation.

Subsequently, one of the more significant findings to emerge from this study is that there is a constant need for new models or recipes that are locally created. Although very important principles and implications emerge from the research findings, the application of the former in developing countries strictly depends on the legal, political, economic, socio-cultural and technological conditions of each country.

Thomas Edison had once defined innovation as 'one per cent inspiration and ninety-nine per cent perspiration'. Considerably more work still needs to be done to determine the country recipes for boosting local pharmaceutical innovation. Nonetheless, the power of that one per cent should not be underestimated in efforts to move forward.

Bibliography

BOOKS

Andersen, B. (2006) *Intellectual Property Rights, Innovation, Governance and the Institutional Environment*, Cheltenham, UK and Northampton, MA, USA: Edward Elgar.

Angell, M. (2005) *The Truth about the Drug Companies: How They Deceive Us and What to do about It*, New York: Random House.

Arup, C. and W. van Caenegem (2009) *Intellectual Property Policy Reform, Fostering Innovation and Development*, Cheltenham, UK and Northampton, MA, USA: Edward Elgar.

Aubert, J.E. (2004) *Promoting Innovation in Developing Countries: A Conceptual Framework*, Washington DC: World Bank Institute.

Baumol, W. (2002) *The Free-Market Innovation Machine*, Princeton, NJ: Princeton University Press.

Beer, J.J. (1959) *The Emergence of the German Dye Industry*, Urbana, IL: University of Illinois Press.

Bessen, J. and M. Meurer (2008) *Patent Failure*, Princeton, NJ: Princeton University Press.

Bishop, M.J. (2003) *How to Win the Nobel Prize: An Unexpected Life in Science*, Cambridge, MA: Harvard University Press.

Boldrin, M. and D. Levine (2008) *Against Intellectual Monopoly*, New York: Cambridge University Press.

Borkin, J. and C.A. Welsh (1943) *Germany's Master Plan: The Story of the Industrial Offensive*, London: John Long.

Breznitz, D. (2007) *Innovation and the State: Political Choice and Strategies for Growth in Israel, Taiwan and Ireland*, New Haven, CT: Yale University Press.

Chang, H.J. (2008) *Bad Samaritans: The Guilty Secrets of Rich Nations and the Threat to Global Prosperity*, New York: Bloomsbury Press.

Chang, H.J. (2002) *Kicking Away the Ladder – Development Strategy in Historical Perspective*, London: Anthem Press.

Chaudhuri, S. (2005) *The WTO and India's Pharmaceuticals Industry: Patent Protection TRIPS and Developing Countries*, New Delhi: Oxford University Press.

Cohen, W.M. and S.A. Merrill (2003) *Patents in the Knowledge-Based Economy*, Washington, DC: NRC.

Correa, C.M. (1999) *Intellectual Property Rights and the Use of Compulsory Licences: Options for Developing Countries*, Geneva: South Centre.

Correa, C. (2010) *Designing Intellectual Property Policies in Developing Countries*, Kuala Lumpur: TWN.

Correa, C. (2000) *Integrating Public Health Concerns into Patent Legislation in Developing Countries*, Geneva: South Centre.

Correa, C. (2003) *Protection of Data Submitted for the Registration of Pharmaceuticals: Implementing the Standards of the TRIPS Agreement*, Geneva: South Centre.

Correa, C. (2007) *Trade Related Aspects of Intellectual Property Rights: A Commentary on the TRIPS Agreement*, Oxford: Oxford University Press.

CTIETI, (1983) *The Competitive Status of the US Pharmaceutical Industry: The Influences of Technology in Determining International Industrial Competitive Advantage*, Washington, DC: National Academy Press.

Davis, H. and D. Davis (2005) *Israel in the World: Changing Lives through Innovation*, London: Weidenfeld & Nicolson.

de Carvalho, N.P. (2005) *The TRIPS Regime of Patent Rights*, 2nd edn, The Hague: Kluwer Law International.

Dhar, S. (2006) *Case Studies on Growth Strategies – Volume II*, Hyderabad, India: ICFAI Books.

Dransfield, R. and D. Needham (2005) *GCE AS Level Applied Business Double Award for OCR*, Oxford: Heinemann.

Dutfield, G. (2003) *Intellectual Property Rights and the Life Science Industries*, Dartmouth, NH: Ashgate.

Fagerberg, J., D. Mowery and R. Nelson (2005) *The Oxford Handbook of Innovation*, New York: Oxford University Press.

Gassmann, O., G. Reepmeyer and M. von Zedtwitz (2008) *Leading Pharmaceutical Innovation*, 2nd edn, Heidelberg, Germany: Springer.

Gervais, D. (2007) *Intellectual Property Trade and Development: Strategies to Optimize Economic Development in a TRIPS-Plus Era*, New York: Oxford University Press.

Gervais, D. (2003) *The TRIPS Agreement: Drafting History and Analysis*, London: Sweet & Maxwell.

Gollin, M. (2007) *Driving Innovation, Intellectual Property Strategies for a Dynamic World*, New York: Cambridge University Press.

Hippel, E. Von (1988) *The Sources of Innovation*, London: Oxford University Press.

Jackson, J. (2000) *The Jurisprudence of GATT and the WTO*, New York: Cambridge University Press.

Jaffe, A. and J. Lerner (2004) *Innovation and Its Discontents, How Our Broken Patent System is Endangering Innovation and Progress, and What to do about It*, Princeton, NJ: Princeton University Press.

Jeffreys, D. (2005) *The Remarkable Story of a Wonder Drug Aspirin*, New York: Bloomsbury Publishing.

Khan, Z. (2005) *The Democratization of Invention: Patents and Copyrights in American Economic Development, 1790–1920*, New York: Cambridge University Press.

Kim, L. (1997) *Imitation to Innovation: The Dynamics of Korea's Technological Learning (Management of Innovation and Change)*, Boston, MA: Harvard Business Press.

Kingston, W. (2003) *Innovation: The Creative Impulse in Human Progress*, Washington, DC: The Leonard R. Sugerman Press Inc.

Ladas, S. (1975) *Patents, Trademarks and Related Rights – National and International Protection*, Cambridge, MA: Harvard University Press.

Lessig, L. (2001) *The Future of Ideas*, New York: Random House.

Lundvall, B. (2002) *Innovation, Growth and Social Cohesion*, Cheltenham, UK and Northampton, MA, USA: Edward Elgar.

Macfarlane, G. (1984) *Alexander Fleming: The Man and the Myth*, Oxford: Oxford University Press.

Malerba, F. and S. Brusoni (2007) *Perspectives on Innovation*, New York: Cambridge University Press.

Maskus, K.E. (2000) *Intellectual Property Rights in the Global Economy*, Washington, DC: Institute for International Economics.

Matthews, D. (2002) *Globalising Intellectual Property Rights*, London: Routledge.

Maxwell, R. and S. Eckhardt (1990) *Drug Discovery: A Casebook and Analysis*, Totowa. NJ: Humana Press.

May, C. and S. Sell (2006) *Intellectual Property Rights: A Critical History*, London: Lynne Reiner.

Merill, S. and R. Levin (2004) *A Patent System for the 21st Century*, Washington, DC: National Academic Press.

Moe, E. (2000) *Governance, Growth and Global Leadership: The Role of the State in Technological Progress*, Aldershot: Ashgate Publishing.

Mowery, D. (1999) *US Industry in 2000: Studies in Competitive Performance*, Washington, DC: National Academy.

Murmann, J.P. (2003) *Knowledge and Competitive Advantage: The Co-evolution of Firms, Technology and National Institutions*, New York: Cambridge University Press.

Neal, H., T. Smith and J. McCormick (2008) *Beyond Sputnik: US Science Policy in the Twenty-First Century*, New York: University of Michigan Press.

Nunn, A. (2009) *The Politics and History of AIDS Treatment in Brazil*, New York: Springer.

Odagiri, H., A. Goto, A. Sunami and R. Nelson (2010) *Intellectual Property Rights, Development and Catch-up*, New York: Oxford University Press.

Palombi, L. (2009) *Gene Cartels, Biotech Patents in the Age of Free Trade*, Cheltenham, UK and Northampton, MA, USA: Edward Edgar.

Penrose, E.T. (1951) *The Economics of the International Patent System*, Baltimore, MD: The Johns Hopkins Press.

Pigou, A.C. (1924) *The Economics of Welfare*, London: Macmillan.

Roberts, E. (1987) *Generating Technological Innovation*, Oxford: Oxford University Press.

Ryan, M.P. (1998) *Knowledge Diplomacy: Global Competition and Politics of Intellectual Property*, Washington, DC: Brookings.

Saha, T. (1980) *Research, Development and Technological Innovation*, Lanham, MD: Lexington Books.

Scherer, M. and D. Ross (1990) *Industrial Market Structure and Economic Performance*, 3rd edn, Boston, MA: Houghton Mifflin.

Schumpeter, J. (1939) *A Theoretical, Historical and Statistical Analysis of the Capitalist Process*, Vol.1, New York: McGraw Hill.

Schumpeter, J. (1939) *Business Cycles*, V.I–II, New York: McGraw-Hill.

Schumpeter, J. (1934) *The Theory of Economic Development: An Inquiry into Profits, Capital, Credit, Interest and the Business Cycle*, Cambridge, MA: Harvard University Press.

Schumpeter, J. (1942) *Capitalism, Socialism, and Democracy*, New York: Harper Brothers Publishers.

Sell, S. (2002) *Private Power, Public Law: The Globalization of Intellectual Property Rights*, Cambridge: Cambridge University Press.

Shargel, L. and I. Kanfer (2005) *Generic Drug Product Development: Solid Oral Dosage Forms*, New York: Dekker.

Smith, A. (1776) *The Wealth of Nations*, Oxford: Clarendon Press.

Taylor, C.T. and A.Z. Silberston (1973) *The Economic Impact of Patent System: A Study of the British Experience*, Cambridge: Cambridge University Press.

Vogel, E.F. (1991) *The Four Little Dragons: The Spread of Industrialization in East Asia*, Cambridge, MA: Harvard University Press.

BOOK CHAPTERS

Andersen, B. (2006) 'If "Intellectual Property Rights" is the Answer, What is the Question? Revisiting the Patent Controversies' in Andersen, B. (ed.) *Intellectual Property Rights, Innovation, Governance and the Institutional Environment*, Cheltenham, UK and Northampton, MA, USA: Edward Elgar, pp. 109–48.

Caracostas, P. (2007) 'The Policy-Shaper's Anxiety at the Innovation Kick: How Far Do Innovation Theories Really Help in the World of Policy?' in F. Malerba and S. Brusoni (eds) *Perspectives on Innovation*, New York: Cambridge University Press, pp. 464–90.

Cockburn, I., R. Henderson, L. Orsenigo and G. Pisano (1999) 'Pharmaceuticals and Biotechnology' in D. Mowery (ed.) *US Industry in 2000: Studies in Competitive Performance*, Washington, DC: National Academy, pp. 363–99.

Cohen, W., R. Florida, L. Randazzese and J. Walsh (1998) 'Industry and the Academy: Uneasy Partners in the Cause of Technological Advance' in R. Noll (ed.) *Challenges to Research Universities*, Washington, DC: Brookings Institution, pp. 171–200.

Dasgupta, P. (1986) 'The Theory of Technological Competition' in J. Stiglitz and G. Mathewson (eds) *New Developments in the Analysis of Market Structure*, Cambridge, MA: MIT Press, pp. 519–48.

Drahos, P. (2009) 'The Jewel in the Crown: India's Patent Office and Patent-Based Innovation' in C. Arup and W. van Caenegem (eds) *Intellectual Property Policy Reform, Fostering Innovation and Development*, Cheltenham, UK and Northampton, MA, USA: Edward Elgar, pp. 80–101.

Edquist, C. (2005) 'System of Innovation: Perspectives and Challenges' in J. Fagerberg, D. Mowery and R. Nelson (eds) *The Oxford Handbook of Innovation*, New York: Oxford University Press, pp. 181–209.

Fagerberg, J., and M. Godinho (2005) 'Innovation and Catching-up' in J. Fagerberg, D. Mowery and R. Nelson (eds) *The Oxford Handbook of Innovation*, New York: Oxford University Press, pp. 514–43.

Fagerberg, J. (2006) 'Knowledge in Space: What Hope for the Poor Parts of the Globe?' in B. Kahin and D. Foray (eds) *Advancing Knowledge and the Knowledge Economy*, Cambridge MA: MIT Press, pp. 217–35.

Gervais, D. (2009) 'Policy Calibration and Innovation Displacement' in N. Netanel (ed.) *The Development Agenda*, New York: Oxford University Press, pp. 51–78.

Granstrand, O. (2006) 'Intellectual Property Rights for Governance in and of Innovation Systems' in B. Andersen (ed.) *Intellectual Property*

Rights, Innovation, Governance and the Institutional Environment, Cheltenham, UK and Northampton, MA, USA: Edward Elgar, pp. 311–45.

Kim, L. (1993) 'National System of Industrial Innovation: Dynamics of Capability Building in Korea' in R. Nelson (ed.) *National Innovation Systems*, New York: Oxford University Press, pp. 357–83.

Kingston, W. (2003) 'Antibiotics, Invention and Innovation' in W. Kingston (ed.) *Innovation: The Creative Impulse in Human Progress*, Washington, DC: The Leonard R. Sugerman Press Inc.

Kingston, W. (2009) 'Why Patents Need Reform, Some Suggestions for It' in C. Arup and W. van Caenegem (eds) *Intellectual Property Policy Reform: Fostering Innovation and Development*, Cheltenham, UK and Northampton, MA, USA: Edward Elgar, pp. 11–29.

Lee, K. and Y.K. Kim (2010) 'IPR and Technological Catch-up in Korea' in H. Odagiri, A. Goto, A. Sunami and R. Nelson (eds) *Intellectual Property Rights, Development and Catch-up*, New York: Oxford University Press, pp. 133–67.

Lundvall, B. and S. Borras (2005) 'Science, Technology and Innovation Policy' in J. Fagerberg, D. Mowery and R. Nelson (eds) *The Oxford Handbook of Innovation*, New York: Oxford University Press, p. 599–631.

Mansfield, E. (1987) 'Microeconomics of Technological Innovation' in B. Guile and H. Brooks (eds) *Technology and Global Industry*, Washington, DC: National Academy Press, pp. 307–26.

Maskus, K., S. Dougherty and A. Mertha (2005) 'Intellectual Property Rights and Economic Development in China' in C. Fink and K. Maskus (eds) *Intellectual Property and Development*, Oxford: Oxford University Press, pp. 295–304.

Moir, J.H. (2009) 'What are the Costs and Benefits of Patent Systems' in C. Arup and W. van Caenegem (eds) *Intellectual Property Policy Reform: Fostering Innovation and Development*, Cheltenham, UK and Northampton, MA, USA: Edward Elgar, pp. 29–55.

Mowery, D. (2010) 'IPR and US Economic Catch-up' in H. Odagiri, A. Goto, A. Sunami and R. Nelson (eds) *Intellectual Property Rights, Development and Catch-up*, New York: Oxford University Press, pp. 31–62.

Mowery, D. (2001) 'The United States National Innovation System after the Cold War' in P. Laredo and P. Mustar (eds) *Research and Innovation Policies in the New Global Economy*, Cheltenham, UK and Northampton, MA, USA: Edward Elgar, pp. 15–46.

Mowery, D. and B. Sampat (2005) 'Universities in National Innovation Systems' in J. Fagerberg, D. Mowery and R. Nelson (eds) *The Oxford Handbook of Innovation*, New York: Oxford University Press, pp. 209–40.

Murmann, J.P. and R. Landau (1998) 'On the Making of Competitive Advantage: The Development of the Chemical Industries in Britain and Germany since 1850' in A. Arora, R. Landau and N. Rosenberg (eds) *Chemicals and Long-Term Economic Growth: Insights from the Chemical Industry*, New York: John Wiley & Sons, Inc.

Narula, R. and A. Zanfei (2005) 'Globalization of Innovation: The Role of Multinational Enterprises' in J. Fagerberg, D. Mowery and R. Nelson (eds) *The Oxford Handbook of Innovation*, Oxford: Oxford University Press, pp. 318–48.

Nelson, R. and N. Rosenberg (1993) 'Technical Innovation and National Systems' in R. Nelson (ed.), *National Innovation Systems*, New York: Oxford University Press, pp. 3–28.

Odagiri, H., A. Goto and A. Sunami (2010) 'Introduction' in H. Odagiri, A. Goto, A. Sunami and R. Nelson (eds) *Intellectual Property Rights, Development and Catch-up*, New York: Oxford University Press, p. 12.

Odagiri, H., A. Goto and A. Sunami (2010) 'IPR and the Catch-up Process in Japan' in H. Odagiri, A. Goto, A. Sunami and R. Nelson (eds) *Intellectual Property Rights, Development and Catch-up*, New York: Oxford University Press, pp. 95–132.

Odagiri, H. and A. Goto (1993) 'The Japanese System of Innovation: Past, Present and Future' in R. Nelson (ed.) *National Innovation Systems*, New York: Oxford University Press, pp. 76–114.

Park, G.W. (2008) 'Intellectual Property Rights and International Innovation' in K. Maskus (ed.) *Intellectual Property Growth and Trade*, Amsterdam: Elsevier, V.2, pp. 289–327.

Pugatch, M., M. Teubal and O. Zlotnick (2010) 'Israel's High-Tech Catch-up Process' in H. Odagiri, A. Goto, A. Sunami and R. Nelson (eds) *Intellectual Property Rights, Development and Catch-up*, New York: Oxford University Press, pp. 208–46.

Teubal, M. (1993) 'The Innovation System of Israel: Description Performance and Outstanding Issues' in R. Nelson (ed.) *National Innovation Systems*, New York: Oxford University Press, pp. 477–97.

West, J. (2006) 'Does Appropriability Enable or Retard Innovation' in H. Chesbrough et al. (eds) *Open Innovation: Researching a New Paradigm*, Oxford: Oxford University Press, pp. 109–33.

JOURNAL ARTICLES

Arora, A., M. Ceccagnoli and W. Cohen (2008) 'R&D and the Patent Premium', *International Journal of Industrial Organization*, V.26, I.5, pp. 1153–79.

Blumenthal, D., N. Causino, E. Campbell and K. Seashore (1996) 'Relationships between Academic Institutions and Industry in the Life Sciences – An Industry Survey', *The New England Journal of Medicine*, V.334. N.6, pp. 368–74.

Boetinger, S. and A. Bennett (2005–2006) 'The Bayh-Dole Act: Implications for Developing Countries', *IDEA*, V.45, pp. 261–81.

Breznitz, D. (2007) 'Industrial R&D as a National Policy: Horizontal Technology Policies and Industry-State Co-evolution in the Growth of the Israeli Software Industry', *Research Policy*, V.36, I.9, pp. 1465–82.

Burk, D.L. and M.A. Lemley (2003) 'Policy Levers in Patent Law', *Virginia Law Review*, Vol. 89, pp. 1575–688.

Caffrey, A. and J. Rotter (2004) 'Consumer Protection, Patents and Procedure: Generic Drug Market Entry and the Need to Reform the Hatch-Waxman Act', *Virginia Journal of Law and Technology*, V.9, N.1, pp. 4–44.

Charnovitz, S. (2001) 'The WTO and the Rights of the Individual', *Intereconomics*, V.38, pp. 98–108.

Chen, Y. and T. Puttitanun (2005) 'Intellectual Property Rights and Innovation in Developing Countries', *Journal of Development Economics*, V.78, I.2, pp. 474–93.

Cohen, J. (2007) 'AIDS Drugs: Brazil, Thailand Override Big Pharma Patents', *Science*, V.316, pp. 816–20.

Cohn, C. (1990) 'Compulsory Licensing in Israel under Pharmaceutical Patents – A Political Issue?', *Patent World*, V.27, I.22, pp. 22–7.

Collier, R. (2009) 'Drug Development Cost Estimates Hard to Swallow', *Canadian Medical Association Journal*, V.180, I.3, pp. 279–80.

Correa, C. (2006) 'Implications of Bilateral Free Trade Agreements on Access to Medicines', *Bulletin of the World Health Organisation*, V.84, N.5, pp. 399–404.

Debackere, K. (2000) 'Managing Academic R&D as a Business at KU Leuven: Context, Structure and Process', *R&D Management*, V.30 N.4, pp. 323–28.

Dimasi, J., R. Hansen and H. Grabowski (2003) 'The Price of Innovation: New Estimates of Drug Development Costs', *Journal of Health Economics*, V.22, pp. 151–85.

Dooley, L. and D. Kirk (2007) 'University-Industry Collaboration: Grafting the Entrepreneurial Paradigm onto Academic Structures', *European Journal of Innovation Management*, V.10 N.3, pp. 316–32.

Dove, A. (2000) 'Betting on Biogenerics', *Nature Biotechnology*, V.19, pp. 117–20.

Drahos, P. (2002) 'Developing Countries and International Intellectual Property Standard-Setting', *JWIP*, V.5, pp. 765–89.

Drahos, P. (2007) 'Four Lessons for Developing Countries from the Trade Negotiations over Access to Medicines', *Liverpool Law Review*, V.28, pp. 11–39.

El-Said, M. (2007) 'Editorial: Free Trade, Intellectual Property and TRIPS-Plus World', *Liverpool Law Review*, V.28, pp. 1–9.

El-Said, M. (2005) 'The Road from TRIPS-MINUS, to TRIPS, to TRIPS-Plus: Implications of IPRS for the Arab World', *JWIP*, V.8, pp. 53–62.

Engelberg, A. (1999) 'Special Patent Provisions for Pharmaceuticals: Have They Outlived Their Usefulness? A Political, Legislative and Legal History of US Law and Observations for the Future', *IDEA: The Journal of Law and Technology*, V.39 N.3, pp. 389–426.

Epstein, R. (2007) 'The Pharmaceutical Industry at Risk: How Excessive Government Regulation Stifles Innovation', *Clinical Pharmacology & Therapeutics*, V.82, N.2, pp. 131–2.

Faunce, T.A. and J. Lexchin (2007) '"Linkage" Pharmaceutical Evergreening in Canada and Australia', *New Zealand Health Policy*, V.4, I.8, pp. 1–11.

Fersko, R.S., E. Trogan and P.M. Harinstein (2005) 'Hatch Waxman: A work in Progress, Responding to the Conundrum: How to Encourage Innovative New Drugs While Reducing the Cost of Access', *Journal of BioLaw and Business*, V.8, N.3, pp. 20–7.

Freeman, C. (1995) 'The "National Innovation System of Innovation" in Historical Perspective', *Cambridge Journal of Economics*, V.19, pp. 5–24.

Gallini, N. (1992) 'Patent Policy and Costly Imitation', *RAND: Journal of Economics*, V.23, N.1, pp. 52–63.

Godin, B. (2006) 'The Linear Model of Innovation: The Historical Construction of an Analytical Framework', *Science, Technology & Human Values*, V.31, pp. 639–67.

Gray, N. (2006) 'Drug Discovery through Industry – Academic Partnerships', *Nature Chemical Biology*, V.2, N.12, pp. 649–53.

Griffiths, S. (2004) 'From the Analyst's Couch: Betting on Biogenerics', *Nature Reviews, Drug Discovery*, V.3, pp. 197–98.

Held, S., C. Bolte, M. Bierbaum and O. Schöffski (2009) 'Impact of "Big Pharma" Organizational Structure on R&D Productivity', *Schriften Zur Gesundheitsokonomie*, pp. 1–16.

Helpman, E. (1993) 'Innovation, Imitation and Intellectual Property Rights', *Econometrica*, V.61, N6, pp. 1247–80.

Jaeger, K. (2006) 'America's Generic Pharmaceutical Industry: Opportunities and Challenges in 2006 and beyond', *Journal of Generic Medicines*, V.4, pp. 15–22.

Jaffe, A. (1989) 'Real Effects of Academic Research', *The American Economic Review*, V.79, pp. 957–70.

Janicke, P.M. and L. Ren (2006) 'Who Wins Patent Infringement Cases?', *American Intellectual Property Law Association Quarterly Journal*, Vol. 34, pp. 1–37.

Joseph, S. (2003) 'Pharmaceutical Corporations and Access to Drugs: The "Fourth Wave" of Corporate Human Rights Scrutiny', *Human Rights Quarterly*, V.25, pp. 425–52.

Julian-Arnold, G. (1993) 'International Compulsory Licensing: The Rationales and the Reality', *The Journal of Law and Technology*, V.33, I.2, pp. 349–400.

Kaitin, K. (2008) 'Obstacles and Opportunities in New Drug Development', *Nature*, V.83, N.2, pp. 210–12.

Katz, M. and C. Shapiro (1987) 'R&D Rivalry with Licensing and Imitation', *The American Economic Review*, V.77, N.3, pp. 402–20.

Kneller, R. (2003) 'Autarkic Drug Discovery in Japanese Pharmaceutical Companies: Insights into National Differences in Industrial Innovation', *Research Policy*, V.32, pp. 1805–27.

Krishnaswamy, S. (2009) 'Mashelkar Report on IP Rights Version II: Wrong Again', *Economic & Political Weekly*, V.XLIV. N.52.

Kuhlman, S. (2003) 'Evaluation of Research and Innovation Policies: A Discussion of Trends with Examples from Germany', *International Journal of Technology Management* V.26. N.2–4, pp. 131–49.

La Croix, S. and A. Kawaura (1996) 'Product Patent Reform and its Impact on Korea's Pharmaceutical Industry', *International Economic Journal*, V.10, N.1, pp. 109–24.

Lee, K.T. (2007) 'Comment on 'From Industrial Policy to Innovation Policy: Japan's Pursuit of Competitive Advantage', *Asian Economic Policy Review*, V.2, pp. 271–2.

Lichterman, B. (2004) 'Aspirin: The Story of a Wonder Drug', *British Medical Journal*, V.329, p. 1408.

Mahoney, R., L. Keun, L and Y. Mikyung (2005) 'Intellectual Property, Drug Regulation, and Building Product Innovation Capability in Biotechnology: The Case of Hepatitis B Vaccine in Korea', *Innovation Strategy Today*, V.1, N.2, pp. 33–4.

Malebra, F. and L. Orsenigo (2002) 'Innovation and Market Structure in the Dynamics of the Pharmaceutical Industry and Bio-technology: Towards a History-Friendly Model', *Industrial and Corporate Change*, V.11, N.4, pp. 667–703.

Mancinelli, L., M. Cronin and W. Sadée (2000) 'Pharmacogenomics: The Promise of Personalized Medicine', *PharmSci*, V.2, E.1, pp. 29–41.

Mansfield, E. (1995) 'Academic Research Underlying Industrial Innovations: Sources, Characteristics and Financing', *The Review of Economics and Statics*, V.77, N.1, pp. 55–65.

Mansfield, E. (1986) 'Patents and Innovation: An Empirical Study', *Management Science*, V.32, N.2, pp. 173–81.

Mansfield, E., M. Schwartz and S. Wagner (1981) 'Imitation Costs and Patents – An Empirical Study', *Economic Journal*, V.91, N.364, pp. 907–18.

Marzo, A. and L.P. Balant (1995) 'Bioequivalence: An Updated Reappraisal Addressed to Applications of Interchangeable Multi-Source Pharmaceutical Products', *Arzneim-Forsch/Drug Res* V.45, pp. 109–15.

Maskus, K., M. Penubati (1995) 'How Trade-Related are Intellectual Property Rights?', *Journal of International Economics*, V.39, pp. 227–48.

Maskus, K. (1998) 'The Role of Intellectual Property Rights in Encouraging Foreign Direct Investment and Technology Transfer', *Duke Journal of Comparative, International Law*, V.9, pp. 109–61.

Masuda, S. (2008) 'The Market Exclusivity Period for New Drugs in Japan: Overview of Intellectual Property Protection and Related Regulations', *Journal of Generic Medicines*, V.5, N.2, pp. 121–30.

Maybarduk, P. and S. Rimmington (2009) 'Compulsory Licences: A Tool to Improve Global Access to the HPV Vaccine?', *American Journal of Law & Medicine*, V.35, pp. 323–50.

Mazzoleni, R. and R. Nelson (1998) 'Economic Theories about the Benefits and Costs of Patents', *Journal of Economic Issues*, V.32, N. 4, pp. 1031–53.

Mazzoleni, R. and R. Nelson (1998) 'The Benefits and Costs of Strong Patent Protection: A Contribution to the Current Debate', *Research Policy*, V.27, pp. 273–84.

Mehl, A. (2006) 'The Hatch-Waxman Act and Market Exclusivity for Generic Drug Manufacturers: An Entitlement or an Incentive?', *Chicago-Kent Law Review*, V.81, pp. 649–77.

Merges, R. and R. Nelson (1990) 'On the Complex Economics of Patent Scope', *Columbia Law Review*, V.90, N.4, pp. 839–916.

Merges, R. (1988) 'Economic Perspectives on Innovation: Commercial Success and Patent Standards', *California Law Review*, V.76, I.4, pp. 803–76.

Mossinghoff, G. (2000) 'National Obligations under Intellectual Property Treaties: The Beginning of a True International Regime', 9 *Federal Circuit Bar Journal*, V.4, pp. 591–603.

Mueller, J.M. (2007) 'The Tiger Awakens: The Tumultuous Transformation of India's Patent System and the Rise of Indian Pharmaceutical Innovation', *University of Pittsburgh Law Review*, V.68, N.3, pp. 491–641.

Mytelka, L.K. (2006) 'Pathways and Policies to (Bio) Pharmaceutical Innovation Systems in Developing Counties', *Industry and Innovation*, V.13, I.4, pp. 415–53.

Nelson, R. (1986) 'Institutions Supporting Technical Advance in Industry', *The American Economic Review*, V.76, pp. 186–94.

Nelson, R. (2006) 'Reflections of David Teece's "Profiting from Technological Innovation ..."', *Research Policy*, V.35, pp. 1107–9.

Opderbeck, D. (2005) 'Patents, Essential Medicines and the Innovation Game', *Vanderbilt Law Review*, V.58, pp. 501–54.

Park, G. and J.C. Ginarte (1997) 'Intellectual Property Rights and Economic Growth', *Contemporary Economic Policy*, The World Bank, V.15, pp. 51–61.

Park, W. (2002) 'Patent Rights and Economic Freedom: Friend or Foe?', *Journal of Private Enterprise*, V.18, N.1, pp. 84–121.

Pretnar, B. (2003) 'The Economic Impact of Patents in a Knowledge-Based Market Economy', *International Review of Intellectual Property and Competition Law*, V.34, N.8, pp. 887–906.

Quinn, J.B. (2000) 'Outsourcing the Innovation: The New Engine of Growth', *Massachusetts Institute of Technology Sloan Management Review*, V.41, N.4, pp. 13–28.

Rader, R. (2008) '(Re)Defining Biopharmaceutical', *Nature Biotechnology*, V.26, N.7, pp. 743–751.

Rader, R. (2007) 'What is a Generic Biopharmaceutical? Biogeneric? Follow-on Protein? Biosimilar? Follow-on Biologic?', *BioProcess International*, V.5, pp. 28–38.

Rai, A. and R. Eisenberg (2003) 'Bayh-Dole Reform and the Progress of Biomedicine', *American Scientist*, January-February, p. 52.

Reichman, J. and R. Dreyfuss (2007) 'Harmonization without Consensus Critical Reflections on Drafting a Substantive Patent Law Treaty', *Duke Law Journal*, V.57, pp. 85–98.

Reichman, J. and D. Lange (1999) 'Bargaining around the Trips Agreement: The Case for Ongoing Public-Private Initiatives to Facilitate Worldwide Intellectual Property Transactions', *Duke Journal of Comparative & International Law*, V.9, I.11, pp. 11–58.

Reichmann, J.H. (2009) 'Compulsory Licensing of Patented Pharmaceutical Inventions: Evaluating the Options', Comment, *Pharmaceutical Regulations*, V.37, I.2, pp. 247–63.

Roberts, C. and S. McCoy (2000) 'TRIPS around the World: Enforcement Goes Global in 2000', *Legal Times*, April 10, pp. 46–50.

Sakakibara, M. and L. Branstetter (2001) 'Do Stronger Patents Induce More Innovation? Evidence from the 1998 Patent Law Reforms', *The RAND Journal of Economics*, V.32, N.1, pp. 77–100.

Scheindlin, S. (2004) 'Copolymer 1: An Off-Beat Drug Development Story', Reflections: *Science in the Cultural Context*, V.4, I.1, pp. 6–9.

Schumpeter, J. (1947) 'The Creative Response in Economic History', *The Journal of Economic History*, V.7, N.2, pp. 149–51.

Schumpeter, J. (1928) 'The Instability of Capitalism', *The Economic Journal*, V.38, N.151, pp. 361–86.

Sell, S. (1995) 'Intellectual Property Protection and Antitrust in the Developing World: Crisis, Coercion and Choice', *International Organization* V.59, pp. 315–49.

Sharma, N.L and S. Goswami (2009) 'The Nuances of Knowledge Creation and Development in the Indian Pharmaceutical Industry', *Journal of Knowledge Management*, V.13 N.5, pp. 319–30.

Sherwood, R. (1997) 'The TRIPS Agreement: Implications for Developing Countries', *The Journal of Law and Technology*, V.37, pp. 491–544.

So, D.A. et al. (2008) 'Is Bayh-Dole Good for Developing Countries? Lessons from the US Experience', *PLOS Biology*, V.6, I.10, pp. 2078–82.

Solo, C.S. (1951) 'Innovation in the Capitalist Process: A Critique of the Schumpeterian Theory', *The Quarterly Journal of Economics*, V.65, N.3, pp. 417–27.

Stiglitz, J. (2008) 'Economic Foundations of Intellectual Property', *Duke Law Journal*, V.57, pp. 1693–1700.

Summers, T. (2003) 'The Scope of Utility in the Twenty-First Century: New Guidance for Gene-Related Patents', *Georgetown Law Review*, V.91, I.2, pp. 475–509.

Teubal, M. (1996) 'R&D and Technology Policy in NICs as Learning Processes', *World Development* V.24, I.3, pp. 449–60.

Thompson, M. and F. Rushing (1999) 'An Empirical Analysis of the Impact of Patent Protection on Economic Growth', *Journal of Economic Development* V.24, I.1, pp. 67–76.

Tomer, G. (2008) 'Prevailing against Cost-Leader Competitors in the Pharmaceutical Industry', *Journal of Generic Medicines*, V.5, pp. 305–14.

Torrence, A.W. and B. Tomlinson (2009) 'Patents and the Regress of Useful Arts', *The Colombia Science and Technology Law Review*, V.10, pp. 130–68.

Trouiller, P. et al. (2002) 'Drug Development for Neglected Diseases: A Deficient Market and a Public-Health Policy Failure', *Lancet*, V.359, 9324, pp. 2188–94.

Tsai, F-S. L.H.Y. Hsieh, S-C. Fang and J.L Lin (2009) 'The Co-evolution of Business Incubation and National Innovation Systems in Taiwan', *Technological Forecasting and Social Change*, V.76, I. 5, pp. 629–43.

Uon, H., K.S. Choi, E. Park and M. Kwak (2009) 'Hepatitis B Vaccinations among Koreans: Results from 2005 Korea National Cancer Screening Survey', *BMC Infectious Diseases*, V.9, pp.185–92.

Vijayaraghavan, B. and P. Raghuvanshi (2009) 'Impact of the Amended Indian Patent Act on the Indian Pharmaceutical Industry', *Journal of Generic Medicines*, V.5, pp. 111–19.

Weinhold, D. and U. Reichert (2009) 'Innovation, Inequality and Intellectual Property Rights', *World Development*, V.37, I.5, pp. 889–901.

Yu, P.K (2006) 'The First Ten Years of the TRIPS Agreement: TRIPS and Its Discontents', *Marques Intellectual Property Law Review*, V.10, pp. 369–400.

ONLINE SOURCES

Angelino, H. and N. Collier (2004) 'Research and Innovation Policies in France and Japan: Similarities and Differences', a presentation of the informatics, accessed 18 May 2008 at http://www.nii.ac.jp/hrd/HTML/OpenHouse/h16/archive/PDF/704.pdf.

Bard, M. (2007) 'The Arab Boycott', Jewish Virtual Library, accessed 22 August 2010 at http://www.jewishvirtuallibrary.org/jsource/History/Arab_boycott.html.

Benoliel, D. and B.M. Salama (2009) 'Towards an Intellectual Property Bargaining Theory: The Post-WTO Era', accessed 2 February 2010 at http://www.escholarship.org/uc/item/4c03k7v7.

Besok, M.: 'A Commentary: Last Days of the Boycott – 01-Feb-94', Israel Ministry of Foreign Affairs, accessed 11 September 2010 at http://www.mfa.gov.il/MFA/Archive/Articles/1994/LAST%20DAYS%20OF%20THE%20OYCOTT%20-%2001-Feb-94.

Block, F.: 'America's Stealth Industrial Policy', accessed 10 August 2013 at http://www.longviewinstitute.org/blockstealth.

Brown, H. (2005) 'Dealing with the Generic Threat', *PharmaFocus*, 14 September 2005, accessed 21 August 2010 at http://www.prophet.com/newsevents/news/story/20050914smith.html.

Chan, M. (2007) Keynote Address Delivered at the Prince Mahidol Award Conference, accessed 14 September 2010 at http://www.who.int/neglected_diseases/dgspeech2/en/index.html.

Coch, R.: 'Robert Koch developed many microbiological techniques', accessed 13 January 2014 at http://www.microbiologytext.com/index.php?module=Book&func=displayarticle&art_id=26.

Drahos, P. (2007) 'Trust Me: Patent Offices in Developing Countries', accessed 10 August 2013 at http://ssrn.com/abstract=1028676.

Edquis, J.B. and B.A. Lundvall (2010) 'Economic Development and the National System of Innovation Approach', Paper presented at the first Globelics Conference, accessed 29 August 2010 at http://www.globelicsacademy.net/pdf/BengtAkeLundvall_2.pdf.

Eurek, S. (2003) 'Hatch-Waxman Reform and Accelerated Market Entry of Generic Drugs: Is Faster Necessarily Better?', *Duke Law & Technology Review*, accessed 13 September 2010 at http://www.law.duke.edu/journals/dltr/articles/2003dltr0018.html.

Feisee, L. (2001) 'Anything under the Sun Made by Man', Biotechnology Industry Organization, Director for Federal Government Relations and Intellectual Property, accessed 12 September 2010 at http://www.bio.org/speeches/speeches/041101.asp.

'From Nobel Prize to Courthouse Battle: Paul Ehrlich's "Wonder Drug" for Syphilis Won Him Acclaim but Also Led Critics to Hound Him', *The Washington Post*, 27 July 1999, accessed 13 September 2010 at http://www.encyclopedia.com/doc/1P2-615079.html.

Fu, X. (2008) 'Foreign Direct Investment, Absorptive Capacity and Regional Innovation Capabilities: Evidence from China', OECD Global Forum on Investment, 27–28 March 2008, accessed 13 September 2010 at http://www.oecd.org/dataoecd/44/23/40306798.pdf.

Gagnon, M-A. and J. Lexchin (2008) 'The Cost of Pushing Pills: A New Estimate of Pharmaceutical Promotion Expenditures in the United States', accessed 13 September 2010 at http://www.plosmedicine.org/article/info:doi/10.1371/journal.pmed.0050001.

Gawlicki, S.: 'IP Litigation is Virtually Assured for Generic Drug Makers', Intellectual Property – A special Report from Corporate Legal Times, accessed 3 September 2010 at www.sutherland.com/files/Publication/.../GenericDrugMakersIP.pdf.

Geroski, P.A. (2005) 'Intellectual Property Rights, Competition Policy and Innovation: Is There a Problem?', SCRIPTed, V.2, accessed 12 August 2010 at http://www.law.ed.ac.uk/ahrc/script-ed/vol2-4/geroski.asp.

Getz, D. and V. Sagal (2008) 'The Israeli Innovation System: An Overview of National Policy and Cultural Aspects', Samuel Neaman Institute for Advanced Studies in Science and Technology, accessed 11 September 2010 at http://www.neaman.org.il/neaman/publications/publication_item.asp?fid=859&parent_fid=488&iid=6819.

Grace, C. (2004) 'The Effect of Changing Intellectual Property on Pharmaceutical Industry Prospects in India and China: Considerations for Access to Medicines', DFID Health Systems Resource Centre, accessed 12 September 2010 at www.dfidhealthrc.org/publications/atm/Grace2.pdf.

Gilbert, J. (2006) 'Competition and Innovation', *Journal of Industrial Organization Education* V.1, I.1, accessed 18 August 2010 at: http://works.bepress.com/richard_gilbert/15.

Gulbrandsen, M.: 'The Role of Basic Research in Innovation', accessed 12 September 2010 at www.cas.uio.no/Publications/Seminar/Confluence_Gulbrandsen.pdf.

Hicks, M.D. (2006) 'A Broad Overview of the US Innovation System', accessed 10 September 2010 at http://crds.jst.go.jp/GIES/archive/GIES2006/participants/abstract/12_diana.pdf.

'India's First Compulsory Licence Upheld, but Legal Fights Likely to Continue', Intellectual Property Watch, 4 March 2013, accessed 12 September 2010 at http://www.ip-watch.org/2013/03/04/indias-first-compulsory-licence-upheld-but-legal-fights-likely-to-continue/.

'Issues Related to Accessing Patented Knowledge for Innovation', Background Paper, accessed 21 September 2010 at www.crdi.ca/.../11829736311Background_paper_on_Accessing_Patented_Knowledge_for_Innovation.pdf.

Jaffe A. (2005) 'Is the US Patent System Endangering American Innovation? A Congressional Briefing Luncheon', accessed 26 August 2010 at http://www.athenaalliance.org/pdf/patent_reform.pdf.

Javorcik, B.S. (1999) 'Composition of Foreign Direct Investment and Protection of Intellectual Property Rights in Transition Economies', accessed 26 August 2010 at http://ssrn.com/abstract=180128 or DOI: 10.2139/ssrn.180128.

Juon H., K. Choi, E. Park, M. Kwak and S. Lee (2009) 'Hepatitis B Vaccinations among Koreans: Results from 2005 Korea National Cancer Screening Survey', BMC Infectious Diseases, V.9, accessed 25 September 2010 at http://www.biomed central.com/1471-2334/9/185.

Kılıç, B., A. Benedict and T. Yang (2013) 'Reversing the "IP Ratchet": Global Implications of the US Supreme Court's Ruling in Myriad', CitizenVox, accessed 26 August 2013 at http://www.citizenvox.org/2013/06/19/reversing-the-ip-rachet-global-implications-of-the-u-s-supreme-courts-ruling-in-myriad/.

Levenson, D. (2005) 'Consequences of the Bayh-Dole Act', accessed 1 September 2010 at http://ocw.mit.edu/NR/rdonlyres/Electrical-Engineering-and-Computer-Science/6-901Fall-2005/D02FDA40-5159-4097-86E4-E66D6E5FAF31/0/bayh_dole.pdf.

Lippoldt, D. (2006) 'Intellectual Property Rights, Pharmaceuticals and Foreign Direct Investment', Groupe d'Economie Mondiale de Sciences Policy Brief, accessed 31 August 2010 at www.gem.sciences-po.fr/.../lippoldt_IPRs_Pharma_FDI1106.pdf.

Love, J. (2003) 'An Agenda for Research and Development', Meeting on the Role of Generics and Local Industry in Attaining the Millennium Development Goals in Pharmaceuticals and Vaccines, The World Bank, Washington DC, 24–25 June 2003, accessed 28 August 2010 at http://www.cptech.org/ip/health/rndtf/.

Luzzatto, K. (2008) 'Pharmaceutical Patents in Israel', accessed 29 August 2010 at www.luzzatto.com/articles/11.12.08(7).pdf.

'Members of US Congress Seek Pressure on India Over IP Rights', Intellectual Property Watch, 20 June 2013, accessed 29 August 2010 at http://www.ip-watch.org/2013/06/20/170-members-of-us-congress-pressure-india-on-ip-rights/.

Mohtadi, H. and S. Ruediger (2009) 'Imitation, Innovation and Threshold Effects: A Game Theoretic Approach', accessed 12 September 2010 at http://www.uwm.edu/~ruediger/Imitation,%20Innovation%20and%20Threshold%20Effects%20A%20Game%20Theoretic%20Approach%20Mohtadi%20Ruediger%202009.pdf.

NSW Board of Vocational Education and Training 'Submission to the Productivity Commission Research Study into Public Support for Science and Innovation', accessed 20 September 2010 at http://www.pc.gov.au/__data/assets/pdf_file/0006/37959/sub067.pdf.

Popper, S. and C. Wagner (2002) 'New Foundations for Growth: The US Innovation System Today and Tomorrow', Science and Technology Policy Institute, accessed 25 September 2010 at www.rand.org/pubs/monograph_reports/...0.1/MR1338.0.1.pdf.

Rafiquzzaman, M. and S. Ghosh (2001) 'The Importance of Patents, Trade-Marks and Copyright for Innovation and Economic Performance: Developing a Research Agenda for Canadian Policy', accessed 11 September 2010 at http://strategis.ic.gc.ca/epic/site/ippd-dppi.nsf/vwapj/03%20EN%20Gosh-Rafiquzzaman.pdf/$file/03%20EN%20Gosh-Rafiquzzaman.pdf.

Shadlen, K. (2004) 'The Politics of Property and the New Politics of Intellectual Property in the Developing World: Insights from Latin America', Paper Presented at the Annual Meeting of the International Studies Association, Canada, accessed 9 September 2010 at http://www.allacademic.com/meta/p72999_index.html.

Sherkow, J. (2013) 'And How: Mayo v Prometheus and the Method of Invention', 122 *Yale Law Journal Online* 351, accessed 11 September 2013 at http://yalelawjournal.org /2013/04/01/sherkow.html.

Sir Alexander Fleming, The Nobel Prize in Physiology or Medicine 1945, The Banquet Speech, 10 December 1945, accessed 11 September 2010 at http://nobelprize.org/nobel_prizes/medicine/laureates/1945/fleming-speech.html.

Sir Howard Florey, The Banquet Speech, The Nobel Prize in Physiology or Medicine 1945, 10 December 1945, accessed 11 September 2010 at http://nobelprize.org/nobel_prizes/medicine/laureates/1945/florey-speech.html.

Stiglitz, J. (1999) 'Knowledge as a Global Public Good', accessed 10 September 2010 at http://www.worldbank.org/knowledge/chiefecon/index2.htm.

Sull, D., A.R. Ruelas-Gossi and M. Escobari (2004) 'What Developing-World Companies Teach Us about Innovation', Harvard Business School, Working Knowledge, accessed 11 September 2010 at http://hbswk.hbs.edu/item/3866.html.

Twyman, R. (2002) 'Rational Drug Design: Using Structural Information about Drug Targets or Their Natural Ligands as a Basis for the Design of Effective Drugs', The Human Genome Project, Wellcome Trust, accessed 11 September 2010 at http://genome.wellcome.ac.uk/doc_WTD020912.html.

Yim, D.S. (2005) 'Korea's National Innovation System and the Science and Technology Policy', Science and Technology Policy Institute (STEPI), accessed 23 September 2010 at www.unesco.org/science/psd/thm_innov/forums/korea.pdf.

Yol-Yu, H. (2008) 'Korean National Innovation System', accessed 23 September 2010 at http://crds.jst.go.jp/GIES/archive/GIES2006/participants/abstract/41_hee-yol-yu.pdf.

REPORTS

A Report on Teva Pharmaceutical Industries Ltd., Funding Universe, accessed 21 December 2009 at http://www.fundinguniverse.com/company-histories/Teva-Pharmaceutical-Industries-Ltd-Company-History.html.

Arundel, A. (2001) 'Patents – The Viagra of Innovation Policy?', MERIT, Internal Report to the Expert Group, accessed 22 September 2010 at www.edis.sk/ekes/patents.pdf.

Berecovitz-Rodriguez, A. (1991) 'Historical Trends in Protection of Technology in Developed Countries and Their Relevance for Developing Countries', Geneva: United Nations Conference on Trade and Development.

European Parliament Report, 'Major and Neglected Diseases in Developing Countries', Committee on Development, 22 June 2005, accessed 26 September 2010 at http:// www.europarl.europa.eu/sides/getDoc.do ?language=EN&pubRef=//EP//NONSGML+REPORT+A6-2005-0215+ 0+DOC+P DF+V0//EN.

'Generic Drugs, Glossary of Globalization, Trade and Health Terms', World Health Organization, accessed 25 September 2010 at http:// www.who.int/trade/glossary/story034/en/index.html.

Gilat, D. (2003) 'Development in Israeli Patent Law 2000–2002', (Report to Institute of Intellectual Property in Asia, 19 October 2003), accessed 17 September 2010 at http://www.institute-ip-asia.org/articles/Israel report.pdf.

Global Forum (2007) Building Science, Technology, and Innovation, Capacity for Sustainable Growth and Poverty Reduction, Washington DC.

Harris, H. (1999) 'Howard Florey and the Development of Penicillin', Notes and Records of the Royal Society of London, V.53, N.2.

IFPMA, 'Encouraging Pharmaceutical R&D in Developing Countries', IFPMA Publication, February 2003.

IndusView 'Special Report: Opportunities for India in Generic Drug Space', V.2, I.8, accessed 11 September 2010 at www.theindus view.com/.../pdf/Vol2Issue8Special_report_NA.pdf.

Kuan, S.: 'The Impact of the International Patent System on Developing Countries', Assemblies of the Member States of WIPO, Thirty-Ninth Series of Meetings, Geneva, 22 September to 1 October 2003.

Lee, B. and D. Vivas: 'Intellectual Property Rights: Challenges for Development ICTSD/UNAIDS', Non-attributed Report, 17 June 2004, Sao Paolo, Brazil, accessed 14 September 2010 at www.iprsonline.org/ unctadictsd/dialogue/2004-06.../2004-06-17_report.pdf.

Lewis, J. (2008) 'Intellectual Property Protection: Promoting Innovation in a Global Information Economy', A Report of the CSIS Technology and Public Policy Program.

Maskus, K. (2006) 'Reforming US Patent Policy: Getting the Incentives Right', Council Special Report, N.19.

Nelson, P. (2002) 'Relationships between Market Structure and Innovation', Presentation to Economists Incorporated, 20 February 2002, accessed 26 September 2010 at www.ftc.gov/opp/intellect/nelson.pdf.

'No bargain: Medicare Drug Plans Deliver High Prices', Report from Families USA, 9 January 2007, accessed 5 September 2010 at http:// www.familiesusa.org/resources/publications/reports/no-bargain-medicare-drug.html.

OECD, Accessing and Expanding the Science and Technology Knowledge Base, Paris, 1994, accessed 22 September 2010 at http://www.oecd.org/pdf/M000014000/M00014640.pdf.

OECD, (2002) Foreign Direct Investment for Development, Maximising Benefits, Minimising Costs, Paris.

OECD, (2006) International Investment Perspectives, Paros, Paris.

OECD, (1997) National Innovation Systems, Paris, accessed 22 September 2010 at www.oecd.org/dataoecd/35/56/2101733.pdf.

OECD, Report on National Innovation Systems, 1993.

OECD, The Knowledge Based Economy, OCDE/GD(96)102, Paris, 1996, accessed 22 September 2010 at www.oecd.org/dataoecd/51/8/1913021.pdf.

'Prescription Drugs: Improvements Needed in FDA's Oversight of Direct-to-Consumer Advertising', GAO-07-54, Washington, November 2006, accessed 8 September 2010 at www.gao.gov/new.items/d0754.pdf.

Reichman, H.J. (2004) 'Undisclosed Clinical Trial Data under TRIPS Agreement and Its Progeny: A Broader Perspective', UNCTAD-ICTSD Dialogue on Moving the Pro-Development IP Agenda Forward, Bellagio.

Science/Business Roundtable Innovation Report, (2006) 'Innovation: The Demand Side, New Ways to Create Markets and Jobs in Europe', accessed 12 September 2010 at www.sciencebusiness.net/documents/demandside.pdf.

Shadlen, K. (2009) 'The Political Contradictions of Incremental Innovation in Late Development: Lessons from Pharmaceutical Patent Examination in Brazil', APSA 2009 Toronto Meeting Paper, August 2009, accessed 17 September 2010 at SSRN: http://ssrn.com/abstract=1449086.

Suh, J. (2000) 'Korea's Innovation System: Challenges and New Policy Agenda', UNU/Intech Discussion Papers.

UNCTAD/DTCI, (1996) Incentives and Foreign Direct Investment, Current Studies, Series A, No. 30, UN Publications, Geneva.

UNCTAD, (1998) World Investment Report, Geneva.

UNCTAD, (2005) World Investment Report, Geneva.

UNCTAD, LDC Report Highlights: LDC Report Series, N.2, December 2007.

UNECE, (2007) 'Creating a Conducive Environment for Higher Competitiveness and Effective National Innovation Systems: Lessons Learned from the Experiences of UNECE Countries', Geneva, New York.

Villareal, M.A. (2001) 'Orphan Drug Act: Background and Proposed Legislation in the 107th Congress', CRS Report.

WIPO, 'Existence, Scope and Form of Generally Internationally Accepted and Applied Standards Norms for the Protection of Intellectual Property', WO/INF/29 September 1988, Issued as GATT Document Number MTN.GNG/NG11/W/24/Rev.1.

WORKING PAPERS

Baskaran, A. and M. Muchie (2008) 'Foreign Direct Investment and Internationalization of R&D: The Case of BRICS Economics', Diiper Research Series Working Paper, N.7.
Baker, J.B. (2007) 'Beyond Schumpeter vs. Arrow: How Antitrust Fosters Innovation', AAI Working Paper 07–04., accessed 23 September 2010 at http://ssrn.com/abstract=1103623.
Balconi, M., B. Stefano and L. Orsenigo (2008) 'In Defence of the Linear Model: An Essay', KITeS, Working Paper 216, accessed 23 September 2010 at ftp://ftp.unibocconi.it/pub/RePEc/cri/papers/WP216BalconiBrusoniOrsenigo.pdf.
Bessen, J and E. Maskin (2000) 'Sequential Innovation, Patents and Imitation', MIT Working Paper, Economics.
Chen, Y. and M. Schwartz (2010) 'Product Innovation Incentives: Monopoly vs. Competition', Georgetown University Working Paper, 29 January 2010, accessed 10 September 2010 at http://econ.georgetown.edu/research/33243.html.
Cohen, W., R. Nelson and J. Walsh (2000) 'Protecting Their Intellectual Assets: Appropriability Conditions and Why US Manufacturing Firms Patent (Or Not)', NBER Working Paper, 7552, accessed 21 September 2010 at http://www.nber.org/papers/w7552.
Drahos, P. (2005) 'An Alternative Framework Fort: The Global Regulation of Intellectual Property Rights', CKGD, Working Paper.
Eicher, T. and C. Penosola (2006) 'Endogenous Strength of Intellectual Property Rights: Implications for Economic Development and Growth', Economics Working Paper, University of Washington.
Encaoua, D., D. Guellec and C. Martínez (2005) 'Patent Systems for Encouraging Innovation: Lessons from Economic Analysis', February 2005, accessed 22 September 2010 at http://eurequa.univ-paris1.fr/membres/encaoua/pdf/The%20ECONOMICS%20OF%20PATENTS%20june%202005.pdf.
Etzkowitz, H.: 'The Triple Helix of University – Industry – Government Implications for Policy and Evaluation', Working Paper 2002–11, Science Policy Institute.
Futagami, K., T. Iwaisako and H. Tanaka (2007) 'Innovation, Licensing and Imitation: The Effects of Intellectual Property Rights Protection

and Industrial Policy', Discussion Papers 07–05, OSIPP, accessed 22 September 2010 at http://www2.econ.osaka-u.ac.jp/library/global/dp/0705.pdf.

Kumar, N. (2003) 'Intellectual Property Rights, Technology and Economic Development: Experience of Asian Countries', RIS Discussion Paper No.25/2003.

Lerner, J. (2002) 'Patent Protection and Innovation over 150 Years', NBER WP 8977.

Levin, R., A. Klevorick, R. Nelson and S. Winter (1987) 'Appropriating the Returns from Industrial Research and Development', Brookings Papers on Economic Activity.

Maskus, K. (2000) 'Intellectual Property and Foreign Direct Investment', Centre International Economic Studies, Working Paper No.22.

Maskus, K. (2006) 'Reforming US Patent Policy: Getting the Incentives Right', Council Special Report, N.19, November 2006.

Menell, P. (2003) 'Intellectual Property: General Theories', Levine's WP Archive (618897000000000707).

Mohtadi, H. and S. Ruediger (2009) 'Imitation, Innovation and Threshold Effects: A Game Theoretic Approach', accessed 21 September 2010 at http://www.uwm.edu/~ruediger/Imitation,%20Innovation%20and%20Threshold%20Effects%20A%20Game%20Theoretic%20Approach%20Mohtadi%20Ruediger%202009.pdf.

Mokyr, J. (2005) 'The Great Synergy: The European Enlightenment as a Factor in Modern Economic Growth', Society for Economic Dynamics, Meeting Papers, 179.

Moser, P. (2005) 'How do Patent Laws Influence Innovation? Evidence from Nineteenth-Century World Fairs', NBER, Working Paper 9909, accessed 23 September 2010 at http://www.nber.org/papers/w9909.

Motohaski, K.: 'Japan's Patent System and Business Innovation: Reassessing Pro-patent Policies', RIETI Discussion Paper Series 03- E-020.

Roper, S. (1999) 'Innovation Policy in Israel, Ireland and the UK – An Evolutionary Perspective', Working Paper Series No. 47, NIERC.

Ramani, S. and V. Mukherjee (2010) 'CSR and Market Changing Product Innovations: Indian Case Studies', UNU-MERIT Working Paper, 2010–026.

Schacht, W. (2000) 'Federal R&D, Drug Discovery, and Pricing: Insights from the NIH-University-Industry Relationship', CRS Report.

Scherer, F.M. (2007) 'Pharmaceutical Innovation', Working Paper 07–13, AEI-Brookings Joint Centre for Regulatory Studies.

Tassey, G. (1998) 'Comparisons of US and Japanese R&D Policies', Strategic Planning and Economic Analysis Group, National Institute of Standards and Technology.

Thomas, J.R. (2009) 'Patent "Evergreening": Issues in Innovation and Competition', CRS, 13 November 2009.

Thomas, J. and W. Schacht (2007) 'Patent Reform in the 110th Congress', CRS Report RL33996Trajtenberg M. (2005) 'Innovation Policy for Development: An Overview', STE Program Working Paper, STE-WP-34-200, p. 5.

UNIDO, (2006) 'The Role of Intellectual Property Rights in Technology Transfer and Economic Growth: Theory and Evidence', Vienna, Working Paper.

Walker, S. (2001) 'The TRIPS Agreement, Sustainable Development and the Public Interest', IUCN Environmental Law Centre, Discussion Paper, p. 23.

World Bank Recommendations for Latin American and Caribbean Countries in Tertiary Education and Innovation, accessed 23 September 2010 at http://web.worldbank.org/WBSITE/EXTERNAL/COUNTRIES/LACEXT/EXTLACREGTOPEDUCATION/0,,contentMDK:20887002~pagePK:34004173~piPK:34003707~theSitePK:444459,00.html.

UNPUBLISHED THESIS

Lee, Y. (2004) 'Patent Rights and Universities: Policies and Legal Framework for Korea', a thesis submitted for the Doctor of Philosophy, Queen Mary, University of London.

NEWS

'An Israeli Giant in Generic Drugs Faces New Rivals: Arab Boycott Gave Teva Edge: Now it's No. 1 in Industry, but US Market Toughens', *The Wall Street Journal*, 28 October 2004, accessed 23 September 2010 at http://online.wsj.com/article/SB109890935431257528.html#articleTabs%3Darticle.

'Azilect – Innovative Drug: Teva Pharmaceuticals', accessed 24 September 2010 at http://www.tevapharm.com/Azilect/.

'Azilect – The One-a-Day Parkinson's Pill', 4 June 2006, Israel21c: Innovation News Service, accessed 24 September 2010 at http://www.israel21c.org/health/azilect-the-one-a-day-parkinson-s-pill.

'Biotech Drugs' Generic Future Debated: Medications are Hard to Afford', *The Washington Post*, 10 February 2005, accessed 24 September 2010 at http://www.washingtonpost.com/wp-dyn/articles/A12377-2005Feb9.html.

'Biotechnology Israel' (2006) Special Report, *Nature Biotechnology*, V.24, N.4.

'China Spurs Pharma Innovation', *News and Analysis, Nature Reviews: Drug Discovery*, V.9, 2010, pp. 581–82.

'Evolving R&D for Emerging Markets', *News and Analysis, Nature Reviews: Drug Discovery*, V.9, June 2010, pp. 417–20.

'Generic Biotech Drugs: Cure or Quagmire?', *Businessweek*, 15 June 2009, accessed 23 September 2010 at http://www.businessweek.com/technology/content/jun2009/tc20090615_361364.htm.

'Hatch-Waxman Compromise Bill in Need of Reform', *Drug Store News*, 17 February 2003, accessed 25 September 2010 at http://find articles.com/p/articles/mi_m3374/is_2_25/ai_97998967/.

'Increasing M&A Activity in the Generics Industry: What Happens Next?', Sci. Tech.Trade Newsletters, 26 June 2008, accessed 25 September 2010 at http://scicasts.com/analysis/1826-bio-it-a-bio technology/1960-increasing-maa-activity-in-the-generics-industry-what-happens-next.

'Indian-TRIPs Compliance Legislation under Fire', *Bridges Weekly Trade News Digest*, V.9 N.1, 2005, accessed 7 February 2011 at http://ict sd.org/i/news/bridgesweekly/7273/.

'Innovation in Israel – Advantages in Generating Ideas', accessed 24 September 2010 at http://innovation.freedomblogging.com/category/innovation-in-israel/.

Israel, National Trade Estimate Report on Foreign Trade Barriers (NTE) 2007, PHRMA, accessed 25 September 2010 at www.sidley.com/db30/cgi-bin/pubs/US-Israel_Business_Law_Developments.

'Life Sciences in Israel', Israel Ministry of Industry Trade and Labor Foreign Trade Administration, accessed 23 September 2010 at http://www.israeleconomicmission.com/index.php?option=com_docman&task=doc_download&gid=18&Itemid=1.

Press Release from Teva Pharmaceuticals, 16 October 2009, accessed 23 September 2010 at http://www.tevapharm.com/pr/2009/pr_876.asp.

Major Overhaul of the Israeli PTE System: Attention and Action Required, accessed 18 March 2014 http://www.rcip.co.il/en/article/major-overhaul-of-the-israeli-pte-system-attention-and-action-required/.

'Public Handouts Enrich Drug Makers, Scientists', *The Boston Globe*, 5 April 1998, accessed 24 September 2010 at http://www.cptech.org/ip/health/econ/bg04051998.html.

Science Business Report, accessed 22 September 2010 at www.sciencebusiness.net/documents/demandside.pdf.

'Technion Research Helps Those with Neurodegenerative Diseases', American Technion Society, accessed 22 September 2010 at http://www.ats.org/site/PageServer?pagename=about_parkinson.

'Teva Increases Generics Leadership Worldwide with Unexpected Acquisition of Barr Pharmaceuticals', *IHS Global Insight*, 21 July 2008, accessed 25 September 2009 at http://www.ihsglobalinsight.com/SDA/SDADetail13398.htm.

'Teva, in Turnabout, Sues to Protect its Multiple Sclerosis Drug Copaxone', accessed 23 September 2010 at http://industry.bnet.com/pharma/10005164/teva-in-turnabout-sues-to-protect-its-multiple-sclerosis-drug-copaxone/.

'Teva May Face Generic Rival to Copaxone', accessed 25 September 2010 at http://www.marketwatch.com/story/teva-may-face-generic-rival-to-ms-drug-copaxone.

'Teva Seeks Deals to Deepen Branded Business in "Niche" Diseases', 23 February 2009, accessed 21 September 2010 at http://www.bloomberg.com/apps/news?pid=20601202&sid=aQhXH2ygDnlk.

'Teva Shares Off: Mylan Files for Generic Copaxone', Marketwatch, 14 September 2009, accessed 25 September 2010 at http://www.marketwatch.com/story/teva-shares-off-mylan-files-for-generic-copaxone-2009-09-14.

'Teva Signs Drug Development Deal with OncoGeneX', 29 December 2009, *Silico Research*, accessed 22 September 2010 at http://silico.wordpress.com/2009/12/29/teva-and-oncogenex-sign-global-licence-and-collaboration-agreement/.

'Teva's Copaxone patent appeal to go unheard, May 2014 generic launch prospects debated', *Financial Times*, 27 August 27 2013, accessed 22 September 2010 at http://www.ft.com/intl/cms/s/2/1657223a-0f24-11e3-ae66-00144feabdc0.html#axzz2gOkj1j00.

'Teva's Growth Strategy 2008–2012', Sholomo Yanai, President and CEO, Teva Pharmaceutical Industries Ltd., 21 February 2008, accessed 22 September 2010 at www.tevapharm.com/pdf/Presentation 21.02.08.pdf.

'Teva's Patent Marathon Runner', Globes, 24 April 2006, accessed 25 September 2010 at http://www.ivc-online.com/ivcWeeklyItem.asp?articleID=6969.

'The Global Use of Medicines: Outlook through 2017' IMS Institute, November 2013, accessed 19 March 2014 at http://www.drugstorenews.com/sites/drugstorenews.com/files/IMS%20Health%20Global%20Use%20of%20Medicines%20FINAL%5B1%5D.pdf

'The Other Side of the Molecule: Teva Seeks to Protect its Patch', Patlit, 19 October 2009, accessed 22 September 2010 at http://patlit.blogspot.com/2009/10/other-side-of-molecule-teva-seeks-to.html.

'Two Marriages and a Funeral', *Outlook Profit*, V.1, N.12, August 2008, p. 50.

'Technion Research Helps Those with Neurodegenerative Diseases', American Technion Society, accessed 26 September 2010 at www.ats.org/site/PageServer?pagename=about_parkinsons.

'US, Israel Resolve Long-Standing Pharma Battle', *PharmaTimes*, 23 February 2010, accessed 24 September 2010 at www.pharmatimes. com/WorldNews/articles.aspx?id=17449.

CASES

Association for Molecular Pathology v Myriad Genetics, 569 U.S. 12-398 (2013).
Bilski v Kappos, 561 U.S. _ (2010).
Diamond v Chakrabarty, 447 US 303 (1980).
Farbenfabriken Vormals Friedrich Bayer & Co v Chemische Fabrik Von Heydon (1905) 22 RPC 501.
Mayo v Prometheus, 566 U.S. _ (2012).
Watson v Henry Bristol Myers Squilibb, 194 F. Supp. 422 (D. Md. 2001).

Index